BUSINESS
REPORT
WRITING

BUSINESS REPORT WRITING

HARRY M. BROWN
Midwestern State University

D. VAN NOSTRAND COMPANY
New York   Cincinnati   Toronto   London   Melbourn

D. Van Nostrand Company Regional Offices:
New York   Cincinnati

D. Van Nostrand Company International Offices:
London   Toronto   Melbourne

Published by D. Van Nostrand Company
135 West 50th Street, New York, N.Y.   10020

10 9 8 7 6 5 4 3 2 1

PREFACE

This book is designed to develop skill in writing clear, well-organized, thorough reports. Skill in writing effective reports may well be a major factor in determining how far a person will advance in the business profession. Out of this purpose comes the structure of the book.

Part I focuses on the communication process and the specific report writing project. Chapters 1 and 2 define the report, point out its significance in business, briefly outline the qualities of good writing, and discuss the specific techniques of writing for the reader. Here students are given a preliminary report framework so that they can practice some report writing while their skills develop through the course to the writing of a full-fledged report. Included are exercises and problems in rewriting, analysis, and the development of selected aspects of report projects.

Part II offers basic tools for writing reports—developing various types of paragraphs as the unit of thought, writing effective sentences, using precise and forceful diction, following a logical and convincing thought process, and using helpful graphics. The chapters are not discursive, but they do give abundant materials to work with—explanations, examples, exercises, and writing projects.

Part III deals with the writing of the full-fledged report. Chapters 8–10 take the writer through the step-by-step process of writing the report—defining the problem clearly, gathering the right materials, analyzing and evaluating the information, actually writing the report, and putting it in the proper format. Exercises and problems allow the student to apply the principles and techniques. Chapter 11 gives practice in writing different kinds of reports for various job assignments. Model reports are provided, along with abundant exercises and materials for report projects.

The Appendix contains checklists and glossaries of useful information, such as business terms, abbreviations, English usage, and punctuation.

The book is flexible. For instance, Chapter 1 is introductory as well as basic. It can be explored deeply. With its definitions, attitudes, and basic report frameworks as checkpoints, the student can undertake one of the large report projects from Chapter 11. Various sections of the book can be studied concurrently, such as "Building Your Ideas Through Paragraphs" and "Shaping Your Thought Processes." The chapters on sentences and words may be dealt with as classroom units or used as reference.

The examples and illustrations that represent quality writing are credited. Those that point out weaknesses or were drawn from student reports have not been identified, but they are not less authentic and valuable expressions of report writing techniques.

CONTENTS

vii

BUSINESS
REPORT
WRITING

PRINCIPLES OF BUSINESS COMMUNICATION

1
Perspectives on Report Writing

DECISIVE DOCUMENTS

Among the most effective of reports is the legendary, "Sighted sub, sank same," from the naval officer to his superior. Another is railroad repairman Flanagan's report about the derailed train: "Off again, on again, gone again. Flanagan." These activity or field reports are clear, complete in the context, concise, and correct. They have presented materials dealing with a solution to a problem.

Ideally, a business report sequence might run in the same clipped style.

Joe:
Please work me up a plan to increase our profits by $250,000 a year.

Bill

Bill:
Here is the plan to increase our profits by $250,000 a year:

$$A + B + C + D = \$250,000$$

Joe

Unfortunately, most reports cannot be as brief and direct as these somewhat imaginative reports, but the principles remain the same. We just extend the simplicity to several factors. For instance, the little formula from Joe could expand to something like this:

$$\text{Labor} + \text{Investment} + \text{Material} + \text{Promotion}$$
$$= \text{New Product} + \text{New Market} = \$250{,}000$$

The extended factors could become the materials for analysis and recommendation and provide the structure for a 30–40 page report on new product development. A problem can be solved, a decision can be made, a course of action can be taken.

The report writer must extend his skill to the several factors that comprise the large report. Skill in writing clear, well-organized, thorough reports may well be a major force in determining how far a businessman or businesswoman will go in a profession. Having good ideas and suggestions is not enough; the person in business must be able to put these ideas and suggestions into writing in order to communicate them to others in higher positions who can put the ideas and suggestions into action. That gives us a definition of a report. It is a written communication conveying business information about research or a situation from one area of business to another to assist in making a decision.

In all but the smallest of businesses, no one person can do all the work. Other minds must be enlisted to help carry responsibility. The efforts of each person sharing that responsibility must be coordinated so that the business can operate smoothly and meet its objectives. The business report is one of the main means by which those efforts are coordinated.

Most business reports go up the chain of command in an organization. Members of a department write reports for their supervisor so that he or she can coordinate their efforts and, in turn, report the department's activities to the executive who coordinates the efforts of the various departments—and so on up the chain of command. Other reports go across the organization from one staff member to another, or from one department to another. Others go down the chain, informing the staff of decisions made or further steps to be taken. Still other reports go outside the organization, like the report from an advertising agency to a client, informing him of progress on a new advertising campaign. Reports can come from the outside in, such as reports from a management consultant who is retained to study a company problem.

Regardless of direction, however, business reports are vital to the coordination of objectives and activities. Effective reports are necessary for all but the most minor decisions in business. Poor reports will cause confusion. Write effective reports and you may be called upon to assume greater responsibilities.

Reports serve three basic functions. All reports convey facts (by definition, they must). Some reports also interpret the facts that they convey. And some reports that interpret also make recommendations in light of those interpretations. Within these three basic functions there are many specific kinds of reports. There are periodic, progress, project, field, laboratory, library, and inspection reports, as well as combinations of some types (such as laboratory–library).

Reports deal with such subjects as sales figures, marketing surveys, employee attitudes, credit ratings, new product development, consumer attitudes, production analyses, profit and loss figures, and plant expansion. These and many other kinds of information are exchanged continually in normal business operations.

Suppose, for example, that a bicycle manufacturing company wants to diversify its production because the current market has become severely competitive, and the faddish nature of bicycles makes the future uncertain. Should the company go into lawn mowers, outboard motors, motorbikes, or various sports novelties? What must the company know before it launches an expensive new production project? First of all, it must know everything about itself and its financial and productive capacity for expansion. It must have knowledge about the market—what products are needed, what competition exists, what distribution channels are available. When we consider the requirements of such an undertaking, the task seems impossible. Yet such activity takes place every day in modern business. Every responsible position in business requires a person who can recognize the need for action, analyze the need, and contribute to the final solution. Finally, people must learn how to record their action in words—words that will be intelligible to those who read the report. This is the job of the report writer. Its importance cannot be overemphasized.

QUALITIES OF EFFECTIVE REPORTS

What makes a report effective? On this both writers and readers agree. An effective report is *clear, complete, concise,* and *correct.*

Clear

First of all, an effective report must be clear. The first purpose of a report is to convey facts and information. If the message is not clear, then nothing else can really count. Consider these examples of unclear writing:

> The saleswoman, Margaret Bernstein, told the complaining customer that the fault was hers. (Who's to blame? Just which woman does "hers" refer to?)

> The kind of thing that he referred to in his memo suggested that his company has been thinking along these lines. (The statement is so vague and general as to be almost meaningless.)

> One cannot praise Billings too highly for his sales efforts. (Is Billings to receive high praise or not?)

These are small statements, perhaps unimportant in themselves, but they tangle the business process. They require additional questions, correspondence, or explanation, or they force the reader to guess at the meaning. Write your report so that the reader will understand clearly. Select your facts, thoughts, and words and put them in such a sentence structure that the reader will understand instantaneously.

Complete

Your report must be complete, according to its purpose and subject. You should not include irrelevancies, but do not leave out anything the reader needs to know. Check the following fragment of information:

> The proposed new Copy Mate 620 makes copies a lot faster than the older 310.

The comparison means nothing. Until we know how many copies per minute (or the equivalent) each machine produces, we cannot sensibly decide to shift to the new 620.

On the other hand, irrelevant elements weaken the thought flow and waste the reader's time.

> Computers, whose memory capacity has been increasing rapidly in recent years, would have had a major influence on the economic recovery of the 1930s if they had existed sooner.

The idea of increasing memory capacity has nothing to do with the point of the sentence. It just makes us juggle conflicting references to the 1930s and the 1980s. The sentence should be shortened and rearranged to bring out the straightforward, precise information.

If computers had been available in time, they would have had a major influence on the economic recovery of the 1930s.

For your reader's sake, give him complete information, but not more than complete.

Concise

Without being curt or telegraphic, your report should be brief and direct. Use just enough words so that your reader will get the information as quickly and easily as possible. The following excerpt makes us wade through too many words to get to the point.

The photograph which is included on page 3 will give you an idea as to the appearance of the building.

The more direct sentence is better.

The photograph on page 3 will show you what the building looks like.

In the following selection, the idea is tangled in so many words that we reach frustration before understanding.

We plan to devote considerable effort to the study of developing requirements and will seek to develop proposed solutions to the various possible needs we can foresee in advance of the time that a decision will be required.

An effective report might have read:

We will try to solve the problem when we find out what it is.

Correct

Correct writing means two things. Your information must be accurate and your grammar must be correct. Incorrect information often springs from incorrect thinking. Fuzzy, hasty, or biased thinking can produce shaky conclusions and opinions.

Four of the six workers were Mexican Americans. So we could hardly expect good work from them. (For such a foregone, and probably biased conclusion, we would want a lot of evidence.)

We do not advocate strikes, but we feel striking is the only way for hospital nurses to get their rights. (*Contradiction:* If you "feel striking is the only way" then you *do* advocate.)

Since presenting information is the first purpose of a report, the report will fail if the information is inaccurate or shaky. You must check facts, figures, names, dates, conclusions, and everything. Errors can be expensive. One digit can make a difference of thousands of dollars (for example, $58,000 instead of $85,000).

Writing should also be correct in grammar, spelling, and punctuation. Not using the accepted standards of English is risky. You may shake the reader's confidence in your competence and responsibility, and you may distract him from the line of thought of the report. Consider the effect of the following inaccuracies and blunders.

We should authorize the cashier to make monthly advances to the new saleswomen. (We are not finally fooled about meaning, but we do have a thought or two about the writer's mental sharpness.)

This sum should be paid in a single amount at the time of the employee's death, which is what they prefer.

Certificates of Deposit are automaticly renewed unless the customer gives instructions to the contrary.

Errors in reports are costly, confusing, and embarrassing. Careful checking can eliminate them.

THINKING YOUR WAY TO SUCCESSFUL COMMUNICATION

Listing the qualities of an effective report is fairly easy; producing them is not so easy. Why is it that we can find the many examples of poor reports that we have quoted in this chapter? What is wrong with report writers? Why don't they write clearly, completely, concisely, and correctly? The elements of the report process are fairly simple. The writer works with just two things—the material and the readers. The purpose of the report process is clear: the responsible report writer gathers information, processes it through his mind, and gets it into the mind of the reader—and does this as precisely and quickly as possible. All this seems clear enough, not mysterious, not sensational, hardly even debatable. Why, then, do so many report writers fail to write effective reports?

The answer to this question is that much business report writing falls short simply because writers do not think. Good writing is always a product of good thinking. When writers are vague or ambiguous or wordy, their thinking is fuzzy and inexact. When they leave out necessary information, they have not thought enough about the purpose it will serve. When they drag on with irrelevant details, they have failed to think about what is really important. If a writer thinks before he writes, thinks while he gathers material, thinks when he writes, and thinks about how he can improve what he has written, then he is likely to come up with an effective report. Here are the basic questions a thoughtful writer will answer.

1 Who is my reader?
2 Just what does he want to know?
3 What do I want to tell him?
4 For what purpose am I writing?
5 For what purpose will my reader use this material?
6 What are the various ways of arranging and writing this particular material?
7 What do I want my reader to do?
8 How would I react if I were in his place?

As you can see from these questions, the way to write effectively is to think carefully about your material and your reader. See how this statement applies to the four qualities of effective writing. *Clear* writing comes from clear thinking. Will my reader understand? Are my sentences clear and my thoughts easy to follow? *Complete* thinking requires thinking about your reader, his purpose, and just what he needs to know to make his decision or solve his problem. *Concise* writing comes from thinking your way through to the essentials, cutting out the irrelevant, and considering how to put your material in the most direct form. *Correct* writing requires a total clear thinking process and a knowledge of the standards of grammatical usage. It also requires a concern for the tastes and perceptions of the reader.

The qualities of an effective report, then, are easy to define. The barriers to effective communication can be pinpointed. What the report writer must do is think his way through the barriers to communication so that his reader gets the message loud and clear.

In Chapter 2, we will discuss how to avoid many of the barriers

MORRIS   ⋈   Communications and
Information Handling

To: James Randall   From: Tom Boone   Date:
April 14, 1978
Data Communications
Division Correspondence

SUBJECT: Removal of Lease Deck Equipment from the Factory

Recently a Recommendation was floated by Product Management covering
write-off of missing off-rent Lease Deck equipment. Included in
the Recommendation was a paragraph or two covering reasons for
disappearance of equipment; however, recently I have discovered a
reason which was not put forth in the Recommendation.

Last week you were observed removing a Morris 1000 from the front
door of the factory and loading same into the trunk of a visitor's
car. Subsequent investigation revealed that the S/N of the
equipment was 21200 and that is was being given to City of Dallas as
a demo replacement for a unit already in their possession. The
unit to be replaced, however, was not returned at the time of pickup
of the replacement, nor has it been returned to date to my knowledge.
Further investigation revealed that you removed the unit from the
storeroom area by having it assigned to an "R" job. This is of
course a refurb job. The unit was not actually removed for refurb
purposes as explained above. Now we have a unit charged to an R
job which is in fact in a customer's hands. If we took a physical
today and you were no longer with us, we would be missing one
terminal since no one but you knew where the terminal ultimately
was sent. The only paperwork available charges it to an "R" job.
In addition, we have another terminal which should be returned, but
only you know about this fact. No shipper has been cut to my
knowledge to cover return of the replaced unit.

Our existing procedures state that a unit may not be shipped to a
customer or prospective customer without a shipper issued by Order
Entry. Also, equipment is to be shipped by Factory personnel
through shipping dock and not delivered at the front door by
Product Managers. I seriously question what authority you have to
violate the existing Company Procedures in this matter. I also
wonder how much of our missing equipment is due to Product Managers
removing equipment without proper paperwork.

I have made Ted Burford aware of the method used to remove the 1000
from the factory and he has advised me that it will not happen again
unless existing Procedures are revised.

I would also appreciate your following up on the City of Dallas for
the return of the replaced unit and, in fact, I feel you should
have Order Entry cut a shipper to cover the return.

Willis Vaughn will be in touch with you in the next few days
regarding the return of this unit.

cc: R. Wallace
W. Vaughn

Figure 1.1

MORRIS   Communications and
Information Handling

To: Tom Boone   From: James Randall   Date
April 19, 1978
Data Communications
Division Correspondence

SUBJECT: Your Memo of April 14 on Removal of Lease Deck Equipment

I would like to commend you for your amazing detective work in
uncovering the facts in this case--considering that you did not
talk to me and, according to your memo, I was the only one who
knew what was going on.

There was a demo order issued for a 1030-11 terminal for the City of
Dallas. This was done through the normal channels, with all the
proper paperwork. Upon installation, there was an interface problem,
and the customer requested a model 1040-11. It was agreed the
best thing to do was physically swap the terminals, then Order Entry
would notify Lease Deck Accounting of the serial number swap against
the existing demo order. Messrs. Goldman, Brinker, Rollins, Myers,
and Gerber were aware of this and the location of the terminal.

The Division is already choking on excess paperwork, including your
memo and this one; but since you have caught me in my underhanded
scheme to deprive the system of the necessary paperwork upon which
it thrives, we will comply.

By copy of this memo, I am instructing Marketing to issue a demo
EOF for a model 1040-11, S/N 21200. Order Entry will then issue a
Manufacturing Work Order. The MID checking the terminal out of
inventory already exists--Order Entry will then issue a "paperwork
only" shipper. Field Engineering should then fill out an EIR.

Marketing must also generate a cancellation of order 21954-10,
model 1030-11, S/N 10495. Order Entry will then issue a return
shipper for this terminal and Field Engineering a removal EIR.

This assumes that the customer does not purchase one of the
terminals in the meantime, and further complicate the paperwork.
Should this happen, however, I am sure you have procedures to cover
it, since we are in business to sell terminals, as well as generate
documents.

cc: H. Goldman
     M. Brinker   W. Vaughn
     N. Rollins   R. Wallace

Figure 1.2

to communication by writing for the reader. Subsequent chapters will continue with special devices for making your report clear, complete, concise, and correct.

Analyze the memo exchange in Figures 1.1 and 1.2 as examples of barriers to communication. The memos illustrate how failure to use accurate data can bring about a lot of disturbance. The names of the company and people involved have been changed; otherwise, the memos are intact as actually sent. Tom Boone wrote his suspicious memo without gathering exact and sufficient data, and he made a fool of himself. Not only did he get Randall's witty, sarcastic reply, but he must have suspected what the gossip was about him—especially among those to whom Randall sent carbon copies.

Consider how much time and effort was wasted in this need to "generate documents." Consider also the bad feelings that must have existed for at least a little while between Randall and Boone. If Boone had spent just 30 seconds on the phone, he could have gathered enough exact information to prevent the costly blunder.

EXERCISES AND PROBLEMS

1. Rewrite the following sentences, clearing up ambiguities, vagueness, and contradictions.
   a. It was twenty minutes before three, maybe less.
   b. Billings told Tillman that he should have written a follow-up letter.

   c.   DAILY COFFEE SHOP HOURS
                  Breakfast—7:30–9:30
                  Lunch—12:00–2:30
                  —Closed Mondays—

   d. Nobody uses Vesper Nature Lotion anymore.
   e. Low conversation annoys most customers.
   f. Add the cleaner to the water when it reaches 185 degrees.
   g. She almost typed 25 letters before lunch.
   h. Bursting suddenly, three men were killed by the gas tank.
   i. Your dog will not shrink from being washed with Doggy Foam.
   j. All pamphlets from suppliers should be sent to the head buyer.
   k. A hurricane hit the Gulf Coast that day, although in St. Petersburg, Florida, the weather was calm.
2. The following sentences lack factual precision because essential

information has been omitted or irrelevant information h\(\)
included. Rewrite the sentences to include appropriate ...ail
and remove irrelevancies.
   a. Parker's is down Main Street, past the post office.
— b. Send us everything you have on your accident, Mrs. Jones,
   and we will expedite your claim immediately.
   c. Thank you for the request for the pamphlet.
   d. Hillside Resort has long been known as the complete conven-
   tion center for business and professional groups such as yours.
   Whatever your preference in the way of sports, Hillside has
   it. There's tennis, golf, tennis, swimming, water skiing, horse-
   back riding, volleyball—you name it. And the big news is
   that it won't be long before we have winter sports too. (Just
   what makes winter sports big news? How long is "long"?)
   e. Your instructions were to ship 300 catalogs to Pittsburgh,
   250 to Cleveland, and 430 to Columbus. I want to see what
   is happening to our shipments.
   f. The Scott Company employs 250 men and 150 women; therefore, Scott discriminates against women.
   g. Wichita Falls, which was named for the waterfall seven miles
   up the Wichita River, is the center of a large oil industry.
   h. Also enclosed in our letter are two well-known customers
   of ours.
   i. Mae earned her promotion through hard work, and she graduated from Briarcliff in 1975.
   j. High-Guard Doors can be installed on any normal-sized garage.
3. Check these sentences for misspellings or incorrect words and
   figures.
   a. Be sure to write down the name and phone number of every
   perspective buyer.
   b. The bad news did not effect her optimism.
   c. Nothing can change the appearance of a living room quite
   as much as an undraped widow.
   d. We are shipping you ½ dozen (6) green Sportsman jackets,
   size 38, at $11.25 each. Please send your check for $76.50.
4. Assume that you have written the first draft of a report for
   the Customer Service Manager in the home office of Auto General, Inc. There have been several complaints from customers
   (managers of retail auto parts stores) that checks due them for
   exchange parts (brake shoes and generators, for example) and
   return merchandise are slow in reaching them. They say your
   competitors are much faster.
   You investigate and wish to recommend that each district

office of Auto General should prepare its own refund checks so that customers will get them sooner. Here is the final section of your report. It is clumsy, wordy, and hard to read. Rewrite it specifically for the Customer Service Manager so that he will find it easy to read.

Therefore, I recommend that we instruct all district managers that effective May 1 and thereafter they issue all checks for any amount written out to customers for exchange parts and for returned merchandise from their office directly to the customer without having to go through the home office.

I feel that this plan and procedure will not only help to improve customer relations substantially but will also close the gap on one of the important areas where our company compares unfavorably with other companies in its contact with customers.

However, the district managers may or may not find in their previous or committed routine that this is feasible. This new practice may be too time-consuming. Comment on same shall be returned to me. This should be done by return mail, as we ought to effectuate this new procedure immediately.

2
Writing for the Reader

REPORTS

The report you write is important. Decisions are waiting upon it, the Company's future will be shaped by it, and your own future will be affected. As business and industry expand and as government agencies multiply, the need for effective information and control systems becomes even more critical than ever. The report you are doing is needed. It was probably requested by a superior or a colleague who wants to base an important decision on it—to open a branch store, to shift personnel, to manufacture a new product, or to make any number of moves that will affect the Company and you.

Unfortunately, many reports are less than effective. They are a mass of dull, wandering words and sentences dragging along compilations of undigested data that confuse and frustrate the reader. Why does such an outrageous thing happen? Probably the main reason for poor reports is that the writer does not write for his reader but for himself. The poor writer is likely to be one of two extremes—the torture rack or the ego trip.

If his problem is the torture rack, then he just wants to get an assigned job done and get it off his back. His poorly written report is just a desperate attempt to compromise. Because writing is painful to him, he tries to avoid it. When he can't avoid it, he puts it off, evidently hoping it will go away like some psychosomatic pain.

Or he delays in frustration, because he doesn't know how to begin, or continue.

Therefore, the writer's common approach is to wait until the deadline is this coming Friday. Then, as though he's been carrying his data around in a 200-pound sack, he dumps it on paper in a disorganized mass, not really concerned with the reader, but delighted to get something down on paper. In the process, he disgorges every piece of information that vaguely relates to the subject, and for good measure may even toss in a few unrelated facts, unsupported opinions, and troublesome inconsistencies. When he feels the pile of rough draft looks impressively high, he stops writing. He's done his job. He's finished the report. With this torture rack kind of report writing, however, he can write thousands of words and hardly convey a single thought.

In the other extreme, the poor report may be the result of an ego trip. The report writer may fall in love with his own grandiose use of words and programs. He may pour out data, charts, and generalities in huge gobs that get to the reader like an uncharted wilderness or a warehouse shaken by an earthquake. Here is an example of a writer who tries to be impressive by putting a simple, straightforward concept into high-sounding language. Such an explanation may seem to be making a point, but a reader has a hard time finding any clear meaning.

> It would be an impossible task to categorically state the functional factors pertaining to the interrelationship of the functional field of highway planning and traffic engineering. Yet a relationship exists. This might be illustrated by the use of traffic-engineering analysis of the existing operational characteristics of a channelized intersection during the conduct of a complete inventory. The reversal of this interdependency and use of information can be further illustrated by highway planners' use of these data in analyzing the significance of the type problem in the process of project priority determinations.

The writer seems to be saying something like this:

> Highway planners and traffic engineers must work together to solve traffic problems.

But the writer has lost sight of both the reader and the significance of the report itself.

The standard of a good report is the reader. But the difficulty is not that of agreeing on standards but of interpreting them. For example, both writers and intended readers agree that reports should be clear, complete, concise, accurate, appropriate, and readable. But the two often differ in their interpretation of these qualities. To the writer, everything is clear because he is closest to the subject; to the reader nothing may be clear.

How then can standards be made clear? Very simply, by measuring them against the reader. He occupies the most important position in the communication hierarchy, because he is the reason why the report is prepared. Therefore, to be meaningful, the standards must be related to the reader's education, experience, areas of responsibility and interest, and purpose in requesting the report.

When a report doesn't measure up to standards—that is, when it doesn't meet the needs of the reader—the fault is almost surely the writer's. At least he must take the blame. The writer must consider the reader, figure out just how to satisfy him, and not attempt to satisfy someone other than the intended reader. Instead of considering his report a painful job or an ego trip for himself, the report writer should write for his reader.

He can produce a piece of material that he can take pride and joy in—a job well done, a supervisor or colleague helped or pleased, a decision or direction for the Company's future supported, and a feather or two in his own credential cap. "That Paul Mason is one of the sharpest men we've got. We sure need him."

Consider a case in point. Tim Thompson is Director of Market Research at Monarch Chemicals, Inc. In October 1980, he received the following memo from C. J. Barton, Executive Vice President:

> What about acetone? Let's take a look at the domestic market for the principal uses of acetone over the next five years to see if we should consider becoming a supplier. I'd like a summary evaluation as soon as possible.

Tim assigned the project to Paul Mason, and several weeks later received the following report.

```
                    THE ACETONE MARKET


      This summary report is submitted in response to your
request for a market study on the U.S. demand for acetone
through 1980 to include principal end-use breakdowns.
```

Most of the information from which the conclusions were
drawn was obtained by field work, although a statistical
approach also proved valuable. The end-use patterns and
growth that can be expected over the next five years have
been estimated. Since acetone is used primarily as a paint
solvent, this particular end-use and its growth through 1985
is of major importance.

The major end-use of acetone--as a paint solvent--will
grow some 90 million pounds over the next five-year period
from 420 million pounds in 1980. It is estimated that acetone
in the cosmetics industry will remain essentially unchanged
over the next five years, although within the next three years
consumption in this end-use may grow from a current 50 million
to some 60 million pounds. The over-all economics of wood
derivatives as a raw material for acetone is not expected to
change. In 1980, acetone as a solvent accounted for some 86%
of total consumption, including both industrial and military
end-uses. The cosmetics end-use accounted for about 10%.
The over-all market for acetone is expected to grow from some
485 million pounds in 1980 to about 608 million pounds in 1985.
The other major end-use for acetone--as a glue synthesizer--is
relatively small and is expected to remain unchanged during
this period as a level of 7-8 million pounds.

Although current installed capacity is some 625 million
pounds, 90 to 95 million of this is now inactive; effective
producing capacity is thus reduced to 530 million pounds.
The majority of this is produced from crude wood spirits and
some from distillation of certain acetates and sugar. Domestic
consumption of acetone in 1980 was some 485 million pounds.
Of this, some 62 million pounds represents imported materials,
yielding an indicated domestic production of 423 million pounds.

It is concluded that over the next five-year period imports
will represent some 14% of total domestic consumption. It is
therefore estimated that of the 608 million pounds expected to
be consumed in 1985, only some 518 million pounds will come
from domestic production. This is substantially below installed
producing capacity, as indicated above.

Recent price reductions by all domestic producers of
acetone to 22.25¢ per pound in tank-car quantities brings
profitability to an all-time low. It is believed that
marginal producers of acetone will find it extremely difficult
to operate effectively in the field with this low profit
margin (e.g., sales coverage, technical service, competition
from fully amortized plants).

Therefore, although growth is indicated, it will be
nominal and a portion will be absorbed by imported acetone.
For these reasons, it is concluded that it is inadvisable for
Monarch to consider entering the market as a new supplier at
this time.

Tim Thompson, like so many executives, was constantly trying to find time to give to the many reports he had to write, review, or digest. But he was steadily losing ground. Reports such as the one Paul Mason submitted only made the problem worse, for it gave him two more jobs. He had the horrendous task of reading and rereading the confusing material to try to extract some meaningful information, and he would have to spend extra time reworking it.

Faced with such a task, Tim felt much like a person who ordered a tape recorder so that he could tape an important conference, but received a box filled with tubes, wires, wheels, transistors, resistors, and a multitude of other electronic components. He was confused because the supplier forced him to segregate and reconstruct components that might be unfamiliar. He was annoyed because what he wanted to do was to use the product, not construct it.

Some writers don't see their work in relation to what it's all for—the reader. They seem oblivious to the problems they create. Paul Mason, for example, believed that the conclusion of the market study was clear and that all the necessary detail had been included. What he failed to recognize, however, is that like a person confronted with a multitude of tape recorder components, the reader of a disorganized report cannot tell whether all the parts included are necessary or extraneous until he has reconstructed the product.

Paul could have satisfied the reader's requirements, saved his boss a great deal of work and anxiety, and perhaps enhanced his own position if he had arranged the data in some kind of logical order, struck out tangential thoughts, deleted redundancies and meaningless statements, restructured the presentation, and made it livelier by using the active voice more. For example, he might have prepared the report somewhat along the following lines.

The Advisability of Entering the Acetone Market

This report, submitted in response to your request in September, 1980, summarizes the results of a study of the U.S. market for the principal end-uses of acetone over the next five years.

The results indicate that it is inadvisable for Monarch Chemicals to become a supplier of acetone at this time for the following reasons:

1.   Domestic consumption during the next five years will be substantially less than total current domestic installed capacity.

2.   Recently reduced prices of acetone have brought profitability to an all-time low.

CONSUMPTION AND CAPACITY

The overall market for acetone is expected to grow from about 485 million pounds in 1980 to 608 million pounds in 1985. A breakdown of consumption by end-use is given below.

End-Use	1980	1985
	(Millions of Pounds)	
Paint Solvent	420	510
Cosmetics	50	50
Organic Synthesizer	8	8
Miscellaneous	7	40*

*The dynamic growth in this category will be accounted for principally by the use of acetone to clean electronic component parts.

Part of the increase in consumption will be negated by a proportional increase in imports. The volumes supplied by imports and domestic production are shown below.

	1980	1985
	(Millions of Pounds)	
Total domestic consumption	485	608
Supplied by Imports	62	90
Supplied Domestically	423	518

> Current effective producing capacity is only 530 million pounds,
> but another 95 million pounds is inactive. Thus, total current
> installed capacity is 625 million pounds, substantially more than
> the 608 million that will be required in 1985.
>
> All domestic producers of acetone recently reduced their prices to
> 22.5¢ per pound in tank car quantities. This action has brought
> profitability to an all-time low, and it is expected to remain close
> to this level over the period studied. Marginal producers--and
> Monarch would be a marginal producer--will undoubtedly find it
> difficult to operate at this very low profit level, especially
> in the face of competition from fully amortized plants.

Many poor reports are rooted in linguistic naiveté. People think they communicate simply because they talk or write. But no one just communicates; he communicates *something* to *someone*. The main difference between the two versions of the summary report on the acetone market is that the original merely presents information on paper, whereas the revision provides C. J. Barton with a brief evaluation of the market. The revision recognizes that Barton's principal need was to know whether the company should consider becoming a supplier of acetone. Therefore, it answers that question immediately with supporting statements. Then to make the material easy to read and grasp, it provides supporting details under categories relating to the recommendations. In addition, it displays the necessary quantitative information in a tabular form that clearly points out relationships and makes comparison easy. Information tailored to meet the needs of C. J. Barton may not have ruled out questions, but at least the questions would arise from Barton's appraisal of the market, not his appraisal of the presentation.

If the communication effort is a trying experience for people such as Tim Thompson, it is equally trying for the Paul Masons. Reputations are built piece by piece, and it takes only a few reports such as the original version of the market evaluation to establish a Paul Mason as one of the less brilliant communicators in an organization. But reports like the revised version soon mark Paul Mason as "one of the sharpest minds we've got."

The rest of this chapter presents three techniques for getting your message across to your reader.

1 Start him in the right direction.
2 Give him a design for easy reading.
3 Keep him with you by using the right language pace.

START YOUR READER IN THE RIGHT DIRECTION

What do your readers look for first when they begin reading? You can carry on a little experiment to find the answer. Draw some strange symbol or scrawl some indecipherable doodles, letters, or figures on a sheet of paper and leave the paper where your roommates or classmates will see it. What is the first reaction? If your friends are typical, they will gather around the paper trying to decipher it. Soon, one of them will say, "What is this all about?"

That is exactly the question in your reader's mind when he begins your report. *What is this all about?* If your report is as obscure as the scribblings just given, your reader may never find out what it is all about. As a report writer, you have the obligation to tell your reader what your report is about. In almost every form of business report, your task is to lead your reader from his lack of knowledge or his lack of understanding to knowledge and understanding. In this process you have to begin where he is by giving him enough background so that he can read intelligently. You can do this in a variety of ways, many of which will be discussed in successive chapters as they apply to special kinds of reports.

In short memorandum reports, for instance, the standard memo heading may supply adequate information.

TO: Tim Thompson   DATE: November 12, 1980
FROM: Paul Mason
SUBJECT: Advisability of Entering the Acetone Market

In letter reports, you can casually give adequate directions by referring to the letter you are answering in a brief opening sentence.

Dear Tim:
Here is the report on the acetone market you asked for in your letter of September 28.

In long reports, you will probably go into far greater detail, orienting your reader by answering such questions as these:

1 Who did the report and the investigation?
2 What methods were used?
3 How long did the investigation take?
4 What is the central purpose?
5 How does it relate to other research or projects that have to be carried on?

There may be other information your reader needs to get his bearings.

Don't make the mistakes of assuming, first, that the answers to such questions are superfluous or too elementary or, second, that the reader knows as much about the subject as you do. Both of these errors arise from a trait common to all of us—when we are thoroughly familiar with a subject or when we have made an intense study of it, we tend to assume that our readers are at the same point we are now instead of where we *were* when we first started studying the subject. Lead your reader into your subject clearly rather than plunge him in somewhere past the beginning.

There's a lot of fast traffic on the freeway. You'd better let your reader enter at a normal entrance—with a well-marked road sign—and tell him where he's headed.

We can come close to the proper beginning for a business report by a comparison with journalistic techniques. First, there's a headline, whose only purpose is to tell readers in the briefest possible space what the story is about so they can decide whether they want to read it. Then there's the lead, which usually answers the five w's and one h: *What, Who, When* (How long), *Where, Why,* and *How.* These questions make an excellent checklist for your beginnings. You won't always use all six, but if you use those which are appropriate to your readers' needs, you will be starting them on the right road. And that road always begins by giving the answers relevant to the natural question: "What's this all about?"

GIVE YOUR READER A DESIGN FOR EASY READING

Now that you have your readers started on the right road, you have to consider where you are going to take them and how you will take them there. This *where* and *how* takes planning and a good road—or what we call *good design.*

Good Design

When we say a report has good design, we mean the same thing we mean when we say a product has good design. Two things are implied: the product has a functional arrangement of its parts to serve its purpose, and it has an artistic or emotional appeal to merit the approval of the user.

That's what is meant by your writing being designed for easy reading—it should have both an orderly arrangement of parts and an appeal for its readers.

Your design does not have to be too obvious. Your readers do not have to be made highly conscious of the way you have arranged the parts of your writing, but they will be very conscious if the arrangement *isn't* there. The marks of designed writing are that the readers have a sense of going somewhere, that they can follow you easily along the map you've drawn, that they know the difference between your major points and the details, and that they have achieved their purpose. To reach these goals, your writing must have design, which really means that you will have to follow these principles:

1 Begin by telling your reader what the report is about and what its purpose is.

2 Think your way through the best arrangement of parts to serve that purpose.

3 Keep your reader in mind so that you can win his interest, attention, and approval.

Here is an example of a memo report from the head of the Records Department to Jack Bitner. The report lacks design. Note how frustrating it is to read the details without knowing how they fit into an overall pattern. What is the purpose of the report? What are the major points? What is the relationship between the parts? We need a road map with destination, major stations, and road signs.

TO: Jack Bitner   DATE: October 6, 1980

FROM: Ed Turk

SUBJECT: Telephone Survey

During the week of September 22-26, 1980, a survey of telephone inquiries to the main office was conducted. The incoming calls to the Records Department totalled 590. The source of these calls was as follows: approximately 68% from main office clerks and branch

office personnel; approximately 32% from all other
main office personnel.

Due to the fact that the survey was conducted during
a period of reduced activity, the findings were not
representative of the peak periods throughout the
year. Based on an analysis of weekly activity for the
first half of 1980, the volume of telephone inquiries
is projected at 850-900 per week during the peak
periods, which occur during the first part of each
quarter.

During the period of the survey an average of 115-120
calls per day were serviced by Records. Even at this
level, the telephone activity is becoming heavy enough
to be disruptive of the other work routines in the
department.

It is recommended that another employee be hired and
assigned to the Records Department primarily for the
purpose of servicing telephone inquiries.

A revision builds effective design into the report and makes it
easy to read and interesting. The writer identifies the subject at
the very beginning. In the *introduction*, he gives the problem,
the method used, the purpose, and the plan of presentation. In
the *text*, he lists the highlights of the survey findings before giving
an interpretation. The *terminal section* suggests a course of action.
Underscoring the subject line and the use of headings further improve the reading.

TO: Jack Bitner   DATE: October 6, 1980

FROM: Ed Turk

SUBJECT: Need for Additional Employee in Records Department

Introduction   Because telephone activity is disrupting other work routines in
                        the Records Department, I conducted a survey of telephone inquiries

Text

to the main office during the week of September 22-26, 1980. This
report gives the findings of the survey and makes a recommendation
to correct the problem.

Findings

During the week of September 22-26, 1980:

1. Incoming calls to the Records Department totaled 590.

2. Records serviced an average of 115-120 calls daily. Even
    at this level, telephone activity disrupts other work.

3. Sources of these calls are as follows:

        68% from main office clerks and branch office personnel.

        32% from all other main office personnel.

The findings are not representative of peak periods throughout the
year because the survey was conducted during a period of reduced
activity. Yet based on an analysis of weekly activity for the
first half of the year, projected volume of telephone inquiries
is approximately 850-900 weekly during peak periods (first part of
each quarter).

Since the present employees already have duties to keep them busy
throughout the day, this additional activity in the department will
require additional help.

Recommendation

Terminal

We should hire another employee and assign this individual to the
Records Department primarily for servicing telephone inquiries.

Structural Patterns

The structure of the report from Turk provides a framework
you can use for all reports at this stage of our study. The main
part of a report is its body, which includes, or implies, three parts—
introduction, text, and *terminal section.*

Introduction

The introduction captures the reader's attention and presents
a general idea of the topic. You must tell your reader the *purpose*
of the report. You may also explain its *scope* and *limitations,* make
necessary *definition of terms,* tell your *plan* of presentation, and
give a general *overview* of your subject. In short, you prepare the
reader for the information he is about to receive.

Text

The text is the detailed presentation of all the facts and details
of the investigation; therefore it is most important that this section

be organized clearly and logically. It is the heart of the report. Paragraphs should be well developed; transitions between ideas, in both sentences and paragraphs, should show clearly the relationship of these ideas. Meaning can be made clearer by dividing the content into such major areas as theory, procedure, history of the subject, apparatus, etc. It is also good practice to use labels or subject headings to identify the areas of discussion.

Terminal Section

The last major part of the body of a report is the terminal section. Like your introduction, it should emphasize the most important ideas in your report. So make your concluding section as strong as your introductory section. The most common functions of formal end sections to the body of your report are (1) to summarize the major points of your report, (2) to state the conclusions you came to, and (3) to state your recommendations.

1 *Summarize the major points.* Help your readers make sense of the mass of details presented in the text of your report by recalling the essential ideas covered. Just as the introduction offers a preview, the terminal section offers a postview.

2 *State your conclusions.* When your report draws conclusions from the results you have observed and discussed, use the terminal section to list the logical implications of your findings. Sometimes the end section combines a summary of the major points and the conclusions reached.

3 *State your recommendations.* Recommendations go a little further and suggest a course of action based on the conclusions. If you make recommendations throughout the report, you will probably summarize them here.

An informative report will restrict itself to a summary. For an analytical report, your terminal section will contain conclusions or recommendations, or both.

Of course, the terms summary, conclusions, and recommendations need not be used. If your purpose calls for them, just be sure the material is there. You may call them benefits, suggested course of action, merits of the plan, etc. Nor do conclusions and recommendations always have to be located last. There may well be times when you want to achieve immediate input and put your conclusions and recommendations at the beginning of the report, before the text.

Of course, you must have a title, and you may have numerous

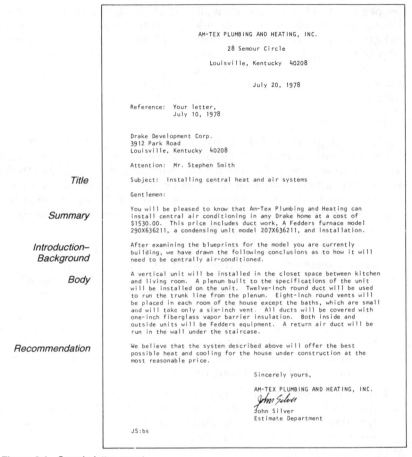

Title

Summary

Introduction–
Background

Body

Recommendation

Figure 2.1   Sample letter report

other sections, such as a title page, table of contents, or bibliography. These possible parts will be discussed in detail later. What we need now is a basic plan that can be adapted to most reports— whether it be the brief informal report or the longer formal report. Let's look at how this three-part plan adapts to standard types of report formats—letter form, memo form, and report form.

Letter Form

An informal report in letter form is addressed to a specific person who usually is not a part of the writer's own company. The letter includes the standard parts of a business letter: heading, date, inside address, salutation, body, complimentary close, and signature. (See Figure 2.1.) The letter may also include an attention line, a reference line, a subject line, typist's initials, and notice of enclosures and carbon copies mailed to others.

The title of the letter report in Figure 2.1 is included in the subject line. The body of the letter includes the content or text of the report, and it follows the three-part plan outlined.

Memorandum Form

The brief informal report may also be presented in the form of a memorandum. The memo report includes the standard parts of the memo plus the elements in the basic plan for a report. You will use a heading for TO, FROM, SUBJECT, and DATE. (See Figure 2.2.) You may possibly use REFERENCE. The title of the memo report in Figure 2.2 is in the subject line. The body of the memo includes the parts of the basic plan.

Standard Report Form

The standard report form is built on the basic plan. The longer report will usually include additional parts. The short report in Figure 2.3 illustrates the basic plan. The title page is shown along with the main ideas and headings, but supporting detail has been left out.

WRITE FOR YOUR READER'S LANGUAGE PACE

After you have started your reader in the right direction and prepared a design or road map that he can follow easily, your problem is to regulate your speed limit. Match your flow of information to your reader so that you can carry your reader at the language pace that he travels best. Too slow, and he will go to sleep or impatiently wander off. Too fast, and he will drop out from exhaustion. Too cumbersome and bumpy, and he will doubt your sincerity and competence.

To keep your reader with you, you must check three features of your language:

1 The limits of expansion
2 The limits of compression
3 The limits of difficulty

Let's look at each of these three features in detail.

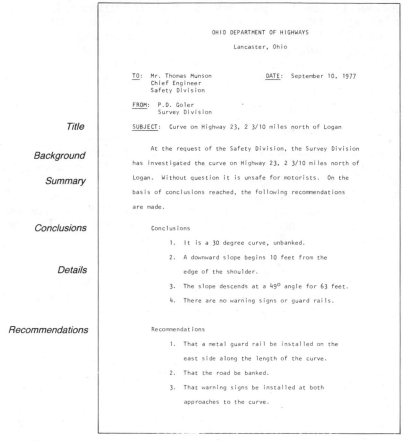

Figure 2.2   Sample memo report

Limits of Expansion

You must not travel too slowly. If you use long strings of words
to carry a few facts or ideas, your reader might impatiently toss
the report aside. Here is an example from a business report that
crawls along through a jungle of words.

From the very beginning of large-scale research programs on
automatic controls, there has been a need for simple but rapid
tests to evaluate these controls. These methods of evaluation

INVESTIGATION OF THE FEASIBILITY OF INSTALLING

XENO 250 ELECTRO-WELDERS IN PLACE

OF THE PRESENT HAND-SOLDERING JIGS

Prepared for

Gerald H. Thompson, Vice-President

General Electronics, Inc.

by

Carl Swanson, Director of Production

July 28, 1980

Figure 2.3 Sample standard report

INVESTIGATION OF THE FEASIBILITY OF INSTALLING

XENO 250 ELECTRO-WELDERS IN PLACE

OF THE PRESENT HAND-SOLDERING JIGS

Introduction

Purpose

The purpose of this examination is to determine whether or not the automatic welder recommended will be profitable to our company.

Conclusions

Conclusions

The hand-soldering process now in use is slow and costly. The output of the Xeno 250 Electro-Welder is over five times that of our present equipment. The cost of changeover would be recovered within six months.

Recommendations

Recommendations

1. Six Xeno 250 Electro-Welders should be purchased.

2. The entire division should be shut down for one week while the new equipment is being installed.

Text

Test of Present Equipment

After conference with the shop foreman and thorough personal checking, I found the hand-soldering process to be slow. It took two minutes for the worker to install and connect the components on one circuit board.

The cost of this hand-soldering process is $3.78 per circuit board.

Test of Recommended Equipment

With a Xeno 250 Electro-Welder, a worker can install the components of one circuit board in 27 seconds.

The cost of installing the components by this method is $2.76 per circuit board.

Cost

The Xeno 250 Electro-Welders cost $5500 each. Installation would cost an additional $400 each. This would bring the cost of all six welders to $35,400.

The increased speed would mean an increase of production which would bring in approximately $98,000 per year, making the welders pay for themselves within the first five months of operation.

Recommended Installation Procedure

Recommendations

I believe that because of the large amount of rewiring needed, it would be advisable to shut this department down for one week while the installation is being made.

must be easy to use and fast. They should also give a definite answer. What is needed is a method which says "yes" or "no" to a specific problem of using automatic controls. The current emphasis on these controls has posed a difficult problem in the field of their evaluation. We therefore need evidence which will give us a method of deciding when to use them.

Slow-paced writing such as this raises a knotty problem for the reader. When he reads it for the first time, he gets a vague impression that the writer is actually saying something significant. Then, because he is after ideas, he goes back to examine what has been said and finds that six sentences and 95 words have been used to express one simple idea:

Because of widespread use of automatic controls, we must develop a simple, fast method of evaluating their use.

Such slow-paced writing is a bane to fast business. Repetition, padding, and wordiness are its earmarks, and the reader's reaction could be an annoyed comment like "Why in the world doesn't he get to the point?" For the intelligent reader, no one can camouflage a scarcity of ideas under a barrage of words.

Check the following examples of verbal expansion and see how crisply they can be brought into proper limits:

SLOW-PACED	ACCELERATED
Your claim that the information submitted to you by us contained certain inaccuracies has prompted us to undertake a careful re-evaluation of the data submitted, with the result that the original information has been determined to be accurate in all instances.	We rechecked our data and found it to be accurate.
In a situation where inefficiency exists, it is normally characterized by supervisory procedures which tend to be lax.	Lax supervision breeds inefficiency.
Following an initial assessment of data availability and requirements, we will organize our data-gathering efforts related to requirements.	As soon as we find out what we need, we'll go out and get it.

A serious disadvantage of this technique is that it assumes the relationship between indicators and the quantity of interest will continue to be of the same nature in the future as it has been in the past.	A serious disadvantage of this technique is that it assumes no change.

The length of the sentences in the left-hand column above points to their wordy, meandering construction. But shorter sentences can also show the same weakness, even though we can't see it right away. For example, the following sentences, taken from a paragraph on lamp improvement, contain the same type of wordiness as do the previous examples.

> Because of improvements in design, the light output of incandescent lamps is certain to increase. This increase will be at least six percent for household sizes and 15 percent for industrial and commercial lighting. A better filament for household lamps will be mounted in an axial manner; high-wattage bulbs for the first time will have a filament which is axial and which is doubly coiled.

We can make the thought crisper and easier to understand by reducing the words 30%.

> Improved filament design will increase the light output of incandescent lamps at least 6% in household sizes and 15% in industrial and commercial sizes. The filament in household lamps will be mounted axially, while that in high-wattage lamps will be axial and double-coiled.

Eliminate the obvious. Some messages don't really carry any information. For example, if a normal person is told his own name, no information is transmitted. Likewise, statements such as the following contribute only words, not information, when included in reports.

> A swivel hitch can be ordered through normal procurement channels. When 300 of the 600 swivel hitches ordered have been manufactured, one can legitimately view the order as being half complete.

> The U.S. Census Bureau recently announced the fact that the United States has reached a population of 220 million. Clearly, this is a substantial growth from the 4 million people counted in the first census of the United States in 1790.

Travelers are people; the size of the population of the market areas directly influences the number of trips that will be taken. Increases in the population result in increases in the number of people who can travel. However, the size of the travel market is also dependent on the urge and ability of the population to travel. In brief, factors that have an impact on the size of the markets are population size, inclination to travel, appeal of destination, and restrictions on travel.

Limits of Compression

Another kind of poor pacing is trying to say too much in too few words. This is exceeding the speed limit. Whenever you see someone puzzling over how to work a sandwich machine or how to follow a receptionist's direction on how to get to somebody's office, the pacing may be at fault. It goes too fast for the reader or listener, it tries to say too much in too few words, or it wrongly assumes that everybody understands the shortcuts in language. Here is a typical example of pouring out ideas and facts too fast for the reader to grasp.

Our classic models have stainless steel, rubber-insulated fixtures for durability, economy, and easy maintenance, and convenient controls to cut down on installation costs and necessary adjustments. They operate on ac and dc current and incorporate the latest principles of electronic controls which means flexibility in their use, better adjustment of the thermal units, less chance of error, and reduced labor costs per unit of production, leading to greater profit margin and more accurate finished products.

Such speed will give your reader mental indigestion because it packs too many facts and ideas in too short a space. One idea or major fact to a sentence is a good rate of forward speed for most readers.

In the following sentence the thought is so compressed that the intended meaning is squeezed out and escapes. It leaves the reader bewildered.

India would like to use concentrated fertilizer to ease harbor congestion and inland transportation.

We think the emphasis is on "concentrated" and that fertilizer in compact form would reduce tonnage and thus traffic in the transportation system. But we are not sure. We need more details.

Likewise, the omission of key phrases in the following sentences creates confusion.

TOO FAST: The Elmsmere Tunnel, extending six miles under Springhill Harbor, represents a great engineering feat. It was dug from both ends simultaneously, and the two sections missed each other by only three inches.

REVISED: The Elmsmere Tunnel, extending six miles under Springhill Harbor, represents a great engineering feat. It was dug from both ends simultaneously, and the two sections were only three inches off center.

TOO FAST: A typical 161-kilovolt line has seven towers per mile with an insulator cost of three times $55, or about $1155 per circuit mile.

REVISED: A typical 161-kilovolt line has seven towers per mile, and each tower has three insulators valued at $55 each. Thus insulator costs are $1155 per circuit mile.

In writing you can control speed by forcing the reader to pause or stop whenever you wish. Useful devices are punctuation marks, short sentences, signal words, and paragraph breaks. Note how the following statement about helium runs on and on as one sentence without a break.

The advances made in the low-pressure liquefaction of helium based on the principles of work extraction to reduce the energy content and therefore the temperature of the gas by expansion engines with subsequent Joule–Thompson expansion make this type of process an attractive alternative.

The pace of the section can be easily slowed. Just break the one long sentence into several shorter ones, separate the units with strategic punctuation marks, and insert signal words like "In this process" and "thus."

Low-pressure liquefaction is an attractive process. In this process, which has been used successfully to liquefy helium, work is extracted from the system by expansion engines; thus, the energy content (and therefore the temperature) of the gas is reduced. The gas is then further cooled by Joule–Thompson expansion.

In the next example, the reader's progress has been stopped just before the significant idea in the sentence. The strategically placed "however" makes the two parts of the idea stand out.

The profits of the rubber companies do not depend, however, solely on tire sales.

Punctuation is the device used in the next example. The dash regulates the pace.

The problem of providing for recreation is not so much one of available space as it is one of allocation—and location.

A writer may also make his pace easier to follow by separating long paragraphs into shorter, more readable units. The following paragraph on packaging requires the reader to swallow a lot of information in one serving.

> Packaging is a major industry today. Although not classified as a separate industry, it has grown into a multi-million dollar enterprise offering a well-coordinated service to the entire economy. Packaging operations and raw materials were valued at $30 billion in 1978, or 3.6% of the Gross National Product for that year. The total volume of packaging materials shipped in 1978 amounted to $16.2 billion, with 45 different "industries" engaged in the manufacture of containers and packaging. At present, packaging is not growing as fast as the economy as a whole, and there are two basic reasons for the lag. First, the percentage of income spent on packaging is limited because consumers' needs for goods remain fairly constant and increases in income are usually spent on more services and leisure activities. Second, packagers have already exploited almost every possible new opportunity. Over 70% of all the packaging materials produced in 1978 were used for consumer goods. The food industry uses 45% of all packaging materials, the chemical industry—including cosmetics, soaps, toiletries, and most drugs—13%, and the remaining 42% is used in a wide range of other industries.

Since the paragraph developed two substantial ideas, it can easily be broken into two paragraphs for easier reading. The phrase "At present" begins the second thought. For even easier grasp, you could begin a third paragraph at "Second," adding a key word or two to make a topic sentence.

> Packaging is a major industry today. Although not classified as a separate industry, it has grown into a multi-million dollar enterprise offering a well-coordinated service to the entire economy. Packaging operations and raw materials were valued at $30 billion in 1978, or 3.6% of the Gross National Product

for that year. The total volume of packaging materials shipped in 1978 amounted to $16.2 billion, with 45 different "industries" engaged in the manufacture of containers and packaging.

At present, packaging is not growing as fast as the economy as a whole, and there are two basic reasons for the lag. First, the percentage of income spent on packaging is limited because consumers' needs for goods remain fairly constant and increases in income are usually spent on more services and leisure activities.

The second reason for the packaging lag is that packagers have already exploited almost every possible new opportunity. Over 70% of all the packaging materials produced in 1978 were used for consumer goods. The food industry uses 45% of all packaging materials, the chemical industry—including cosmetics, soaps, toiletries, and most drugs—13%, and the remaining 42% is used in a wide range of other industries.

Sometimes, brevity and compression of several ideas into one sentence or paragraph do produce effective results as a change of pace. Consider the following example:

> In Chilliwack, B.C., Mrs. Edna Fenton walked into police headquarters and asked the desk constable how she might get herself jailed to escape her angry husband, was advised to hit a cop, did, was.
>
> (*Time*, February 18, 1952, p. 116)

But generally you'll do well not to bewilder your reader by packing your sentences too tightly or by making him travel too fast. In writing, your reader is traveling with you through your ideas. When you arrive at something you want him to observe closely, slow down. Apply the brakes or the regulator by means of punctuation marks, short sentences and paragraphs, or signal words.

Limits of Difficulty

You are writing for your reader so you must use your reader's language. It should be obvious that if you use difficult words beyond his comprehension or vague words beyond tangible meaning, you will lose your reader. Likewise, if you use inflated, insincere language, you will turn him off. There are three useful rules for keeping your language within the limits of easy comprehension.

1 Use standard rather than technical language.
2 Use concrete and specific terms rather than vague generalities.
3 Be direct and natural rather than pompous and inflated.

Let's look at these guides in more detail.

Use Standard, Not Technical Language

The first rule of word selection is to use standard, familiar words. Of course the definition of "familiar words" differs from one person to another. What is everyday usage to some people is high-level talk to others. Know your reader and write for him. If he is a specialist, use specialist's language. If he is not a specialist, why throw up a barrier to communication? A doctor writing to doctors may refer to a "cerebral vascular accident." But he would do well to use *stroke* in writing to non-physicians. An accountant writing to accountants may effectively use *accounts receivable, liabilities,* and *surplus.* In writing to laymen, he might consider using *how much is owed the company, how much the company owes,* and *how much is left over.*

Shoptalk is the term applied to the specialist's language. Shoptalk denotes the private language of a particular profession, trade, or branch of science, technology, industry, or government. Predominantly technical, it is a mixture of figurative language, abbreviations, and conventional terms with unconventional meanings. Those in electronics, for instance, speak of *breadboard circuits, floating grids,* and *one-puff diodes.* Computer specialists use *macro codes, subroutines, algorithm,* and *FORTRAN.* Those in the chemical industry speak of plants coming *on stream;* economists, of *saturated markets* and *softness;* physicians, of *EKG's* and *PEG's;* those in the rubber industry of *factice* and *whizzing.*

Shoptalk is not necessarily an obstacle to communication. In many reports it is useful, in some even indispensable. To members of the same profession, industry, or other special group, special terminology can convey in a single word or phrase a concept or procedure that otherwise might require several sentences or paragraphs to explain. For example, to those familiar with computer language, the terminology in the following memorandum is not an obstacle. By compressing information into two short paragraphs, it speeds communication without clouding the message. But to those who don't know the language of computer technology and operation, the abbreviations and other shoptalk make the memo confusing.

When our two 2311 disk drives are installed in early July, we will reassign SYSRES, SYSLWK, SYS001, SYS002, and SYS003 to the disks on the second selector channel. This will improve our compilation and link edit times.

Under level 7 TOS device assignments it will be necessary to reassign SYS003 to 181 in order to do a four-way tape sort with input on 181 and output on 182.

Shoptalk, then, is only a barrier when the writer fails to consider the reader. If the writer has the slightest doubt about the reader's ability to understand the special technical vocabulary, he should not sacrifice clarity in the interest of speed. He should either express the concept in nontechnical language or define the jargon before using it routinely. Unless the terms are familiar to the reader, the statement is meaningless. Consider the following:

> Without the basic elements of transistors, valves, special klystrons, antennas, transformers, magnets, capacitors, resistors, connectors, traveling-wave tubes, meter movements, without benefit of wiring-systems technology, information handling, and printed circuit technology, and without knowing how electrons perform in circuits, electronics would certainly not exist as it does in the world today.

Whatever the thought originally intended, the writer seems to have buried it in shoptalk. Despite the inflated attempt at impressive language, all the writer has said is

> Without the elements of modern electronics there would be no modern electronics industry.

Although the thought is valid, it is obvious.

Although jargon is often a product of thoughtlessness and laziness, it is commonly used by writers who are trying to be profound. As a result, simple and straightforward concepts are needlessly overcomplicated by a code language that imitates the language of science.

> Let m_j denote the jth member of a string of lexemes; let C_N denote the substantive subcategory of the total lexeme inventory; let op(P,x) be an operation acting on a unitary lexeme to transpose it into a nonunitary lexeme; then we may state with a probability in excess of 0.95 that
>
> $$\text{if } E(m_j),\ m_j \supset C_{N'} \text{ then } \text{op}(P,m_j) = (m_j) + s.$$
>
> (In R. F. Stengel, "Jargoneering: Causes, Cases, Cure," *Design News*, October 12, 1966, p. 293.)

Without losing very much in translation, this learned mathematical exposition simply tells us what we already knew—that we form the plurals of most English nouns by adding "s."

Use Concrete and Specific Words Rather than Vague Generalities

Report writing which communicates with force and clarity is marked by concrete and specific words. Such words are the opposite of abstract and general words, which are fuzzy and vague. Concrete words stand for things the reader perceives—things he can see, touch, hear, taste, or smell. In writing up the results of an experiment, the chemist might say the "substance had a nauseating odor." He would communicate much more sharply if he said, "The hydrogen sulfide smelled like rotten eggs."

The specific word also makes a clearer image than the general word; for example, a "lathe-operator" instead of a "factory worker," a man's "gray pin-striped sharkskin suit" instead of a man's "garment." One of the best examples of the concrete and specific is the famous advertising claim that Ivory Soap is "99 44/100 percent pure." Not so many people would have been impressed with the words "Ivory Soap is very pure."

In the following lists, note how much more vivid the terms in the right-hand column are.

Abstract	Concrete
the majority	53%
in the near future	by Friday noon
a work-saving machine	does the work of eight men
a sizable profit	a 26% profit
good accuracy	pinpoint accuracy
the leading student	top student in a class of 120
light in weight	feather-light

Be Direct and Natural Rather than Pompous and Inflated

Your purpose is to give information and analysis to your reader. Don't try to impress with your ability and importance. You can sell yourself best by giving a clear, direct, substantial report. Some writers believe that long, involved sentences and many-syllable words will somehow impress the reader. But they are no substitute for direct, natural impression. Consider the example of the communications consultant being shown through the company offices by a vice president. When they came to the room which housed the company records, the consultant asked one of the file clerks, "How long do you keep things in these files?" The clerk answered, "Usually, we don't keep forms any longer than three years. Then we can either tear them up ourselves or give them to the janitor." The consultant turned to the vice president, "When we get back to your office, let's see if the Procedures Manual communicates any better."

Here is what the Manual said.

At the end of the established retention period, which is normally three years, mutilate the forms or carbons to be destroyed by tearing them into small bits or pieces or by shredding them, and dispose of the resulting waste in accordance with the procedures established for the Maintenance Department.

Whoever wrote the statement for the Procedures Manual was trying to make a fairly simple task sound impressive and complex. The words of the file clerk are a more effective explanation, because they try to express an idea, not impress a listener or reader.

EXERCISES AND PROBLEMS

1. What kind of information would you put in the first paragraph of a report on each of these subjects?
   a. The 10% decrease in sales at a branch store in a report to the manager of the main store.
   b. An investigation of the poor service in the company coffee shop in a report to the Personnel Manager.
   c. An analysis of three different makes of typewriters or copying machines, with the purpose of recommending purchase for office use.
2. Drawing upon your knowledge of your hometown or some other city you are familiar with, describe the appeals you would use to attract a new industry to locate a plant there. First prepare a list of appeals aimed at executives of the company, then a list aimed at their wives. Draw up a tentative structural pattern for the report.
3. Select a simple mechanism or tool involving a process that you know well, such as an opaque projector, a tape recorder, or a camera. Describe the mechanism or tell how it works:
   a. For a reader who knows little or nothing about it.
   b. For a reader who understands all the technical terms.
4. You are assistant manager of the regional division of Surety Insurance Company. Until the building for the new branch office is finished—in about nine months—the company plans to lease a particular suite of offices in the area. Ted Larkin, regional manager, has given you the job of inspecting the proposed partially furnished suite to see if it is adequate. There will be two secretary–typists and a field representative in the temporary facility. You will need a small reception area.
   Describe the office layout and make recommendations to Ted Larkin. You may wish to make a simple sketch or drawing. Don't forget lighting, window space, air-conditioning, and parking space. Be concrete and specific in your description.

5. Rewrite the following sentences to make them less pompous and more direct.

    a. This complete and definitive work was not written for lay-men, or for the man on the street, or for the average man, but it was intended for experts in the field of statistics.

    b. You will undoubtedly be interested to know that it has come to my attention through channels that I am unable to divulge because I am still verifying the data that a rival photographic studio will be opened close to ours.

    c. After a comprehensive survey of all the milk consumers in a certain New England city, it was found that the average daily consumption of milk per family in that city was less than two quarts per day.

    d. In response to your communication which was dated March 14, I can only say at this time that we shall have to take more time to make an investigation and to carry on the necessary research.

    e. The new handbook was written for the man who practices accounting, for the individual who runs his own business, for the man who keeps his own accounts, and, in short, for anyone who keeps financial records for himself, his company, or anyone else.

    f. Our each and every wish, then, should be to assist our customers in every way possible, to help them with those difficult problems which they have trouble in solving themselves, and to render every possible service so that we may both prosper mutually.

    g. This situation to which you referred in your letter of October 14 is in my judgment, if I may express a personal opinion, not only dangerous to our hope of expansion in the next year but also renders it practically impossible to enlarge the scope of our organization.

6. Change the following samples to make them easier to read and more appropriate to their purpose.

    a. In preparing the employee opinion report you asked for, we thought we would find out the answers by going directly to our employees. We will show you just what employees think by showing you (1) the 15 questions we asked and the answers, (2) the summary of these answers, (3) the methods we used in collecting and assembling the data, (4) our worksheets, graphs, and tally sheets, and (5) how we arrived at our conclusions. While our question-by-question analysis does not indicate any definite trends of opinion, we hope that you will find it useful. If there are any other conclusions or information you need, we shall be pleased to supply them.

b. It is requested, therefore, that you have the three carbons signed by you or your agent, notarized, and keeping one for your files, return one to us and send the other to the bank which is the transfer agent along with the stock certificate which must be signed by you and sent preferably by registered mail.

c. In this report our purpose is to direct the attention of all employees to the necessity for drastic changes in our precautions for attaining better safety measures. Statistical analysis of last year's lost-time accidents shows an increase of 5.1% over the preceding year and it becomes apparent that here has been a relaxation of our efforts in this respect. For that reason, certain new regulations as outlined below are recommended to correct this situation. After all, this is a subject which directly affects the welfare of every employee and we should, therefore, be able to expect complete cooperation. These new regulations, stated in the following paragraphs, should take effect immediately.

d. This is the report which you requested on June 6. Its subject is "The Need for a More Effective System of Recruiting College Graduates." It therefore deals with a matter of great importance to the Baker Company and all supervisory employees. For that reason, it should be read with care and especially because we have spent two months in interviews and assembling data. Last year, for example, we employed 12 college graduates against our projected needs, as you know, for 38. This shows the importance of the report and why something had to be done about it. That decision is not our prerogative since the authorization for our investigation asked us to institute "a fact-finding survey" as you will recall.

e. In answer to your request for information to send to our sales representatives about the development of Bensolide, I would say its chief advantages are its resiliency, its impermeability, and its durability. While its price is slightly higher than that of competitive products, these advantages more than offset the price factor, a fact which should be obvious to our sales representatives. With increased volume, it is entirely possible that our production costs can be reduced although this is contingent on further developments in the polymerization process. For the time being, thus, our representatives should stress the many uses of Bensolide in the home.

II

TOOLS OF EFFECTIVE REPORT WRITING

3
Building Your Ideas
Through Paragraphs

The basic unit of business reports is the paragraph. Your big idea, or investigation, or analysis is developed through a total report composed of several paragraphs, but the report builds one paragraph at a time. The paragraph is indeed an idea block. It is a single thought or main point developed so that the reader can grasp it clearly. We may think in sentences, and the sentence may state the minimum concept, but the paragraph is the group of sentences used to explain the idea, to open it up, to put it across.

Once you have signaled the topic of your paragraph, usually in the first sentence of your paragraph, logic and the reader demand that you support that *topic sentence.*

The idea must be developed enough to put the point across. There are two general kinds of materials for backing up the idea:

1 *Clarifying details* and examples explain or make clear a difficult or unknown idea so that the reader will understand. He can say, "I see what you mean."
2 *Confirming details,* such as reasons and facts, back up an opinion or debatable idea so that the reader will be persuaded. He can say, "I agree" or "There may be something to what you say."

For example, note the reader's expectation set up by the following topic statement from a report:

Local anesthesia can be produced through three sites of injection.

Even if only for review, the reader expects the three sites to be identified.

Consider another topic idea and the expectation it sets up.

The Havensport plant should be relocated.

Here the reader's natural question is "Just why should the Havensport plant be relocated?" And the report writer is obligated to give reasons in the rest of the paragraph.

Let's follow through on the expectations set up by the topic ideas just given and see how a whole idea block expands into a paragraph. Note the mental satisfaction it gives you to have the three injection sites explained and to know the reasons for relocating the plant.

Local anesthesia can be produced through three sites of injection. Infiltration is the injection of the drug into the tissues. Block anesthesia is produced by the injection of the drug around the main nerves leading to the operation area. These main nerves are blocked from transmitting sensory impulses. Spinal anesthesia results from the injection of the drug into the space surrounding the spinal cord. Because spinal anesthesia causes complete insensitivity to pain and muscular relaxation to the part of the body below the site of injection, it can be used only below the level of the cord that gives rise to spinal nerves aiding in breathing and heart action.

The Havensport plant should be relocated. First, building rock in the Havensport area is questionable. The failure of recent geological explorations in the area confirms suspicions that the Havensport deposits are nearly exhausted. Second, distances from Havensport to major consumption areas make transportation costs unusually high. Obviously, any savings in transportation costs will add to company profits. Third, obsolescence of much of the equipment at the Havensport plant makes this an ideal time to relocate. New equipment could be moved directly to the new site, and obsolete equipment could be scrapped in the Havensport area. These reasons seem sufficient to warrant the move.

Some kinds of reports, such as annual reports and public relations reports, may use very short sentences, even one-sentence paragraphs. Since such reports go beyond informational and analytical purposes, they make use of persuasive and emotional appeals. The quick grasp and appeal of the short sentence and paragraph are often preferred to the sustained concentration required by a long paragraph.

If your report on "Facts You Need to Buy Gold" is a promotional report going outside the company, aimed at encouraging prospective gold investors to use your company's services, then your paragraphs should be short, like this.

The less gold you can afford to buy at a time, the less likely you are to break even. What you'll have to pay above the quoted market price to cover all the costs of buying, holding, and selling gold will vary with the amount you buy. These costs are proportionally higher for small purchases. If you buy less than, say, 50 ounces, the quoted price of gold bullion probably will have to rise 25 to 35 percent for you to recover your total buying and selling costs.

That means that if you buy gold when the quoted price is $180 an ounce, the price will probably have to rise to the range of $225 to $240—an increase of $45 to $60 an ounce—before you can recover all your costs of buying and selling.

If you buy more, the buying and selling costs will be proportionally lower, and you probably will be able to recover your costs with a smaller increase in the quoted price. The less you buy, the greater the drawbacks of gold as an investment.

(Bank of America, "Gold: Facts You Need to Know Before You Buy Gold," December 1974, p. 3)

But if your report is for your boss, who is considering the feasibility of the company's investing in gold as a hedge against inflation, then your data will build ideas that require clusters of sentences.

The less gold you can afford to buy at a time, the less likely you are to break even. What you'll have to pay above the quoted market price to cover all the costs of buying, holding, and selling gold will vary with the amount you buy. These costs are proportionally higher for small purchases. If you buy less than, say, 50 ounces, the quoted price of gold bullion probably will have to rise 25 to 35 percent for you to recover your total buying and selling costs. That means that if you buy gold when the quoted price is $180 an ounce, the price will probably have to rise to the range of $225 to $240—an increase of $45 to $60 an ounce—before you can recover all your costs of buying and selling. If you buy more, the buying and selling costs will be proportionally lower, and you probably will be able to recover your costs with a smaller increase in the quoted price. The less you buy, the greater the drawbacks of gold as an investment.

Note how well the idea block ties together with the final sentence echoing and clinching the opening sentence.

The usual report is a decisive document. It was likely asked for. Decisions are to be based on it—problems solved, directions changed. The idea presented must be valid, clearly explained, and fully backed up. Length and a jumble of words and sentences are not enough. For example, here is a paragraph poorly designed and illogically developed.

The manager with foresight is a teacher too. While college professors frequently lack business experience, they have had experience in teaching. Managers in business, however, do not normally think of themselves as teachers, but they are. Many a young man starting his career wishes that his first supervisor had been a better teacher. His whole career might have been different if only the supervisor had learned to train him properly. In fact, business wastes time, money, and future potential by not learning to teach.

From the topic idea of managers as teachers, the paragraph shifts to comments on college professors, to opinions of young men in business, to waste in business.

Now read the paragraph after it has been given design and development.

The manager with foresight will also be a teacher. Actually, he has two major functions—training an understudy for his job and helping young employees to start their careers effectively. In both these functions, he is essentially a teacher. By learning to instruct those he supervises, he can save time for himself and money for the company. In training an adequate understudy for himself, he is actually preparing himself for greater responsibilities in the future; in helping young men to start their careers properly, he is developing the potential human resources of the company.

The paragraph is designed with consistency of viewpoint, logical analysis of the two functions of the manager, and adequate development of each of the functions.

A paragraph is not just an assemblage of words and sentences, any more than a display window is a heap of objects tossed in from the salesfloor or an automobile engine is a pile of various pieces of metal. The impressive display window, the functioning engine, and the effective report are all thoughtfully designed units carefully put together from specific materials.

The main purpose of this chapter is to get you to analyze the design of paragraphs. Use your pencil; mark up and dissect paragraphs. When you discover that a paragraph has parts and structure and that it builds from a central idea, then you will gain skill at developing your own paragraphs and building them into a clear and effective report.

USING THE THREE KINDS OF MATERIALS

The usual paragraph is made up of three distinct kinds of materials. There are central ideas, details to clarify or confirm the ideas, and devices to connect the parts. If you distinguish these kinds of materials, you can keep control of things as you construct a paragraph.

KINDS OF MATERIALS IN A PARAGRAPH: CHECKLIST

Ideas

These are the points you want to make or the information you want to get across.

Topic sentence or topic idea
Restatement
Summary
Clincher

Supporting Material

This is kind of material that will explain, clarify, validate, or undergird the central idea of the paragraph. These are the workhorses. Here are some of the common kinds.

Statistics	Facts
Examples	Qualifications
Definitions	Illustrations
Explanations	Specific instances
Analogies	Points of comparison

Anecdotes	Points of contrast
List of kinds or types	List of causes and effects
List of component parts	A sequence of causes and
A sequence of events	effects
Reasoning	A sequence of steps or stages

Connective Devices

These are words and phrases that connect and show relationships between parts; they are the bridges, the links, the glue. Here are some common kinds.

Repetition of key words
Synonyms
Pronouns and demonstratives (such as *this* and *that*)
Transitional expressions (such as *first, next, however*)
Restatement
Summary
Logical arrangement of parts

The following paragraph illustrates the three kinds of materials that make up the usual paragraph.

Idea: topic sentence   In psychology, behavior refers to any overt action on the part of an animal organism. The action

Supporting material: may be simple or complex. At one extreme, it may
qualification
Connection be blinking an eye, flexing a finger, tilting the
Supporting material: head, swallowing some water, taking a step, utter-
examples ing a sound, or putting a mark on a sheet of paper.

Connection At the other extreme, it may be singing a song
on a television show, attempting a ten-foot putt
on the eighteenth hole of a golf tournament, bar-
gaining for an automobile on a used car lot, taking

Supporting material: a final examination in a freshman history course,
examples painting a still life in an attic studio, or piloting
an ocean liner from New York to Liverpool. In

Idea and connec- psychology, behavior is used to designate an overt
tion: restatement action.

(William S. Ray, *The Science of Psychology,*
Macmillan, New York, 1974)

It will be helpful to look at each of these three kinds of materials in detail.

Central Idea

An effective paragraph is usually built around one central idea with enough details to put the idea across. This controlling idea is often put into a single sentence called the *topic sentence*. It usually comes first or near the beginning of the paragraph, but it may be placed in the middle or at the end. The topic sentence may be implied rather than stated, especially in a chronological account. Occasionally the paragraph will be built on a sequence of ideas, and the topic idea will progress throughout the paragraph.

Three principles are especially helpful in framing an effective controlling idea: (a) use a single central idea per paragraph; (b) place the topic sentence first; (c) don't let the supporting material divert you from your idea.

Use a Single Central Idea Per Paragraph

To convey information in easy-to-grasp units, the report writer must be sure that each paragraph contains just one main idea. All other thoughts should grow out of the main idea and expand upon it until the paragraph is factually and logically complete. Note in the following paragraph how each sentence contributes to the unity of the whole by advancing the main idea.

The first finding of our survey of new product development was that records and reports are hopelessly inadequate. The strongest impression created by the survey was that it's difficult to know who's winning the game if no one is keeping score. We had assumed that the divisions maintained reasonably systematic records of work progress, costs, time requirements, and results of new product development. We found, however, that all but two did not. As a result, we had to delay our analysis while the divisions tried to pull together information from memory and from various files. Moreover, when this information was finally supplied, no one could vouch for its accuracy or completeness. Our analysis, therefore, reflects these shortcomings.

In contrast, here is a paragraph that does not stay with a single idea. Instead, it just piles one idea on another without backing up or clarifying any. As a report on information, it is a fraud. It is a paragraph only in appearance. It is a series of undeveloped topic sentences, and thus just a group of one-sentence paragraphs run together to look like a paragraph with an idea development. Actually, there has been little sorting or arranging of thoughts.

About 92% of the power consumed in this country is generated and distributed by the hundred largest utilities. The total number of electric utilities is about 3800. Electric power consumption has been growing steadily at a rate of about 8% a year. This growth is expected to continue into the future. Economics associated with larger generation facilities are producing a trend to network interchange of power and to higher transmission and distribution voltages; 500-kV and 700-kV lines are currently being installed and will be installed in the next few years, and 345-kV lines have been growing faster relative to lower-voltage lines over the past several years.

Another way the report writer can throw the reader off the track is to start with one idea, then abruptly shift to another and never get back to the first. In the following paragraph, the reader expects the discussion to relate somehow to chemical treatment of wood and the use of surface coatings. When it does not, he becomes confused. If the author intended the first sentence to be the topic sentence, the rest of the discussion is irrelevant.

Chemical treatment of wood, and the use of surface coatings, may help the forest products industry hold its present markets and regain some old ones. Last year, some 30 billion board feet of lumber were used in the United States, about the same as in 1920. Per capita consumption actually decreased over the interval from 482 to about 240 board feet. Industrial uses, once a major outlet for lumber, account for only about 10% of consumption; building and construction applications are now the largest single use, taking 72% of the total.

Place the Topic Sentence First

Because of the special way most readers read reports, you will generally do well to place the topic sentence at the beginning of the paragraph. By posting this sign in the most conspicuous position, you help the reader who wants only your main ideas, without supporting material, as well as the reader who reads for all the detail. Your topic sentences sort the details into logical units for both kinds of readers.

Here is a typical paragraph with the topic sentence placed first as a signal to what follows.

Many prehistoric finds suggest attitudes of affection. A Stone Age tomb contains the body of a woman holding a young child in her arms. Caves in North America that were occupied some 9,000 years ago have yielded numerous sandals of different sizes; those of children's sizes are lined with rabbit fur, as if to express a special kind of loving care for the youngest members of the community.

(René Dubos, "The Humanizing of
Humans," *Saturday Review/World*,
December 14, 1974, p. 77)

However, it is possible to place the topic sentence somewhere else and still be clear and effective. In this chronological account, the topic sentence is last, after being prepared for by the anecdote.

There is a story, possibly apocryphal, about a psychologist who shut a chimpanzee in a soundproof room filled with dozens of mechanical toys. Eager to see which playthings the ape would choose when he was all alone in this treasure house, the scientist bent down on his knees and put his eye to the keyhole. What he saw was one bright eye peering through from the other side of the aperture. If this anecdote isn't true, it certainly ought to be, for it illustrates the impossibility of anticipating exactly what an animal will do in a test situation.

(Frank A. Beach, "Can Animals
Reason?," *Natural History*,
March 1948, p. 116)

Sometimes an idea may be split into two or more parts and progress through the paragraph, with supporting material between the parts. This design is especially useful with a series of causes or events or with contrasting ideas.

On paper our parties look like armies. They have the form of a pyramid, with millions of party members and thousands of local party officials at the base, and national party heads at the top. Like the army, they have a hierarchy of leaders and followers, running from the national committee at the top down to town and precinct committees at the bottom. *Actually, the analogy is a false one.* The essence of an army is discipline from the top down. This sort of central discipline is precisely what our parties lack. They have been well described as "loose associations of state and local organizations, with very little national machinery and very little national cohesion."

(James Burns and James Peltason,
Government by the People, Prentice Hall,
Englewood Cliffs, N.J., 1952)

Knowing how your reader reads is important in constructing paragraphs. If you even suspect that your reader skims, you should not risk creating a paragraph in which the apparent topic sentence is counterbalanced by another thought which carries the discussion beyond the boundaries of the apparent topic sentence, and may even contradict it. Consider, for example, this paragraph, which shifts at "Unfortunately":

> Much effort has been given to planning land use near airports. Zoning has been advanced to ensure that surrounding development is compatible with airport operations. Metropolitan planning has been encouraged so that public improvements such as highways will be well located to serve airports. Unfortunately, these planning measures have not succeeded very well. Few metropolitan planning agencies have completed comprehensive plans, and most of these are not binding on constituent jurisdictions or state highway departments. Moreover, showing a site for a new airport on a master plan does not reserve the land; in fact, it may stimulate development in anticipation of the airport.

If there is a chance of being unclear, rebuild the paragraph. The writer could have divided the thought into two paragraphs or expressed the topic thought in a sentence which included the counterbalancing idea. In either case he would not risk conveying only a portion of the thought to the hasty reader who glances merely at the first sentence or two in a paragraph. If he chose to divide the paragraph, a new paragraph could begin with "Unfortunately, these planning measures. . . ." If he chose to combine the two thoughts, the paragraph could begin this way:

> Much effort has been given to planning land use near airports, but it has not succeeded very well. Zoning has been advanced to ensure that surrounding developments are compatible with airport operations, and metropolitan planning has been encouraged so that public improvements such as highways will be well located to serve airports. Unfortunately, however, few metropolitan planning agencies . . .

Don't Let the Supporting Material Divert You from Your Idea

Sometimes digression begins innocently enough as an attempt to clarify the topic idea by an analogy or supporting detail. Sometimes, however, the writer becomes captivated by the lively detail and deserts the very idea he is developing.

The kinds of people who must work together in establishing community colleges—educators, local officials, state legislators, and citizen's groups—often do not realize that they are operating under different sets of assumptions about the nature of the college. Failure to recognize that their premises are different often creates the same kinds of conflicts that have sprung up for years between state legislatures and state universities over the issue of academic freedom. One manifestation of academic freedom is criticism of existing social and political systems. Legislators and industrialists are unwilling to allow universities to train "subversives." Proponents of academic freedom, however, regard society as an abstraction that has no validity apart from the individuals who are its constituent elements; and since social arrangements are designed to benefit the individual, he has the right to criticize their shortcomings.

Such digressions are not a problem of writing skills but of thinking skills. If material in your paragraphs seems irrelevant to you, rethink your topic idea, and stick with it. Don't let supporting material or other ideas get you off the track.

Other Kinds of Idea Sentences

Although we have been discussing the all-important topic sentence for paragraph control, there are other kinds of sentences you may use in your paragraph to express ideas. These are signal or groundlaying sentences, restatements, summaries, and clincher statements. These can be very useful in giving design to a paragraph and thus promoting the clarity and force of your idea development. Here are some examples of different kinds of idea sentences.

Ground Layer and Restatement

Ground layer *Topic sentence* *Restatement*	This is the real crux of the issue. Like all environmental concerns, marine pollution boils down to a question of austerity—global austerity. It's a problem of willingness to make do with less. Two cars in every garage, even only one, means continued pollution of the seas. Or, as one marine biologist in Boston put it, "The solution is really very

simple. You've just got to be prepared to walk
to work."

(Richard Bernstein, "Chaos at Sea,"
Saturday Review/World,
November 20, 1970, p. 16)

Restatement

When, in the spring, a young man chances to look up and exclaim,
"What a gorgeous blonde!" it should be recognized that his words
tell us precious little about the young lady to whom he is presumably
referring, but that they do tell us something about himself. He is
projecting; the "gorgeousness" is inside him. When a hospital patient,
somewhat the worse for imbibing, tells us in agitated tones that
there are pink elephants on the wall, he is not telling us anything
about the wall; he is informing us of his own internal state. He is
projecting; the pink pachyderms are in his own head. When a friend
greets you with the cheery announcement that it is a fine day, he
is not informing you about the weather; he is only telling you that
he has had a good night's rest and a satisfactory breakfast. He is
projecting; the "fineness" is not of the day so much as it is of his
own body. When a man says ruefully, "I didn't know it was loaded,"
he is informing you that he sometime previously projected his own
notions about a gun into the gun.

(Wendell Johnson, *People in
Quandaries,* Harper & Row, New York, 1946)

Summary Statement—Clincher

Standardization and the collective utilization of energy have had
the effect of knitting the population of a huge community together.
A metropolis is a colossal organism, which is composed of such elements as skyscraper office buildings, apartment houses and hotels,
subways, telephones, water and gas mains. Millions in homes, factories, and offices are enmeshed in the hidden wires of a single electric
powerhouse. Let an accident occur like one of about 20 years ago
which crippled a substation on New York's East Side, and lights
go out, elevators stop running, ice cubes are no longer made in
refrigerators, vacuum cleaners are impotent, candles have to be
burned, homes and offices are cut off from one another, each fending
for itself. Without the telephone the skyscraper would be impossible;
with the telephone metropolitan cities like London, Paris, New York,

and Chicago develop into regions. Some remnants of sectionalism remain in the United States, but when ten million persons scattered between San Francisco and New York or St. Paul and New Orleans listen to the same radio program or when one friend in Boston telephones another in New Orleans to wish him a Merry Christmas the effect cannot but be one of unification.

(Waldemar Kaempffert, *Explorations in Science,* Viking Press, New York, 1953)

A paragraph should be so developed that it ends not merely with a restatement of the topic thought, but with a conclusion which pins down the topic thought. The resolution doesn't have to be specifically stated, any more than the topic thought has to be stated explicitly, but the reader should know what the point is and be convinced that it has been made clearly, completely, and conclusively.

Supporting Material

After you have clarified a central controlling idea for a pargraph, you must say enough about the idea to put it across. So the next step in writing is to select materials, according to your purpose and the best methods of accomplishing that purpose.

In selecting and arranging materials to develop your idea, you are likely to have one of two purposes in mind for your reader— *to inform* or *to persuade.* If your purpose is to inform, as in an informative report, then you must use clarifying details, such as definition, analytical parts, descriptive details, explanations, examples, analogies, illustrations, and so on. If your purpose is to persuade, as in an analytical or interpretive report, then you will make use of evidence, statistics, specific instances, examples, reasons, reasoning, and so on. The materials for the two purposes overlap, just as the two purposes often combine. The point is to gather appropriate material to back up your idea.

Inform

In the following paragraph, in order to inform, the author clarifies by using definition, analysis into types, and examples. At the end of the paragraph we are ready to say, "Yes, you have made it clear. I understand what you mean by 'needs'."

Topic sentence: def-
inition of needs
Type: physical
3 examples

Type: nonphysical

5 examples

By "needs" I mean the inherent demands that men make because of their constitution. Needs for food and drink and for moving about, for example, are so much a part of our being that we cannot imagine any condition under which they would cease to be. There are other things not so directly physical that seem to me equally engrained in human nature. I would mention as examples the need for some kind of companionship; the need for exhibiting energy, for bringing one's powers to bear upon surrounding conditions; the need for both cooperation with and emulation of one's fellows for mutual aid and combat alike; the need for some sort of aesthetic expression and satisfaction; the need to lead and to follow; etc.

(John Dewey, "Does Human Nature Change?," *The Rotarian,* February 1938, p. 8)

Convince

In the following paragraph, in order to convince, the writer validates his opinion by citing specific instances which show that his generalization covers a widespread occurrence.

Topic sentence:
opinion
Specific instance

As the United States comes up against severe shortages in a lengthening catalog of raw materials, the economics of recycling used products becomes increasingly attractive. In Fort Worth, Texas, for instance, the price of scrap paper has risen from $9.25 a ton to $23.00. By salvaging for resale more of the paper that makes up some 50 percent of its municipal garbage, Public Works Director Jack Graham expects to increase the city's paper profits from $50,000 a year to $250,000.

(Anthony Wolff, "World Progress Report," *Saturday Review/World,* January 12, 1974, p. 8)

The paragraph on p. 48 recommending the relocation of the Havensport plant has the purpose of persuasion. To support his recommendation, the analyst cites three very tangible and convincing reasons. In contrast, here is a paragraph that has appearance only, not function. It is just a group of sentences surrounded by white space with no idea given development. It poses the topic idea in the form of a question, but the following material does not answer the question. Instead, it consists of nothing more than a series of nonstatements.

Will it be profitable to build a recycle reactor for energy production? For countries like England it would seem necessary; for others like Canada, which has plenty of natural uranium, the answer was quite evident. For all others, it seemed a matter of national economy and thus a detailed study would be required in each case.

Here is another paragraph which has only the appearance of persuasive force. The writer ends with a strong "therefore," apparently convinced that he has developed the thought powerfully and logically. Actually, however, three topics are introduced, but none is developed. Just restating the first topic at the end is not enough to rescue the paragraph.

The cause of most automobile accidents is mental failure rather than mechanical. In many instances, drivers travel at such high speeds and so close to other cars that their reflexes are not fast enough to avoid a collision when the car in front stops suddenly. "Tailgating" is all too frequent in heavy traffic. Although our road construction and improvement programs have been greatly expanded to relieve traffic congestion, they have not been able to keep up with increased use of automobiles. Moreover, with cutbacks in passenger service on railroads in some sections of the country, automobile travel will undoubtedly continue to increase. Therefore, drivers will have to be even more alert in order to avoid accidents.

What the reader wants is evidence of "mental failure." Slow reflexes are cited in sentence 2, but we need more on mental failure—statistics on sleep, drunkenness, poor eyesight, emotional disturbance, poor judgment, etc. By sentence 4, we are off on a new topic.

In contrast to the two preceding paragraphs which do not clearly develop an idea, check the following paragraph with its solid design and support. After a firm opening topic sentence, the writer undergirds his assertion by a fitting illustration, by contrast, and by reasoning. He clinches his argument with an apt quotation. The reader is inclined to say, "I think you've got something there."

And so, precisely because the businessman's drive for profitability is identical with his drive for lower costs, his profit is a pretty good measure of social welfare. Suppose two companies make similar products and sell them at about the same price. Company A nets $10 million, but Company B nets twice as much because it is run by a tough crew of hardheaded, no-nonsense, endlessly striving managers motivated by abundant bonuses—the kind of men corporate critics often like to describe as s.o.b.'s. To an individual consumer, the two companies might seem to offer little choice. But so far as society at large is concerned, Company B has done a much better job, because it has used $10 million less of our resources, i.e., raw material and manpower, in doing the same job. So, obviously, the s.o.b.'s have been better for society than easygoing and irresolute managers would have been. As the Lord remarked of Faust, "He who strives endlessly, him we can redeem."

> (Gilbert Burck, "The Hazards of Corporate Responsibility," *Fortune Magazine*, June 1973, p. 214)

Another writer uses several methods to form a basis for his topic idea—that certain groups are "barriers in the way of a workable world" and will have to become less exclusive. He blends definition, contrast, illustration, and causal analysis in a tight design. Note the definition opening sentence, the restatement towards the end ("will have to be softened . . . generalized"), and the powerful final clincher sentence.

Topic sentence	Clubs, fraternities, nations—these are the beloved barriers in the way of a workable world, these will have to surrender some of their rights and
Definition	some their ribs. A "fraternity" is the antithesis of *fraternity*. The first (that is, the order or organiza-
Contrast	tion) is predicated on the idea of exclusion; the second (that is, the abstract thing) is based on a feeling of total equality. Anyone who remembers back to his fraternity days at college recalls the
Illustration	enthusiasts in his group, the rabid members, both old and young, who were obsessed with the mystical charm of membership in their particular order. They were usually men who were incapable of genuine brotherhood or at least unaware of its implications. Fraternity begins when the exclusion formula is found to be distasteful. The effect of any organization of a social and brotherly nature

Cause and effect is to strengthen rather than to diminish the lines which divide people into classes; the effect of states and nations is the same, and eventually these lines will have to be softened, these powers will have to be generalized. It is written on the wall that *Restatement* this is so. I'm not inventing it, I'm just copying *Clincher* it off the wall.

(E. B. White, *One Man's Meat*, Gollancz, London, 1943)

Many specific methods and materials may be used to develop the idea of the paragraph. Some of these are statistics, lists, examples, illustrations, definitions, points of constrast, and reasoning. Check the list on p. 51. Use any of these and others. The principle is to use enough definite material to make your idea clear to your readers or to persuade them of its validity. Formulate your central idea clearly. Then build your paragraph under it.

Connective Devices

Not only must your paragraph have a clear central idea and sufficient supporting material, it must also have tight connections between the parts. The relationships between the parts must be clear, smooth, and logical. If your reader cannot follow the direction of thought, of course you will lose him. There are two main ways to achieve a smooth flow of thought in your paragraphs: (a) a logical sequence of ideas and (b) the use of transitional devices such as key words, repetition, parallel structure, and transitional signals.

A Logical Sequence of Ideas

There are several common ways to arrange the ideas and sentences of a paragraph in logical order. Depending on your subject and supporting material, you can move in (1) a time sequence or (2) a spatial sequence. You can move (3) towards a climax, from least important to most important. You can move (4) from general to particular or (5) from particular to general. Or you can move (6) from the familiar to the unfamiliar. You may begin (7) with a general statement which is then supported by specific details, or, in reverse, you may begin (8) with a series of details and conclude with the generalizing or summarizing statement.

The following paragraph on "Learning in Animals" is built on an order of climax, moving from the least important idea to the most important: ant, earthworm, rat, cat, and higher apes. Note the disjointed effect if the sentence on cats were to be placed second, between the ant and the earthworm.

> An ant cannot purposefully try anything new, and any ant that accidentally did so would be murdered by his colleagues. It is the ant colony as a whole that slowly learns over the ages. In contrast, even an earthworm has enough flexibility of brain to enable it to be taught to turn toward the left or right for food. Though rats are not able to reason to any considerable degree, they can solve such problems as separating round objects from triangular ones when these have to do with health or appetite. Cats, with better brains, can be taught somewhat more, and young dogs a great deal. The higher apes can learn by insight as well as by trial and error.
>
> (George R. Harrison, "How the Brain
> Works," *Atlantic Monthly*,
> September 1956, p. 58)

An order of visual space is useful when a writer wishes to report what he or she has observed. The movement of the paragraph would follow the movements of the observer. The following paragraph begins by giving us a front view of some station buildings. Then it describes the roofs as seen from a distance. Next we move closer to identify the separate buildings. From there we focus on the hut and move closely enough to touch the eaves and windows to crawl inside. Once inside, the writer notes the floor and furnishings and finally narrows his observation to just one corner of the room.

> The station buildings were long, low huts, made of sun-dried, mud-colored bricks, laid up without mortar (*adobes*, the Spaniards call these bricks, and the Americans shorten it to *'dobies*). The roofs, which had no slant to them worth speaking of, were thatched and then sodded or covered with a thick layer of earth, and from this sprung a pretty rank growth of weeds and grass. It was the first time we had ever seen a man's front yard on top of his house. The buildings consisted of barns, stableroom for twelve or fifteen horses, and a hut for an eating-room for passengers. This latter had bunks in it for the station-keeper and a hostler or two. You could rest your elbows on its eaves, and you had to bend to get in at the door. In place of a window there was a square hole about large enough for a man to crawl through, but this had no glass in it. There was no flooring, but the ground was packed hard. There was no stove, but the fireplace served all needful purposes. There were

no shelves, no cupboards, no closets. In the corner stood an open sack of flour, and nestling against its base were a couple of black and venerable tin coffee-pots, a tin tea-pot, a little bag of salt, and a side of bacon.

(Mark Twain, *Roughing It,* Harper &
Bros., New York, 1913)

Study the logical structure of this paragraph on "business jargon." The opening question, "Why," makes the reader look forward to the answer. First comes a statement of general reasons, then a narrowing down to a specific reason: status. Then status is amplified to describe first the man with insecure status and then the man with secure status.

Why do people who in private talk so pungently often write so pomp-ously? There are many reasons: tradition, the demands of time, care-lessness, the conservative influence of the secretary. Above all is the simple matter of status. Theorem: the less established the status of a person, the more his dependence on jargon. Examine the man who has just graduated from pecking out his own letters to declaim-ing them to a secretary and you are likely to have a man hopelessly intoxicated with the rhythm of business. Conversely, if you come across a blunt yes or no in a letter, you don't need to glance further to grasp that the author feels pretty firm in his chair.

(William H. Whyte, "The Language of
Business," *Fortune Magazine,*
November 1950, p. 115)

Signals of Movement

With a complex idea, the logical movement can be made easy to follow by certain words which signal the movement. The central idea of the paragraph that follows is that freedom of speech occurs "only when opinions are expounded in the same hall to the same audience": a heavy idea, but the writer carries you along by certain transitional signals.

If the democratic alternative to the totalitarian one-way broadcasts is a row of separate soapboxes, then I submit that the alternative is unworkable, is unreasonable, and is humanly unattractive. It is above all a false alternative. It is not true that liberty has developed among civilized men when anyone is free to set up a soapbox, is free to hire a hall where he may expound his opinions to those who are willing to listen. On the contrary, freedom of speech is established to achieve its essential purpose only when different opinions are expounded in the same hall to the same audience.

> (Walter Lippmann, "The Indispensable Opposition," *Atlantic Monthly*, August 1939, p. 186)

Try underlining the signal words in the paragraph and see how clear the logical movement is.

If

then

It is

above all   It is not true

when

On the contrary

only when

Signals of movement are often more mechanical than the organic, logical structure of the thought pattern and can often be added during the final editing of the paragraph without much rewriting. If the writer, however, does not put in the signals, his reader may be lost. Concerned mainly with developing ideas in the first draft, writers often concentrate on paragraph unity and pay little attention to coherence. There is nothing wrong with this method as long as they put in the necessary traditional signals during revision. When they fail to do so, their reports may contain paragraphs like the following:

> Several factors may keep Colburn Company from entering the new product area. The company is not convinced that its already busy sales force could handle the additional work. It does not want to increase its sales force. Its sales costs are already quite high. Its R & D staff may not be able to devote adequate time to the new area. The staff is hard pressed to perform all the work necessary on existing products. Recently the department was almost halved. Some six senior members left the company. Further work on new products is unlikely. The R & D staff may well have to be built up just to handle the necessary work on existing products.
> Benton, Inc. already manufactures products quite similar to the product under development. Its sales force could sell the new product along with the current line without much

additional effort. The company needs to expand its product line somewhat. Some of its products are being replaced by synthetic devices. Benton's development efforts on this product are more advanced than Colburn's. It stands to lose more if it discontinues work in this area. It wants to keep its large R & D staff busy. It wants to maintain its reputation for technological leadership. Benton is much more likely than Colburn to develop the product.

At first reading, the paragraphs may seem clear and easy to read because of the simplicity of the sentence structure. Simplicity alone, however, does not guarantee clarity. For example, the hasty reader might think that the first paragraph offers at least six reasons why Colburn Company is reluctant to enter new product areas. A more careful reader, however, may recognize that there are not six reasons. Actually, the paragraph gives three basic reasons for Colburn's reluctance. What appears as additional reasons is intended as elaboration on the basic reasons.

The reader also may misunderstand the first sentence in the second paragraph. He might assume that Benton, Inc. is likely to offer such strong competition that Colburn Company would be unwise to enter the market. As he reached the end of the paragraph, however, he might become less sure of the original interpretation. The ending of the second paragraph merely *implies* that Benton will enter the market, but this idea should be *stated explicitly* because market entry is the key thought of the comparison in both paragraphs. If the writer had reviewed his draft and added helpful signals, he could have made the paragraphs clearer, more emphatic, and more readable, as shown below.

Several factors may keep Colburn Company from entering the new product area. *First,* it is not convinced that its already busy sales force could handle the additional work. It does not want to expand the sales force, *however, because* sales costs are already high. *Second,* its R & D staff may not be able to devote adequate time to the new area; *in fact,* the staff is hard pressed to perform all the work necessary on existing products. Recently the department was almost halved *when* six senior members left the company. *Consequently,* further work on the new product is unlikely. *Instead,* the R & D staff may well have to be built up just to handle the work on existing products.

Benton, Inc., *on the other hand,* already manufactures products similar to that under development. Its sales force could handle the new product without much additional effort. *Moreover,* the company needs to expand its product line, *because* some of its products are being replaced by synthetic devices. *In addition, since* Benton's development efforts on this product are more advanced than Colburn's, it stands to lose more if it discontinues work in this area. *Finally,* Benton wants to keep its large R & D staff busy *and* maintain its reputation for technological leadership. *Thus,* Benton is much more likely than Colburn to complete development of the product and enter the market.

The following list supplies some words and phrases frequently used to provide continuity between parts of sentences and paragraphs.

Additional detail	Moreover, furthermore, in addition, besides, first, second, third, finally
Causal relationship	Therefore, because, accordingly, thus, consequently, hence, as a result, so
Comparison	Similarly, here again, likewise, in comparison, still
Contrast	Yet, conversely, whereas, nevertheless, on the other hand, however, but, nonetheless
Condition	Although, if
Illustration	For example, in particular, in this case, for instance
Time sequence	Formerly, after, when, meanwhile, sometimes
Intensification	Indeed, in fact, in any event
Summary	In brief, in short, to sum up
Repetition	That is, in other words, as has been stated

SPECIAL KINDS OF PARAGRAPHS AS TOOLS

We have been looking in general at the idea block of the report, the paragraph, and how to put your idea across through clear idea statement, supporting material, and connective devices. We now need to look at certain kinds of paragraphs as special tools. At times, your report assignment will call for you to develop a paragraph in a certain way, according to your subject, your purpose, and the thought process involved. You might, for instance, want to trace a trend, define a term, compare sets of specifications, describe a machine operation, make a general statement more vivid and specific, back up a recommendation by reasons, give proof for an opinion by examples. These are just some of the tools you must have at your command as you present the information of your report.

Let's look at some of these special paragraphs to see how they are designed.

Proof by Example

An opinion becomes convincing when we can show it in practice. In the following paragraph, the idea that "San Francisco is changing" is backed up by detail after detail. When we finish reading the paragraph, we can say "It sure is."

> San Francisco is changing. Like other central cities throughout the country, it has been losing manufacturing firms and employment to its suburban areas. The family with children is leaving the city, primarily for the suburbs, and is being replaced by unrelated individuals—the widow, the widower, the bachelor, and the working girl. While the city continues to play its traditional role as Bay region reception center for immigrants, the racial and ethnic character of the immigrants has changed: Negro and Mexican–American families are now replacing the Irish and Italian immigrants. Much of the city's physical plant—its houses, schools, streets, stores and factories—is aging, in some instances at a faster rate than the city's considerable effort to restore or replace it.
>
> *(San Francisco Community Renewal Program,* Report to City Planning Commission, Little, Inc., San Francisco, 1965)

Note how the following paragraph uses three different examples to build from the topic sentence. The topic sentence sets up the big ideas of "close attention" and "impact." Then the details of wall decorations are examples of "attention," and the two employees are examples of opposing kinds of "impact."

The company pays close attention to the environmental impact of its construction program, energy conservation in its buildings, and the furnishing of interior space. At Mt. Pleasant, for example, the walls are decorated with lucite-enclosed cases containing stamps, coffee beans, dolls, and flags by graphics designer Ivan Chermayeff. All this care seems to have been lost on some employes; one remarked he didn't care what his office looked like if it were quiet. At Santa Teresa, however, an employe was so taken with the art collection that she visited an art museum for the first time.

(James Carberry, "The Corporation as Patron of Architecture," *Wall Street Journal*, October 27, 1978, p. 23)

Specifics Behind the General

Sometimes the topic sentence is just a general statement, and the paragraph simply clarifies the generalization by giving it in specific terms. For a thoughtful executive preparing to make a decision, the term "majority" may not be precise enough. He may say, "Okay, I'm glad for the conclusion. But just what are the figures?"

A majority of economists consulted believe that there will be a drop in business activity during the first quarter of next year. Of the 195 economists interviewed, 12% looked for continued increases in business activities, and 27% anticipated little or no change from the present high level. The remaining 16% looked for a recession. Of this group, nearly all (88%) believed the down curve would occur during the first quarter of the year.

Testimony of Authority

Quoting an expert in the field is a good way to back up an opinion. Specialists are important in business and industry. An expert speaking on the subject of his or her greatest information persuades us. His or her knowledge, experience, and opinion are solid. You undergird your appeal if you cite the opinions of experts on your product or services. If the writer is regarded by the reader as an expert, the writer's opinion will carry weight. If you are not an expert, you can call on those who are. A letter from a shop mechanic evaluating the condition of your car's engine is more valid than the opinion of a car salesman. If a cigarette advertisement suggests that Spring Green cigarettes with menthol are sure to give you zest and health, you are less persuaded than by the opinion of the Surgeon General, who has determined that "cigarette smoking is dangerous to your health."

Whether you are the specialist or you draw on others who are specialists, you can make use of respected opinion to promote your appeal. The following excerpt makes use of the testimony of authority:

> I believe we should shift Sam Pullman from the lathe department. Carl Wilson, the labor-relations analyst, studied the situation carefully and thinks we're in for increasing friction with the employees as long as Sam is their foreman.

In the following two-paragraph section on causes of shortages of hotel rooms, the report writer draws upon two different people who are likely to know what they are talking about. One is a vice president of a motor-hotel chain. The other is officer of a company that sponsors a lot of business travel.

> The shortage of hotel rooms is severe because of several factors, says Walter Biegler, vice president, finance, at La Quinta, a motor-hotel chain concentrated in the Southwest. "During the 1974–75 recession years," he explains, "travel was down due to inflation and the energy crisis, and hotel chains stopped expansion. Now, the overall economy is better, airlines have started discount fares, and more people are traveling. But there is the same number of hotel rooms." Primarily as a result of heavy business travel, Mr. Biegler adds, on "Monday through Thursday, we're 100% full," and La Quinta has an average annual occupancy rate of 89%.
>
> William A. Ibach, an investment officer for Northwestern Mutual Life Insurance Co., Milwaukee, believes business travel has grown because "corporations are loosening up their purse strings. The average businessman is going for a high-quality hotel and motel room." And Monsanto Co., the giant chemical concern based in St. Louis, says it has found lodging there for 611 people so far this year, up from 525 a year ago.
>
> ("Full House," *Wall Street Journal*,
> October 25, 1978, p. 1)

Tracing a Process

Because business and industry are much concerned with processes, you will frequently be called upon to report on a process.

A process is essentially a chronological account—a sequence of events or steps. The sequence may be a marketing trend, the sales history of the Acme engine, the steps in getting tuna from the sea to the supermarket customer, or the percentage of increase in suburban homes since 1950.

The method of reporting is that of the story teller—recounting the significant events or stages from beginning to end. In the following paragraph, the report writer gives us a perspective on the U.S. fertilizer industry by tracing its origin and growth.

The U.S. fertilizer industry began with phosphate on the East coast and in the Southeast. It was made up of a large number of phosphate manufacturing and mixing plants. Each of these plants served a local area of 100–300 miles in diameter and sold its product either directly or through wholesalers to retail stores. As the industry expanded into other kinds of fertilizer and extended to other areas of the country, the share of the market held by the East coast and the Southeast steadily decreased from 75% in 1940 to about 30% today.

Here is another section of a report that traces a marketing process.

To understand these functions, let us consider how one product is marketed. How about a thick, juicy T-bone steak?

The marketing of steak commences when the farmer decides that his cattle are ready to leave the farm. The animals are loaded into a truck and hauled to the nearest livestock market. Here, after being graded and weighed, they are sold to a packer. The cattle are then moved into the packer's pens, where they await slaughter. After the animals are butchered, the meat is graded, inspected by government personnel, and placed in refrigerated storage. During this time the salesmen of the meat packer have been taking orders from butchers, restaurateurs, and other wholesale meat buyers. To assist in this selling activity, the packer has been advertising in magazines and newspapers.

After an order has been placed, one of the packer's trucks delivers a side of beef to your favorite restaurant. Outside, a flashing sign announces "Sizzling Steaks!" You go in, place your order, and receive a delicious, 16-ounce T-bone. The marketing process is now complete.

(J. T. Cannon and J. A. Wichert, *Marketing: Text and Cases*, McGraw-Hill, New York, 1953)

You will usually make it easier for your readers to follow the explanation of a process if you give them an overview first. Divide the process into major steps, and list them in the order in which they occur. The process may involve many separate actions; so to keep you readers from getting lost in the forest of little steps and to protect them from a monotonous "and–then" sequence, closely group related steps into a single main step. For instance, preparing burley tobacco for market involves dozens of activities, but the major steps of the process are five: (1) removing the tobacco from the barn, (2) stripping and sorting the leaves, (3) pressing and bulking the stripped leaves, (4) loading the stripped leaves, and (5) unloading the stripped leaves at the warehouse. Each step consists of several substeps. The second step—stripping and sorting the leaves—consists of sorting the plants, grouping the leaves, and tying the leaves into "hands."

You may present the overview in two ways—by list or flow chart. Let's first look at a couple of examples of sentences that list the major steps of a process:

Making paper consists of four major steps: preparing the pulp, removing impurities from the pulp, turning the pulp into paper strips, and wrapping the paper around a roller or cutting the paper into separate sheets.

For quick clarity, listing the major steps in a column makes them easier to see, to remember, to refer to—primarily because of the attention drawn to them by the surrounding white space.

Making paper consists of four major steps:

1 preparing the pulp
2 removing impurities from the pulp
3 turning the pulp into paper strips
4 wrapping the paper around a roller or cutting the paper into separate sheets

Quite often a flow chart or other graphic device gives an overview of the general activity of the process. The block diagram, the simplest form of flow chart, shows the steps of a process by means of labeled blocks connected by arrows. The arrows indicate the direction of the activity flow.

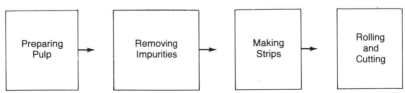

Pictures or schematic symbols are useful in showing activity at specific stages in the process.

Classification and Division

Groupings like kinds and breaking a unit down into component parts are common thought processes and ways of developing paragraphs. Once you have itemized the kinds or thought out the component parts of something and then listed them in a topic sentence, the paragraph builds naturally. Just describe each kind or part in turn, showing relationships to one another in the whole scheme. The writer of the following paragraph classifies three common steel manufacturing processes. The principle of relationship and interest of the writer is the quality of steel produced.

> The common processes of manufacturing steel are the Bessemer, the open-hearth, and the electric-furnace. Bessemer steel, which is of low quality, is used where the steel will not be subjected to corrosive influences or high impact. Open-hearth steel, which is of high quality, is used as structural steel. Electric-furnace steel, which is of the highest quality, is used in tools, crankshafts, and bearings.

We may classify a group of items, or divide one item into parts differently according to our particular interest at the time. For instance, with politics as the focus you may classify Americans as Republicans, Democrats, or Independents. With an economic interest, you may classify people as consumers or producers. A sociological focus could use an ethnic or minority principle of classification. Minority groups could be classified in terms of race or nationality, such as Spanish-American, Negro, Puerto Rican, etc., on one hand, or in terms of sex, ethnic groups, age, etc., on the other hand. Apples could be classified by different principles of interest: for an artist, color and form; a farmer, variety; a grocer, price; or a cook, taste.

Two rules are important in classifying and dividing:

1 *Follow one principle of interest consistently.* Do not cross classify or mix two different principles. For example:

Consistent: Low income, middle income, high income.
Inconsistent: Low income, middle income, self-employed.

2 *Be complete.* Do not leave out an important part or kind. You do not necessarily have to discuss all aspects of something,

but you must justify your limits if you leave out an important item.

Complete: Kindergarten, elementary school, junior high school, high school, college.

Incomplete: Kindergarten, high school, college.

Look at the following paragraph as an example of easy development. First, the writer divided his large item, bonds, into three consistent and complete categories. Then he further clarified each part in turn by explanation and descriptive detail. The principle of interest is the degree of safety.

There are three main categories of bonds—government, municipal, and corporation. Of the three, "governments" are easily the safest. U.S. bonds are backed by the full faith and credit of the United States government, and if it goes bankrupt, we're all going to be in deep trouble anyway. Municipal bonds rank second in safety, although, like "corporates," they come in a wide range of credit ratings. The best are rated "triple A," while the worst are rated "C" or "D." Municipal bonds are issued by states, counties, cities, or special taxing districts. They are backed by the taxing provisions of that entity's government. Corporate bonds, of course, are issued by corporations, and thus are backed by the faith and credit of that company.

Definition of Terms

Definition is one of the most frequently used paragraph tools. No matter what other methods of paragraph development you use, you will often need to interrupt to define a term. Deciding what terms to define is not easy. You don't want to insult your reader. On the other hand, you must give him all the help he needs to understand what you say. If the term has a special meaning in your trade or profession, and those outside your field will read it, define it. If the term is not widely used, define it. If the term is widely used, but there is a chance that its meaning is vague, define it. Terms like *subsistence income, high standard of living, technical writing, mental cruelty, religious, racist, unemployed,* and *seasonally adjusted* are often used as if everybody knew what they mean. If you are using such a term responsibly and if understanding its meaning is essential to understand your point, define it.
There are two main kinds of definitions. We need brief *clarifying*

definitions to explain an unfamiliar term or to indicate the precise meaning of a word that is to be understood in a particular context. *Extended definition* is a major method of developing an entire subject.

The usual way to give a clarifying definition is to do as the dictionary does and give a synonym (*eleemosynary:* "charitable") or place the word in a class and then distinguish it from others in the class (*slogan:* "a brief attention-getting phrase used in advertising or promotion").

Definitions to clarify may also be *stipulative,* or selected for the moment ("By training I mean on-the-job experience."). Sometimes, informally, we use *operational* definitions ("Circumspection is what you use when you walk into the boss's office.").

Extended definition is useful in clarifying abstract concepts which cannot be defined in a simple formula. Terms such as hedging, liberal, democracy, alcoholic, and high standard of living need the support of examples, explanations, and concrete details.Within reason a person may give his own definition of such abstract and controversial terms, if he lets his reader know that he is doing so. The reader may agree or disagree, but at least he can follow the writer's argument if he says, "By successful person I mean. . . ."

In developing an idea by extended definition, you may use any method—giving details, component parts, examples, etc.—that will clarify the concept.

When the writer of the following paragraph had to refer to the special method used by Diversified Industries, Inc. to recycle copper, he found that Diversified had its own special and unfamiliar term "chopping." So, there was need for a definition.

> Diversified developed the "chopping" method of recovering copper from scrap in 1961. "Chopping" involves a mechanical process through which insulated scrap is cut or shredded. By use of specific gravity a separation is made between nonferrous metals and foreign insulation elements, such as plastic, paper, fiber and glass. Unlike traditional methods of recovering scrap, "chopping" doesn't involve burning and doesn't violate pollution laws.
>
> (*Wall Street Journal,*
> October 27, 1978, p. 7)

Note the various methods used by the writer to make the term clear. He puts it in a class and then distinguishes ("a method of recovering copper from scrap . . . cut or shredded."). He expands on his explanation ("By use of specific gravity . . .") by contrasting with other methods.

One of the clearest ways to define a term is to put it into practice. You can easily give an example or tell a story or anecdote which illustrates the term.

The term *assault* means that someone intended bodily harm to another or put another in fear of bodily harm even though none was inflicted. Let me illustrate: Mr. Wolf and Mr. Lamb got into an argument. At one point Mr. Wolf picked up a club and chased Mr. Lamb up an alley. Some men noticed the altercation and took the club away from Mr. Wolf who is probably now liable for assault.

Comparison and contrast are useful techniques of definition. It can be helpful to say what the term is not, listing the terms that might be confused with it to show their differences, and then winding up with a statement of what it is.

Corpus delicti, contrary to the popular view, does not mean the body of a victim of a murder. It does not mean corpse or proof that there is a corpse. It does not mean charges against a suspect. It means a substantial body of proof that a crime has been committed.

In report writing, a special use of definition is to indicate the boundaries or scope of the report.

The study was designed to

1 evaluate the company's technological capabilities and marketing strategy;
2 review its sales and profit forecasts;
3 determine the potential market for its new product.

To indicate clearly the limitations or the scope of a project, the writer may use exclusion as part of the definition.

Since the project was concerned only with the industrial usefulness of the buildings, we investigated only those which did or could house general factory activities or those directly related. In keeping with our company's needs, we limited the survey to buildings with total floor space of more than 7500 square feet. Thus, all industrial and heavy commercial buildings were surveyed except the following:

1 special-use or single-purpose structures such as refineries, ship piers, and granaries;

   2 buildings that are part of large complexes occupied by firms
with more than 500 employees;

   3 structures which were vacant or to which admittance was
refused.

Comparison and Contrast

One of our most common thought patterns is noting how two
things are alike or different. We use comparison and contrast for
three basic purposes:

1 *To explain two items.* We may want to give information about
both, such as comparing Japanese tractors and Russian tractors.

2 *To explain one item.* We may want to clarify something unfamiliar by comparing it with the familiar, such as comparing
puberty rites in New Guinea with a high-school graduation
in Ohio. Here one item is used merely as a tool to shed light
on the other.

3 *To show one item as better.* We may want to show the superior-
ity of one thing over another, such as the selling ability of
men and women.

Making choices, establishing prices, charting courses of action
require comparison and contrast. We use these methods to decide
which bicycle design to manufacture, which site to use, which
person to hire.

There are two basic patterns of arranging the material. You may
describe all the features of item A and then follow it with all the
similar or differing features of item B. The pattern is $A_{1,2,3}$ then
$B_{1,2,3}$. The second pattern is to alternate the points of comparison
between A and B. The pattern is A_1, B_1, A_2, B_2, and so on. In a
detailed comparison of two automobiles, for example, you might
describe the Dodge in terms of cost, comfort, performance, and
durability, and then do exactly the same thing for the Chevy. Or
you might compare the cost of the Dodge with that of the Chevy,
then the comfort, the performance, and the durability. The two
simple outlines would be like this.

Dodge and Chevy

  I. Dodge
    A. Cost
    B. Comfort
    C. Performance
    D. Durability

II. Chevy
    A. Cost
    B. Comfort
    C. Performance
    D. Durability

Dodge and Chevy
  I. Cost
    A. Dodge
    B. Chevy
 II. Comfort
    A. Dodge
    B. Chevy
III. Performance
    A. Dodge
    B. Chevy
IV. Durability
    A. Dodge
    B. Chevy

Whichever pattern you use, check these points:

1 *Stick to the same principle of comparison.* Be consistent. Give both subjects similar treatment. Points discussed for one subject should be discussed for the other.
2 *Select significant points.* The points of comparison should be significant. That is, they should contribute to your purpose.
3 *Be complete.* All the significant points should be discussed. Don't leave out a main point of comparison.

In the following paragraph, the writer explains the behavior of a "catalyst," a fairly unfamiliar process, by comparing it with a process most readers know about, the way oil works.

The catalyst is in chemistry what oil is in mechanics: an indispensable agent to movement, but not contributing to the motive force. As with oil, consumption of the catalyst is always slight; several liters of oil are enough for a vehicle traveling some thousands of kilometers, and a few kilograms of catalyst allow tons of material to be transported chemically.

(J. E. Germain, "Catalysis,"
Institute of Science Technology,
September 1965, p. 44)

Contrast is the main method used in the following paragraph, show-ing how a tribe and a team differ. The principle of significance is degree of specialization and flexibility.

> It is important to understand that a tribe is not a "team." A tribe is to a team what guerrilla warfare is to conventional warfare. The difference is in the degree of specialization, mobility, coordination, and reaction capability. A team is usually a tightly coordinated group of preprogrammed specialists. (A football team is a good example.) A tribe, however, is a "wider band," with far less specialization and much greater flexibility. Its members, perhaps even more closely united in spirit and action than those of a team, have greater mobility, since a team is programmed only for certain types of actions and conditions.
>
> (Nelson A. Briggs, "Publications Management: The Tribalization of Technical Writers," *Technical Communication*, 3rd quarter, 1976, p. 13)

Another writer wants to give an insight into the emotional impact of advertising. So, he makes an extended comparison with poetry, well known for its emotional force.

> Poetry and advertising have much in common. They both make every possible use of rhyme and rhythm, of words chosen for their connotative rather than their denotative values, of ambiguities that strike the level of unconscious responses as well as the conscious. Furthermore, they both strive to give meaning and overtones to the innumerable data of everyday experience; they both attempt to make the objects of experience symbolic of something beyond themselves. A primrose by the river's brim ceases to be "nothing more" because the poet invests it with meanings; it comes to symbol-ize the insensitiveness of Peter Bell, the benevolence of God, or anything else he wants it to symbolize. The advertiser is concerned with the primrose only if it happens to be for sale. Once it is on the national market, the advertiser can increase its saleability by making it thrillingly reminiscent of gaiety, romance, and aristocratic elegance, or symbolic of solid, traditional American virtues, or sug-gestive of glowing health and youth, depending upon his whim. This is what the writer of advertising does with breakfast food, tooth-paste, laxatives, whisky, perfume, toilet bowl cleaners. Indeed almost all advertising directed to the general public is the *poeticizing of consumer goods.*
>
> (S. I. Hayakawa, "Poetry and Advertising," *Poetry*, January 1946, p. 204)

Note the effective design—the definite opening topic sentence, the use of examples to pin down the thought, the closing line which echoes the opening line and gives a strong sense of resolution. The point has been made.

Tracing Causes and Effects

Much of our thinking deals with tracing causes and effects. We ask "Why?" or "How?" "What will be the outcome?" and then we trace the answer in one of several patterns. We may classify a list of causes, reasons, or effects. We may describe the causal connection between two events, or we may trace a whole series or chain of causes and effects.

The writer traces a chain of events in the following paragraph. How many links are there in the chain from "poor management" to the sharp dip in profits?

> Poor management has created problems for Acme, Inc. Because of careless recruiting and training of personnel, people with little aptitude and experience have been assigned to operate intricate equipment. As a result, equipment breaks down constantly, production has been severely curtailed, and distributors have switched to other sources of supply. The net result is that the company's profits have dipped sharply.

Can you think of any links that might have been left out?

In some instances, we are concerned not with a sequence of causes, but just a list of causes or contributing factors that have no necessary time sequence or relationship to one another.

> Some companies have been virtually forced out of the city by high downtown land prices, traffic congestion, "urban blight," and similar problems. For other firms the pressures to move out have been more gentle but still persuasive. To mention just a few:
>
>> The widespread ownership of private automobiles has vastly increased the worker's mobility and has led to a prevalent distaste for walking to work or even for traveling to work by public conveyance. The worker is likely to prefer even a site that is fairly remote from the area in which he lives if he can drive to it. This has great practical significance to firms bidding for a high-quality work force.
>>
>> Trucking has reduced industry's dependence on the railroad siding but requires access to streets as well as new loading and unloading facilities.

A technological development of major importance has been the increasing use of one-floor production layouts. In the single-story plant or office, no space is lost to stairwells, elevator shafts, or chutes, and no time and power are lost hauling materials in process from one level to another. The one-floor layout envisages cost savings resulting from unloading raw materials at one door, running them through carefully planned processing or assembly lines, and unloading finished goods from another door. Such a layout is incompatible with downtown crowding.

(Richard T. Murphy, Jr. and William L. Baldwin, "Business Moves to the Industrial Park," *Harvard Business Review*, May–June 1959, p. 80)

Descriptive Detail

Too many abstract and general terms are bound to make reports vague and dull. You must at times use abstractions and generalizations to make statements of significance. They are your big ideas. Then you must pin down your generalizations to tangible experience by means of specific and concrete words. It is concrete and specific details which make the idea valid and clear.

Description imitates reality. It brings an object or a scene to life as if the reader were there. It may be a proposed new sports coat, an office layout, a company coffee shop, a traffic accident, a row of slum houses to be redeveloped. Effective description has two main features.

1 *Concrete details.* Description makes use of the five senses. Without the five senses, the mind could acquire no firsthand knowledge. Without sense words and specific, concrete details description is vague and lifeless.

Vague: A little animal was eating some of the food.
Distinct: A bony fox terrier was gulping a piece of bacon and a crust of bread.

2 *A dominant impression.* Effective description selects details and arranges them to give a specific impression. Not every aspect of a subject can be described; you should not drag into your description a hodgepodge of everything about your subject. Usually when you see a thing, you describe it according to your particular interest at the time. In writing, you should select your details carefully and arrange them to emphasize a particular interest, point of view, or controlling idea.

Here is a vivid description of a volcano. Note the concrete words and, in the last sentence, the example which gives a perspective on size.

A volcano is a cone-shaped mountain with a crater in the top that from time to time erupts, spewing gases, rock, ash, and molten lava. The main features of the volcano are its crater (the opening in the earth's surface), and the conduit connecting the opening to the interior of the earth which contains magma (hot, molten lava). The largest active volcano in the world is Mauna Loa in the Hawaiian Islands, which towers more than 13,500 feet above the island floor.

You could draw a picture from the words. Read the following description and see how easily you could draw a sketch of a handsaw.

A hand hacksaw is a metal-cutting saw of three parts: a handle, a C-shaped frame, and a thin, narrow blade about 12 inches long fastened across the open side of the frame.

Graphics can be useful in describing appearance, especially if you want to acquaint readers with something they are unfamiliar with. Photographs and drawings can be useful. Assume, for instance, that you are preparing a manual for a group of beginning drafting trainees. You want to describe an instrument they will have to know forwards and backwards—the hinged ruling pen. You will need to blend as much visual description with functional description as you think necessary to acquaint them with the instrument.

HINGED RULING PEN

        The hinged ruling pen is a precise drawing
instrument used by the draftsman to ink architectural
and engineering drawings. It is designed for drawing
ruled lines only and is not intended for curves or
free handwork. The hinged ruling pen is 4½ inches long
and resembles a surgical knife. The pen consists of
three main parts: the handle, two blades, and the
graduated screw adjustment as shown in the drawing
below.

The Handle

The handle consists of a polished aluminum shaft,
threaded for attachment to the blades. The handle is
cylindrical, having a diameter of 3/8 inch and a length
of 2½ inches. At the point where the handle is attached
to the blades, grooves ½ inch long are placed around the
handle. This grooving provides a textured surface to
hold the pen firmly between the fingers.

The Blades

The blades, made of carefully tempered steel, are
coated with nickel. The width of the blades is ¼ inch
at the handle, tapering to a semi-elliptical point 1/32
of an inch wide. The overall length of the blades is 2½
inches. Both blades must be the same length in order to
hold and deliver the ink properly. The upper blade is
actuated by a spring similar to that of a pocket knife.
The spring permits the upper blade to be held open at
right angles to the fixed blade for cleaning purposes,
or holds it firmly against the other blade.

The Graduated Screw Adjustment

The graduated adjusting screw is steel with a
diameter of 1/16 inch. The adjusting screw is 5/16 inch
long and threaded so that it screws into the upper
blade. Attached to one end of the screw is a cylindrical
head made of steel and nickel plated. The head is 9/32
inch in diameter and 3/32 inch high. The head has
vertical grooves around the outside so that it can be
turned with the fingers to adjust the distance between
the blades and thus regulate the line width.

Sometimes you need to add emotional force to the concrete
words and details, as in a promotional report to the shareholders
or an especially persuasive report to undergird a recommended
action. The following description is more than a three-part listing
of city types and their roles, although they seem quite accurately
described. Note the emotionally toned words ("spat out," "pain
in his heart," "dwarf"). The writer also uses metaphors to make
the description vivid and persuasive ("devoured by locusts," "tidal
restlessness," "embraces New York").

There are roughly three New Yorks. There is, first, the New York of the man or woman who was born here, who takes the city for granted and accepts its size and its turbulence as natural and inevitable. Second, there is the New York of the commuter—the city that is devoured by locusts each day and spat out each night. Third, there is the New York of the person who was born somewhere else and came to New York in quest of something. Of these three trembling cities the greatest is the last—the city of final destination, the city that is a goal. It is this third city that accounts for New York's high-strung disposition, its poetical deportment, its dedication to the arts, and its incomparable achievements. Commuters give the city its tidal restlessness; natives give it solidity and continuity; but the settlers give it passion. And whether it is a farmer arriving from Italy to set up a small grocery store in a slum, or a young girl arriving from a small town in Mississippi to escape the indignity of being observed by her neighbors, or a boy arriving from the Corn Belt with a manuscript in his suitcase and a pain in his heart, it makes no difference: each embraces New York with the intense excitement of first love, each absorbs New York with the fresh eyes of an adventurer, each generates heat and light to dwarf the Consolidated Edison Company.

(E. B. White, *Here Is New York*,
Harper & Row, New York, 1949)

Likewise in the following description, the sharp detail and the emotionally toned words add to the architectural accuracy. A real estate developer might well be persuaded of the feasibility of change in the area.

The country itself is not uncomely, despite the grime of the endless mills. It is, in form, a narrow river valley, with deep gullies running up into the hills. It is thickly settled, but not noticeably overcrowded. There is still plenty of room for building, even in the larger towns, and there are very few solid blocks. Nearly every house, big and little, has space on all four sides. Obviously, if there were architects of any professional sense or dignity in the region, they would have perfected a chalet to hug the hillsides—a chalet with a high-pitched roof, to throw off the heavy winter snows, but still essentially a low and clinging building, wider than it was tall. But what have they done? They have taken as their model a brick set on end. This they have converted into a thing of dingy clapboards, with a narrow, low-pitched roof. And the whole they have set upon thin, preposterous brick piers. By the hundreds and thousands these abominable houses cover the bare hillsides, like gravestones in some gigantic and decaying cemetery. On their deep sides they are three, four and even five stories high; on their low sides they bury themselves swinishly in the mud. Not a fifth of them are perpendicular. They lean this way and that, hanging on to their bases precariously. And one and all they are streaked in grime, with dead and eczematous patches of paint peeping through the streaks.

(H. L. Mencken, *A Mencken Chrestomathy*, Knopf, New York, 1950)

EXERCISES AND PROBLEMS

1. Examine the structure of these paragraphs. Pick out the ideas (such as topic sentences and restatements), the kinds of supporting material (such as examples, causes, comparison), and the connective devices.

   a. Being whipsawed is the option writer's supreme, but rare, indignity. A writer is whipsawed when he loses twice on the same contract and it only happens to a man who writes "straddles." Straddles are contracts which give the buyer two options: one to buy the stock, another to sell it. Thus the writer has two chances to lose.

   For example: Suppose he writes a straddle contract under which he agrees to sell 100 shares of a stock at 70 and to buy it at 70 for a premium of $700—both good for 90 days. Then assume:

   A. The stock rises ten points and is called. The writer has to buy the stock in the market at $8,000 and sell it to the contract-holder for $7,000. Loss: $1,000.

   B. Still within the 90 days, the stock turns around and drops to 60. He has to fulfill the contract by buying the stock from the contract-holder at $7,000 when it is worth only $6,000. Second loss: $1,000.

   To sum up: As against a premium of only $700, the writer has taken a loss of $2,000.

   ("The Hows and Whys of Put and Call Underwriting," *Forbes*, December 15, 1961, p. 21)

   b. People are also stimulated to be impulsive, evidently, if they are offered a little extravagance. A California supermarket found that putting a pat of butter on top of each of its steaks caused sales to increase 15 percent. The Jewel Tea Company set up "splurge counters" in many of its supermarkets after it was found that women in a just-for-the-heck-of-it mood will spend just as freely on food delicacies as they will on a new hat. The Coca-Cola Company made the interesting discovery that customers in a supermarket who paused to refresh themselves at a soft-drink counter tended to spend substantially more. The Coke people put this to work in a test where they offered customers free drinks. About 80 percent accepted Cokes and spent on an average of $2.44 more than the store's average customer had been spending.

(Vance Packard, *The Hidden Persuaders*,
McKay, New York, 1957)

c. We all, in brief, live in and by miracles of community and collaboration. We belong to communities and societies whose threads are woven into the whole pattern of the world since its beginnings. This complex of common interests and purposes and acts and ideas is the most massive fact of man's existence as a social being. Yet it is one of the most neglected in our daily concern with the world. The most formidable political and economic theories of our times take the fact of conflict as the prime mover of history. Our politics are now dominated by the accidents of conflict rather than by our substantial community. We have organized accidents, local in time and place, to declare principles which we now treat as universals. We shall not make sense of our world while we thus misread its evidence.

(Paul McGuire, *There's Freedom for the
Brave: An Approach to World Order*,
Morrow, New York, 1949)

d. A frequent definition of hedging is price "insurance." While that is a reasonably accurate description of the result of hedging, it falls short of explaining how this result is accomplished. While insurance is based on the principle of risk "sharing," hedging is based on the principle of risk "shifting."

Specifically, the risk of potentially adverse price movements is shifted to someone else (who may be either a speculator or another hedger) through the purchase or sale of futures contracts. It is useful to have at least a general understanding of how this works.

The following examples best illustrate the principle of hedging:

Ace manufactures electric motors for household appliances and light industrial equipment. One of its major customers produces washing machines. In selling to this customer, Ace must frequently quote firm prices for electric motors as much as a year in advance.

Since copper wire represents a major cost in the manufacture of electric motors, Ace is highly vulnerable to any significant increase in the price of copper. And Ace management knows that, in the past, copper prices have advanced sharply with no advance warning.

To protect itself against this price risk, they purchase copper futures contracts that closely correspond in quantity and time of delivery to the copper wire required to fulfill its contract with the washing machine manufacturer. In doing so, Ace is hedged against the risk of an increase in copper prices. It uses this fixed price for copper in determining its selling price to its customers.

Should copper prices rise, the profit on its futures contracts will approximately cover the higher price it has to pay for copper wire. The company could, of course, have purchased a large supply of copper wire in advance and stored it until needed, but this would have meant paying storage costs and insurance. And it would have involved tieing up valuable working capital or paying interest on additional debt. Hedging was the most practical and least expensive solution.

("A Frequent Definition of Hedging,"
ContiCommodity Services, Inc., *Wall
Street Journal*, October 25, 1978, p. 5)

2. Compare the effectiveness of these two paragraphs, pointing out what makes one superior to the other.

a. Northwestern could discontinue its financing of dealers, which would reduce expenditures by about $1 million per year. While this approach would reduce capital commitments, it would make dealers hard to come by, since dealers would not have enough equipment to produce a variety of structures. The sales necessary to produce a 15% return without the expense and revenue from financing the dealers were calculated. The sales resulting from this calculation were 16% lower than those shown in Table 2.

b. Northwestern could discontinue its financing of dealers and thus reduce expenditures by about $1 million per year. With these lower expenditures, the company could obtain a 15% return even if sales were 16% lower than those shown in Table 2. This approach, however, would make it difficult to obtain dealers. Moreover, it would probably reduce sales by more the 16%, because dealers would not have enough equipment to build a variety of structures.

3. Pick out the signals of movement in these paragraphs.

a. The significance of inventories in the economic picture must be considered in predicting the movement of the economy.

At present, inventories represent 4.1 months supply. Their dollar value is the highest in history. If considered in relation to increased sales, however, they are excessive. In fact, they are well within the range generally believed to be safe. Thus, inventories are not likely to cause a downward swing in the economy.

b. To the description we have given so far, we must add the impoverishment of the individual in his relationship to the public community. In the first place, the individual finds himself with no meaningful work to do—his job is increasingly frustrating, artificial, and purposeless. In the second place, he finds himself powerless to take action that would have any meaningful impact on society, and on the social evils which are increasingly apparent. Thus, he is not only deprived of "private" experience, he is deprived of a man's role in society. Appearances cannot remove the fact of his impotency, or give him a sense of manhood in the public realm.

(Charles Reich, *The Greening of America*, Random House, New York, 1970)

4. In its original version, the following portion of a report consisted of several separate paragraphs. Here they have been run together into one. As an exercise in paragraph logic, see if you can determine the original paragraph breaks.

Winchester State Bank has announced plans to participate in one of the newest, and, we believe, most interesting trends in banking—the formation of a one-bank holding company. As part of the reorganization, Winchester plans also to convert from a state to a national bank charter. The organization plan, which is designed to provide increased operating flexibility, should improve Winchester's ability to expand its operations geographically and to extend its financial services into areas not permitted under its present charter. Winchester may wish to expand or add mortgage servicing, leasing, factoring, or investment services. Situated in Winchester, Virginia, Winchester is the largest bank in the Southeast and 38th in size in the nation. The bank has offices in 27 cities. Winchester has experienced a superior record of growth among the nation's major banks; net operating earnings per share have increased without interruption at an average annual rate of 10.4% for the first ten years. In the first quarter of 1980, earnings advanced 12%. We estimate that 1980 earnings will be about $3.60 a share (at current tax rates), 10% higher than the $2.79 in 1979. In our opinion, Winchester's prospects for maintaining and perhaps improving its excellent record of growth are enhanced by plans for forming a holding company. We believe that Winchester's above-average price-earnings ratio is justified by the bank's record and prospects, and that the investment-grade shares are attractive for gradual long-term growth.

5. Write a simple paragraph classifying and describing briefly the following:

   a. The main kinds of freight carriers in your city.
   b. The main kinds of advertising media in your city.

6. Select one of the categories in Exercise 5 and write a paragraph comparing or contrasting the different kinds, showing that one is superior to the other.

7. For practice in clarity, describe an office layout, a building site, a part of a machine, or a tool. You may wish to use simple sketches.

8. Assume that you are Director of Personnel of Victor Electronics, Inc. The company coffee shop is in such poor condition that employee morale is seriously damaged. Write a brief report to the company manager recommending that the coffee shop be redecorated and equipment replaced. You should use detail for clarity and some emotionally toned description for additional persuasive force.

9. Write an extended definition of 200–300 words on one of the following terms. Assume your reader is intelligent, but is a layman. You will probably need to use examples and illustrations to explain just what these terms mean in the operation of business.

   electronic data processing   term insurance
   cost accounting   management consultant
   conglomerates   franchise
   mutual funds   diminishing returns

4
Constructing Effective Sentences

The effect of your message is largely determined by the way you put words together into sentences to express your thoughts. If your report is to be clear and forceful, you must go beyond mere correct grammar, though your grammar must be correct for both clarity and force. Your style can follow all the rules of spelling, punctuation, and good usage, and still be cumbersome and weak.

Several kinds of construction commonly creep into the arrangement of sentences and impede the effectiveness of the message. This chapter will identify some bad sentence habits and point out ways to eliminate them. The aim is to make your sentences effective in three areas:

1 Brevity and directness in wording
2 Consistency and connection between parts
3 Emphasis on important ideas

BREVITY AND DIRECTNESS

Without being curt, what you write should be brief and direct. Use only the words you need, and put them in the snappiest order. Your idea should move like an arrow to the target, not lumber like a mud turtle through the underbrush. Every word should contribute to the meaning or to the character of the message. Unnecessary words make your writing flabby and cloudy. The reader finds it too hard to get what you mean and becomes frustrated over the whole report.

Wordiness does not mean using a lot of words. It means using more words than you need. In short, state your idea to the point in the fewest words possible. Here are some guides to being brief and direct.

Repeat for Emphasis Only

Avoid using words whose meanings are clearly implied by other words. Such wordiness is called *redundancy*. Don't say the same thing over and over and over—as I have just done with "over"— except for emphasis. Here are some examples of redundancy:

WORDY: Many of our customers like long, fictional literature. Reading novels is a real pleasure to them.

CONCISE: Many of our customers like reading novels.

WORDY: The contract shall be considered a valid contract if the terms of said contract are not made retroactive to the date on which the contract is signed.

CONCISE: The contract shall be considered valid if its terms are not made retroactive to the date of signing.

Beware of a pair of terms joined by "and" when one of the terms adds no meaning. Here are some examples:

Whatever *help* and *assistance* you need . . .

You are to *go through* the invoices and *separate* them into three piles. (You surely have to "go through" the invoices in order to "separate" them.)

The *worth* and *value* of this merchandise . . .

Jack's *capacity to understand* and his *ability to explain* . . . (If he can "explain," he certainly is able to "understand".)

Avoid double statements in which one term obviously implies the other. Here are some examples:

advance *forward*	visible *to the eye*
tall *in height*	*the month of* August
a *true* fact	his *personal* opinion
red *in color*	*a pair of* twins
when *first* begun	permanently disabled *for life*
surrounded *on all sides*	to combine *together*
consensus *of opinion*	a *complete* monopoly

modern youth *of today*   *absolutely* essential
audible *to the ear*   the *basic* fundamentals

Shorten Clauses and Phrases

When you can, eliminate constructions with "who," "whom," and "that," and reduce prepositional phrases to a key word or two.

WORDY: John Collins, who has been my friend all of my life, wants to work in the dispatching office with me.
CONCISE: John Collins, my lifelong friend, wants to work in the dispatching office with me.
WORDY: The tool which we use in this situation . . .
DIRECT: The tool used in this situation . . .
WORDY: Most of the new styles in this day and age pass quickly.
CONCISE: Most new styles pass quickly.

Check the following examples of common phrases and clauses against their one-word equivalents:

BREVITY: CHECKLIST

in this day and age	today
during the time that	while
a large number of	many
a small number of	few
in the same way	similarly
at an early date	soon
in the near future	soon
at the present time	now (or presently)
due to the fact that	because
most of the time	usually
leaving out of consideration	disregarding
without making any noise	noiselessly
as a result of	consequently
there is no doubt that	doubtlessly
it cannot be denied that	undeniably

The "to" Form of the Verb

Use the "to" form of the verb for a direct route as illustrated in the following examples:

INDIRECT: He was here for the purpose of painting a sign.
DIRECT: He was here to paint a sign.
INDIRECT: In order that enough time be allowed . . .
DIRECT: To allow enough time . . .

Eliminate Unnecessary Articles

If you can use a plural subject instead of a singular subject for general statements, you can eliminate articles *(a, an, the)*.

SINGULAR: A happy customer means a repeat sale.
PLURAL: Happy customers mean repeat sales.

Eliminate Indirectness

Cut out the phrases "it is" and "there is." Direct statements are more effective.

INDIRECT: It is on the first day of a sale that we sell the most.
DIRECT: We sell the most on the first day of a sale.
INDIRECT: There are two trucks that should be replaced.
DIRECT: Two trucks should be replaced.

Avoid Clusters of General Words

Use specific verbs, nouns, and modifiers instead of combinations of general adjectives and adverbs. "Run quickly" means "speed" or "rush." "Turned red with embarrassment" mean "blush." "A person under twenty-one" is a "minor." "A worker in the factory" is a "factory worker." "Extremely tired" is "weary" or "fatigued."

Combine nouns and verbs into one verb. "To give advice" means "advise." "Became the owner of" means "bought" or "acquired."

Combine Short Sentences

A series of short sentences may use a wordy repetition of subjects and verbs. Combine series of short sentences into one reduced, direct sentence.

WORDY SERIES: He typed four letters in the morning. Then after lunch he filed invoices. Then he treated himself to a coffee break.
DIRECT: After typing four letters in the morning and filing invoices after lunch, he treated himself to a coffee break.

Avoid Multiple Hedging

Hedging on a statement causes wordiness and indirectness. A careful writer will not make an absolute statement unless he or she is sure of its validity. He or she will use phrases like "probably," "usually," "it is said that," and "he seems to be." The evasive and unsure writer, however, may hedge more than is necessary. Most evasions produce wordiness. For example, the following sentence contains three hedges.

> I *believe* that market research *seems* to indicate that X-Shine will *probably* go over big.

Such multiple hedging suggests that the writer is unsure of himself. To evade making a direct assertion, he is unnecessarily wordy. One hedge would have been enough.

> I *believe* that market research indicates that X-Shine will go over big.
> Market research indicates that X-Shine *probably* will go over big.

CONSISTENCY AND CONNECTION

Your message will be vague, dull, and maybe even exasperating if the parts of your sentences are not consistent and clearly connected. If your thoughts do not move smoothly and neatly, your reader may not have the time, interest, and energy to labor to get your message. Awkwardness has many causes. Four of the common ones are examined here—fuzzy pronouns and pointers, dangling modifiers, shifts in perspective, and wrenched parallelism.

Fuzzy Pronouns and Pointers

The *customer* told *Sally* that *she* was still confused.

It is risky using personal pronouns like "he," "she," and "they" and pointer words like "that," "this," "which," "the former," and "as mentioned above." These words take their meaning only from other words nearby, and if the connection is not perfectly clear, the communication fails.

Pronouns

Make sure your pronouns point definitely to a noun word. The noun word that a pronoun points to is called an *antecedent* or *referent*. Check these five kinds construction for fuzzy pronouns:

1 *Two Possible Antecedents.* If the pronoun can point to two nouns, change the sentence to leave one clear connection.

FUZZY: James told his supervisor that he had made an error.
CLEAR: James told his supervisor, "You have made an error."
CLEAR: James admitted to his supervisor that he had made an error.
CLEAR: James accused his supervisor of making an error.

2 *Almost Noun.* The word referred to should be the exact form of the noun for which the pronoun is a substitute. Modifiers, possessives, and implied nouns are fuzzy.

FUZZY: Before the repairman could tend to the rabbit cages, some of them ran away.
CLEAR: Before the repairman could repair the rabbit cages, some of the rabbits ran away.

3 *Group of Words as Referent.* The pronouns "which," "that," "this," and "it" are often used fuzzily to refer to a whole idea or group of words. Give them a single noun word or compound word to refer to.

FUZZY: Jones refused to join the office raffle, which was considered as disloyalty to the company
CLEAR: Jones's refusal to join the office raffle was considered as disloyalty to the company.
FUZZY: Mrs. Thompson protested about the new rule, but it didn't change anything.
CLEAR: Mrs. Thompson protested about the new rule, but her protest didn't change anything.

4 *Far-off Nouns.* If the word referred to is too far back in the sentence or paragraph, repeat the noun or rewrite the sentence.

FUZZY: One waitress chased the flies off the counter and then sat down at the table with the other waitresses, but they came back immediately.
CLEAR: One waitress chased the flies off the counter and then sat down at the table with the other waitresses, but the flies came back immediately.

5 *Personal Pronouns in a General Sense.* The pronouns "you," "they," and "it" are usually fuzzy and illogical when they stand for people or things in general rather than for a specific noun word.

FUZZY: At Bay Harbor Resort they treat newcomers courteously.

CLEAR: At Bay Harbor Resort the staff treat newcomers courteously.

CLEAR: At Bay Harbor Resort the residents treat newcomers courteously.

FUZZY: I like courses in economics because they teach you the ideological basis for business.

CLEAR: I like courses in economics because they teach a person (or *me*) the ideological basis for business.

Other Pointers

To save words or sometimes because of laziness, writers may point the reader's attention backward on the page with expressions like these:

the aforementioned   the former
as mentioned above   the latter
the above listed   respectively

For example, a company memo might come through like this:

Parking permits for employees and volunteers are distributed by the Personnel and the Customer Service Departments *respectively.*

The pointer *respectively* is a device for connecting items in the sentence. The trouble, however, is that the reader must jump to the beginning of the sentence to get the meaning clear. And anything that makes the reader stop, stumble, and scramble back through the message to figure out the meaning is a flaw to be removed. The pointer is easily avoided by separate constructions and clear pronoun reference:

Parking permits for employees are distributed by the Personnel Department, those for volunteers, by the Customer Service Department.

Pointers can save a few words, but they should not be used at the expense of a clear connection between parts of the sentence.

Dangling Modifiers

Coming in by plane, the *smog* . . .

A modifier will usually be connected to some word or words that it describes. A dangling modifier, as the term implies, is a modifier given nothing to modify. It just hangs there, disconnected. If the word it should logically modify is not even in the sentence, the part appears to be attached to a nearby word to which it is not logically connected. The reader usually figures out the meaning, but the writer can be left looking rather foolish.

Check the following disconnected meaning with its ludicrous effect.

While *walking* through the showroom, the dirty *windows*. . . . (Halfway through the sentence, the reader gets the image of dirty windows strolling along.)

By following these guidelines, your ability to please customers will improve. (Who's doing the following, *you* or your *ability?*)

He was tired and nervous, causing him to make mistakes. (Not ludicrous, just fuzzy.)

Danglers are easy enough to connect, in one of two ways:

1 Give the phrase its own subject and verb, and it won't need a close attachment.
  While *I walked* through the showroom the dirty windows . . .
2 Insert the right noun or pronoun to tie the phrase together.
  While walking through the showroom, *I* noticed the dirty windows.

The other dangling modifiers can be tightened up the same way.

By following these guidelines, *you* will improve your ability to please customers.
If *you follow* these guidelines, your ability to please customers will improve.
Because *he was* tired and nervous, he made mistakes.
His *tiredness* and *nervousness* caused him to make mistakes.

Shifts in Perspective

When a *person* first realizes his job is important, *they* . . .

When a *person* first realizes a job is important, *he* . . .

Once you have selected your perspective and the kind of construction you are going to use for your message, stick to the pattern—unless you have a very good reason to shift. Your reader is following the trail you have set. Don't throw him off. Here are some checkpoints for shifts to be avoided: person, subject or verb, command and statement, direct and indirect discourse, and tense.

Person

Avoid shifts from third person ("he," "she," "one," "a person," "they") to second person ("you") and from singular ("a person," "he," "one," "she") to plural ("they").

SHIFT: *All personnel* can use Parking Lot C. *You* do not need a permit.

CONSISTENT: *All personnel* can use Parking Lot C. *They* do not need a permit.

CONSISTENT: As a Burns Electronics employee, *you* can use Parking Lot C. *You* do not need a permit.

Subject or Verb

A shift from active verb form to passive verb form changes the subject. In a series keep two subjects either both acting or both being acted upon.

SHIFT: I discovered I was out of typing paper, so a quick trip to Supply had to be made.

CONSISTENT: I discovered I was out of typing paper, so I had to make a quick trip to Supply.

Command and Statement

Make sure that you consistently use either commands or statements. Don't use both in the same sentence.

SHIFT: First read the directions carefully, and then all the parts should be laid out in order of assembly.

CONSISTENT: First read the directions carefully, and then lay out all the parts in order of assembly.

CONSISTENT: First the directions should be read carefully, and then all parts should be laid out in order of assembly.

Direct and Indirect Discourse

Watch especially for shifts between statement and question.

SHIFT: He asked me if I liked the suit and would I like to try it on.

CONSISTENT: He asked me if I liked the suit and if I would like to try it on.

CONSISTENT: He asked me, "Do you like the suit and would you like to try it on?"

Tense

Watch especially for shifts between past and present.

SHIFT: Clemens *is* not fair to Pittman in calling him incompetent. He *cited* only Pittman's failures but *ignored* his successes.

CONSISTENT: Clemens *was* not fair . . . *cited* . . . *ignored* . . .

Wrenched Parallelism

Some words link pairs or series of equal importance, though the ideas may be contrasts or alternatives. Examples of such words are *and, but, or, nor, for, than, not only–but also, both–and, neither–nor, either–or.* Use the same kind of word pattern to express equal or parallel ideas. For example, link word with word, phrase with phrase, clause with clause. Link noun with noun, adjective with adjective, "-ing" word with "-ing" word, etc.

Betty likes   *typing*
               filing, and
               taking coffee breaks.

Betty likes   *to type*
               to file, and
               to take coffee breaks.

The sign words of parallel structure, such as "and," may not always be used, but the parts should still take similar form.

of the people, by the people, for the people
I came, I saw, I conquered.

Parallel structure makes both ideas clear and emphatic. A repeated pattern shows that two or three items are equal and should be grouped. Parallel structure also hits hard because the key words stand out.

WRENCHED: The sales pitch was long, dull, and didn't make any point.
PARALLEL: The sales pitch was long, dull, and pointless.
WRENCHED: I didn't know whether I should become a salesperson or to go into advertising.
PARALLEL: I didn't know whether to become a salesperson or an advertiser.
PARALLEL: I didn't know whether to go into sales work or advertising.
WRENCHED: The foreman was a perfectionist himself and who expected perfection in others.
PARALLEL: The foreman expected perfection in both himself and others.

EMPHASIS

Emphasis is the technique of giving each of your ideas its due weight and of making your ideas hit the reader hard. Emphasis is the result of many skills: (1) clear thinking about your ideas; (2) correct and clear sentence structure; (3) vivid and accurate word choice; and (4) careful use of pronouns and pointers, of perspective, of modifiers, and of parallel structure. Beyond these skills, emphasis is achieved by the following devices:

1 Key positions
2 Order of climax
3 The suspense sentence
4 Delayed subject
5 The strong active verb
6 Unusual word order
7 Repetition of key words
8 The short sentence

Key Position

Last and first are, in that order, the most emphatic spots. End your sentence with the most important idea. Strongest in our minds is what we read last. Lead off with your next most important idea. Bury the minor, dull but necessary ideas in the middle.

WEAK ENDING: Because of careless inspection of the fire extinguishing system, over 200 lives were lost, it was calculated.

EMPHATIC ENDING: Because of careless inspection of the fire extinguishing system, over 200 lives, it was calculated, were lost.

WEAK BEGINNING: In my opinion, apathetic salesmen are the cause of decreased sales.

EMPHATIC BEGINNING: Apathetic salesmen are, in my opinion, the cause of decreased sales.

Order of Climax

Three or more items in a series should be arranged in emphatic order, with the most important item last.

The country's main concerns are hunger, sickness, and death.

While some items usually take a logical order, such as death over hunger, you may choose your own rising order of importance according to context and purpose. For instance, you may wish to stress food problems:

The country's main concerns are sickness, death, and, most immediately, hunger.

Final position is most emphatic. Make sure you put the items in the order of importance called for by your context.

ANTICLIMATIC: The fire in the warehouse killed ten people, injured twenty people, and destroyed two rooms of furniture.

EMPHATIC: The fire in the warehouse destroyed rooms of furniture, injured twenty people, and killed ten people.

Suspense Sentence

The *suspense sentence* withholds its main or completing idea until the very end. A *loose sentence* states the full idea early and then adds qualifiers and other details, often parenthetical. With a loose sentence a reader's attention can lag after he reads the main idea. But a suspense sentence creates suspense and demands attention, because to get the meaning, the reader cannot stop until the period.

LOOSE AND UNEMPHATIC: Maxwell resumed his description of the fire, after standing silently before the committee for a full minute with tears in his eyes.

SUSPENSEFUL AND EMPHATIC: After standing silently before the committee for a full minute with tears in his eyes, Maxwell resumed his description of the fire.

In effective writing most of your sentences should be loose sentences. Too much straining for suspense may give a false sense of melodrama. Here is a standard, loose, effective sentence with the central idea first, where it belongs:

The cashier stopped the flow of blood with a piece of cloth torn from the hem of her dress.

Delayed Subjects

The subject or central idea is delayed in the suspense sentence simply by putting phrases in a certain order. Verbal devices like the expletives "it is" and "there is," "what" clauses, and general synonyms also hold suspense by pointing to the subject to come later. These introductory words are like warning signs to alert the reader: "Important idea just ahead."

STANDARD: An angry crowd was gathering at the cashier's window.

DELAYED: There was an angry crowd gathering at the cashier's window.

STANDARD: Mr. Fleming's curt memo hurt company morale the most.

DELAYED: What hurt company morale the most was Mr. Fleming's curt memo.

Strong Active Verb

Because the active voice expresses the direct action of the subject, it is more emphatic than the passive. As a rule, use the active voice. Use passive, by which the subject is acted upon, only when you can clearly justify it.

WEAK PASSIVE: Fifty dollars was received by each worker.
STRONG ACTIVE: Each worker received fifty dollars.

The active voice is obviously the more direct, concise, and emphatic way of expressing the idea. However, there are two special occasions when you should use the passive voice. The first is when the receiver of the action is more important than the doer:

STRONG PASSIVE: A thin line of black paint is put along the edge of the plate to indicate where the motion block is to be attached.
STRONG PASSIVE: The new showroom was finished in September.
STRONG PASSIVE: The Christmas window was decorated entirely in blue.
STRONG PASSIVE: Cynthia Studdard was arrested, tried, and convicted of the crime of burglary.

The second effective use of the passive is to deliberately deemphasize the normal action of the verb, perhaps to soften the impact of bad news. We can call this the *diplomatic passive.*

DIPLOMATIC PASSIVE: When your check is received . . . (Instead of "When you pay your bill . . .")
DIPLOMATIC PASSIVE: Smoking in the fitting room is prohibited. (Instead of "Don't smoke in the fitting room," or "The management prohibits smoking in the fitting room.")

Unusual Word Order

Any word gains emphasis when it varies from the expected word order. For clarity we usually write a direct line sentence—subject→ verb→any necessary receiver of the action or identifying word. When a word is put in an unexpected place, it gains sudden attention.

NORMAL: We should never have begun such a risky project.
UNUSUAL: Such a risky project we should never have begun.
NORMAL: We could hardly expect prompt payment from a man of his credit rating.
UNUSUAL: Hardly could we expect prompt payment from a man of his credit rating.

NORMAL: The richest market in the country is eagerly waiting for X-90.

UNUSUAL: Eagerly waiting for X-90 is the richest market in the country.

Unusual order must be used sparingly. As a violent means for gaining emphasis, it can easily become artificial and affected. We could well advise, "Sparingly must unusual word order be used."

Repetition of Key Words

Repeating sentence patterns to achieve consistency has been discussed under "Wrenched Parallelism." Key words can also be repeated to emphasize your most important points. Note the double force of the key word "help" in these sentences:

Don't merely ask your client how you can *help* him. Tell him precisely how you can *help* him.

In this passage, the key idea of "new" comes across emphatically.

Everything in the showroom is *new*. The furnishings are *new;* the merchandise is *new;* even the price tags are *new*.

Repetition must be confined to key words or sentence patterns and must be carefully used to gain emphasis. Careless and needless repetition of words leads to dull, flat writing.

WORDY: When *one* studies the *customer, one* will find that the many gestures the *customer* makes will give *one* clues as to what the *customer* is thinking.

The Short Sentence

The typical straightforward sentence runs from 13 to 17 words. You don't need to be a word counter as you write letters, but you should know if your sentences tend to be too long, too short, or monotonously unvaried. If you find that your usual sentence is more than 13 to 17 words long, your style might be cumbersome. Compare the following original with its revision. They both contain the same number of words.

CUMBERSOME: I have carefully checked the personnel records of all our field employees and found only two that I think will be of interest to Mr. Dexter as he faces the difficult problem of selecting the right person for District Manager of the Springfield area.

STRAIGHTFORWARD: I have carefully checked the personnel records of all our field employees and found only two that are promising. Mr. Dexter faces a difficult problem in selecting the right personnel for District Manager of the Springfield area. I think these two will interest him.

The cumbersome first memo has one sentence of 44 words. The snappy second memo has three sentences of 19, 18, and 7 words each.

If, on the other hand, most of your sentences contain fewer than 13 words, your style may sound choppy and juvenile. Compare the following choppy original with the revision, which gains force by combining sentences.

CHOPPY: Martin called today. He said the Model 210s were shipped Friday. They should be here tomorrow. When they arrive, display them in the Elec Room. I'll prepare an ad. I'll let you know when it's ready.

EMPHATIC: Martin called today saying the Model 210s were shipped Friday and should be here tomorrow. When they arrive, display them in the Elec Room. I'll prepare an ad and call you when it's ready.

Variation in sentence length is as important as the average length. Some of your sentences should be short, some average, some long, with no regular pattern of variation. Look again at the revised memo above about Mr. Dexter's search for a district manager. It contains three sentences with an average length of 14.66 words. But note how they vary: 19, 18 (beyond the standard 17), and then a concise, emphatic 7.

Analyze the varied sentence lengths of the following section from a personnel report. The writer wanted to be personal and genial, but forceful.

The Springfield territory, which Maxwell is about to take over, requires a shrewd mind, a facile imagination, and a capacity for downright hard work. Others have tackled it and failed. The last two people took on the job with the same confidence Maxwell shows, only to become frustrated quite quickly with its problems. Both of them underestimated the demands of the territory. I am confident Maxwell will not.

There are five sentences averaging 13.6 words—a fine average. But note the variation: first a long sentence (24 words), then a short one (6 words), another long one (23 words), then a medium short one (9 words), and a final brief one (6 words) that hits like a fist. The ideas gain emphasis through variation of sentence length.

EXERCISES AND PROBLEMS

1. Make the following sentences more brief and direct.
   a. In the event that you can attend the meeting, plan in advance to offer some concrete suggestions on how to reduce the cost and expense of overtime in the Purchasing Department.
   b. Please find enclosed herewith a copy of the report, which is 20 pages in length.
   c. In view of the foregoing facts and figures, it seems appropriate to suggest an entirely new customer-service policy.
   d. You will note when you study the cost of stationery that the expenditure for stationery has gradually and steadily increased for 1977, 1978, 1979, and 1980.
   e. We should make a study of the growing increase in the popularity of bonus compensation systems for personnel in management positions.
   f. Accountants, in studying business procedures and methods of accounting, have been able to classify the business for purposes of their study. They have classified these concerns on the basis of the differences and similarities in the accounting functions.
   g. The mechanization of office records is not a particularly new innovation in the business world.
   h. Are you sending the invitations out in the mail in plenty of time so that those who are being invited will have sufficient advance notice in which to respond?
   i. The accountants in our department individually and collectively agree with the decision arrived at to cease and desist the practice of amortizing product-development costs over a five-year period.
   j. It seems as though the parties concerned might be able to agree on some of the terms we are posing here in this report.
   k. In addition, will you please permit me to state in this letter that we will welcome any suggestions or comments that

you may have at any time if you think of any methods
for the improvement of our service to our customers.

l. Mr. Folk gave a talk on the growing increase in the popularity of bonus compensation systems for personnel in management positions.

m. Permit me to take this opportunity to call your attention
to the fact that we have brought your account up to date.

n. For your information we are attaching hereto a carbon
copy of the letter sent to Mr. Ted Black under date of
July 14.

o. It seems as though we might be unable to agree on some
of the terms you are posing here.

2. Revise the following sentences to eliminate fuzzy pronouns,
dangling modifiers, shifts in perspective, and wrenched parallelism.

Fuzzy Pronouns

a. Gibson told the foreman that he should take the day off.
b. Then a police car arrived, and they arrested the two shop-
lifters.
c. The park which belongs to the city extends over 50 acres
and includes three ball diamonds, a fishing pond, and a
small zoo. It is free to the public.
d. The customer kept interrupting, which annoyed the salesman.
e. The report showed that on the Lower East Side they are
not very sanitary.

Dangling Modifiers

f. Working at top speed in the morning, fatigue may overtake
you in the afternoon.
g. To function smoothly, you must oil the machine every hour.
h. I enjoyed his speech at the dinner, which was very forceful.
i. To be baked just right, you should heat the oven to 375°
before placing the cake inside.
j. We borrowed a calculator from the sales department which
works perfectly.

Shifts

k. Any executive should be considerate of the opinions of
their employees.
l. She resealed the letter after its contents had been carefully
read.

m. First, write a courteous reminder; then if there is no response, you should write an urgent request for payment.
n. Jameson is not fair in calling Miss Olson irresponsible. He mentioned only her weaknesses and overlooked her strengths.
o. All salespersonnel may pick up a new Sun-Ray Kit immediately. You need only show your ID card.

Wrenched Parallelism

p. The personnel manager is responsible for the selection of the right worker, providing appropriate orientation, and the worker's progress.
q. The shipping clerk made three resolutions: (1) to be on time, (2) following instructions carefully, and third, the reduction of waste.
r. The new secretary is good at taking dictation, filing, and ability to type reports.
s. We have three objectives in mind: to finish the job in the shortest time possible, absolute accuracy, and insure that appearance is attractive.
t. The stories in this magazine have three shortcomings:
(1) they appeal only to a small group of teenagers;
(2) too many picture illustrations are employed, and
(3) why must they all be about the bad things in life?
3. Rewrite the following sentences to make them more emphatic according to the principle indicated.

Key Position

a. The markets are in for a period of inactivity, if I can read the signs correctly.
b. On the other hand, the new additive will increase mileage by 20%, tests show.
c. As our lawyer sees it, the trial will be prejudiced against the company from the beginning.
d. Without a doubt, the computer has had a great effect on business.

Order of Climax

e. The news of Betty's winning the Customer Award made her want to shout for joy, to dance, and to laugh.
f. The dog, dragging its chain, raced through the showroom, scraping the paint on the cars, cracking a show window, and overturning a flowerpot.

g. The new credit manager, Jeb Campbell, was president of the Northwest State Bank, chairman of the hospital board, and a member of the Kiwanis Club.

Suspense Sentence

h. Joe finally sold the yacht after three feverish days of phone calls, house calls, and demonstrations.
i. Walter put the the territory in the black after six months of brilliant, tireless work.
j. We will have a better economy only when both management and labor agree that each has a right to its fair share.

Delayed Subject

k. The sarcasm of the office supervisor made the typists nervous.
l. The job can be done in more than one way.
m. To observe a customer being nasty to a salesperson is never very pleasant.
n. Ineffective advertising seems to be the most serious weakness of the Eastland unit.

Strong Active

o. The window has been decorated for the Easter sale.
p. The letter was written by the new assistant to Mrs. Nelson.
q. Your cooperation will be appreciated by us.
r. It is concluded from the marketing survey that a chain of automobile car washes would be highly profitable.

Diplomatic Passive

s. Employees must not take time off for a coffee break until 10:30.
t. You have included much useless information in the report.
u. The manager decided that the factory would operate on Memorial Day.

Unusual Word Order

v. Jack would never make such a quota in a hundred years.
w. You could certainly expect accurate work from a secretary with her sense of responsibility.
x. All the power of that once great industrial empire is gone.
y. We dare not risk such a dangerous lawsuit.
4. Make the following sentence more emphatic by using repetition of the key word "studied."

When Ben Taber took over the Springfield territory, he studied as he had never done before—before work, during lunch hour, at night, and on weekends—until everything in the territory became one piece of knowledge with himself.

5. Improve the clarity and emphasis of these portions of reports by breaking up the one long sentence.

a. Because more than one freight classification may apply to the same type of goods, the traffic manager can effect further savings by a careful auditing or checking of freight bills the company is called upon to pay, since these charges are complicated and involved, and errors are often made in computation as well as in classification.

b. In reference to the transmission damage you reported to your automobile on July 9, 1980, this is to advise after making a thorough inspection of your automobile and after talking with Mr. Thomas, the service manager at Allred's Garage, we have determined that the pump inside your transmission was bad, causing the damage, and not caused from any hole in the pan.

6. The following paragraph has poor sentence structure. Without changing the sequence of ideas, rewrite the paragraph in more effective style.

Advertising agencies offer the skills necessary for companies to have effective advertising programs. The service which agencies provide the companies doesn't cost as much as if the companies did their own advertising. The companies pay for artwork and copywriting. They would have to pay for this anyway if they did their own advertising. Probably they would have to use individual specialists and pay more for them than the agencies pay their own staff to work on one company's advertising. The companies don't pay a dime more for space in the print media or for the time which radio and television have for sale than if they did their own advertising. Here is an example. It would cost a company $11,500 to purchase a full page of advertising space in *Modern Woman* magazine. *Modern Woman* charges an advertising agency $9500 for a full page. This is the standard discount for advertising agencies. The advertising agency charges the company $11,500 for the space. The advertising agency keeps $2,000. You can see why companies are glad to have agencies do their advertising for them. You can also see why agencies compete quite hard for the advertising business of companies.

7. Write the first draft of a paragraph pointing out what could be done to improve the service or to increase sales at one of the local businesses. Make the paragraph at least seven sentences long. After you have finished the first draft, make a copy of it and set the copy aside. Then go to your first draft and experiment with its style, using most of the emphasis techniques discussed in this chapter. When you finally settle on the most effective revision of your original paragraph, turn that revision into a clean, final copy and submit it to your instructor along with the unmarked copy of your first draft.

8. Compare the differences in style between the sentences in each of the following groups.

    a. (1) Three causes of this change are important.
       (2) Three important causes are behind this change.
       (3) There are three important causes for this change.
       (4) This is a change that has three important causes.
       (5) Important in this change are three causes.
       (6) This change has three important causes.

    b. (1) The best buys of yesterday aren't always the best buys of today.
       (2) The best buys of yesterday are not necessarily the best buys of today.
       (3) Yesterday's best buys aren't necessarily today's best buys.
       (4) Yesterday's best buys are not always best buys today.
       (5) Today's best buys aren't always yesterday's.

9. Without changing any of the ideas, rewrite each of the following sentences in several ways. You may use more than one sentence. Then with each version indicate under what circumstances it would be the most effective way to write the sentence.

    a. Jesse Kingman has been under my supervision for over a year and I believe he is one of the most conscientious people in my department.

    b. This report on business bankruptcies must be in by March 28; the chairman has scheduled a press conference on it for April 1.

10. Which version of the following statements is more emphatic? Why? The answers and the authors' names are printed at the end of the exercise.

a. The greatest task before civilization at present is to make machines what they ought to be, the slaves, instead of the masters of men.

b. The greatest task before civilization at present is not to make machines masters of men but to make them the slaves of men.

c. Impatience and laziness are two cardinal sins from which all others spring.

d. There are two cardinal sins from which all others spring: impatience and laziness.

e. It is a mark of genius not to astonish but to be astonished.

f. It is a mark of genius to be astonished, not to astonish.

g. As human history progresses, it becomes nothing but a race between education and catastrophe.

h. Human history becomes more and more a race between education and catastrophe.

i. It is grief that develops the powers of the mind although happiness is beneficial for the body.

j. Happiness is beneficial for the body but it is grief that develops the powers of the mind.

k. Mathematics takes us into the region of absolute necessity, to which not only the actual world, but every possible world, must conform.

l. Not only the actual world but every possible world must conform to mathematics, which takes us into the region of absolute necessity.

m. I believe that man will not merely endure but he will prevail.

n. I believe that man will prevail rather than merely endure.

o. I believe that man will not merely endure; he will prevail.

p. Pass the ammunition and praise the Lord.

q. After you praise the Lord, pass the ammunition.

r. Having praised the Lord, pass the ammunition.

s. Praise the Lord and pass the ammunition.

t. In the beginning God created the heaven and the earth.

u. God began by creating the heaven and the earth.

v. God created the heaven and the earth in the beginning.

w. It is better to ask some of the questions than to know all of the answers.

x. To know all the answers is not better than to ask some of the questions.

Answers: a, Havelock Ellis; d, Franz Kafka; e, Aubrey Mensen; h, H. G. Wells; j, Marcel Proust; k, Bertrand Russell; o, William Faulkner; s, Chaplain (Lieutenant Commander); t, Genesis 1:1; w, James Thurber.

11. Select an article about business from a current periodical. Choose a 500-word passage and analyze it according to the criteria about vigor in this chapter. Clip the passage to your paper before handing it in to your instructor.

12. Find two samples of printed instructions or directions—one that you consider well written and one poorly written. For subjects, you might consider directions for assembling a toy or operating a stereo or procedures for a hospital staff to follow. Analyze the effective sample for techniques of quality. Rewrite the poor sample to improve it.

5

Selecting the Best Words

Individual words are the ultimate building blocks of the report. One word is worth a thousand pictures, if it is the right word. If it's the wrong word, it's worth a lost customer. The effective writer must carefully select and place each word so that it is precise, alive, and direct. People do not read very long that which is sloppy, confused, dull, or hard.

PRECISE

The first principle of your message is to be accurate. It is not enough for your information to be accurate. You must convey that information to the reader. If your words are inaccurate, you will fail.

Choosing precise words has two major problems. First, the relationships between words and their meanings is not one-to-one. Many words have more than one meaning, and your meaning can be expressed by more than one word or set of words. Second, words have two kinds of meaning—the dictionary meaning (or denotation) and the emotional or suggestive meaning (or connotation).

Denotation—The Precise Definition

The denotation of a word is its basic dictionary definition and identifies an idea, an object, or a quality. It is the word's core of meaning and is the first you must consider.

The basic dictionary denotation of "mother" is "female parent."
"War" is "a major armed conflict between nations or between
organized parties within a state." To the extent that a word refers
to the same thing for all people concerned, the meaning is denotative. Some words, such as magnesium, diatom, parallax, and diesel,
have only one denotative meaning with no other suggestive force
or shade of meaning. But most words have different shades of
meaning that different people associate with the word because
of their particular experience with it.

Connotation—The Precise Tone

The connotation of a word is the suggestions, associations, and
emotional responses of the word. Connotations are somewhat different for everyone. But many words have fairly standardized connotations. Thus, "mother" usually means more than the dictionary's
denotation of "female parent." The word often connotes emotional
warmth, security, and comfort. "War" would have different emotional meanings for one who has been maimed by war, for a family
who have fled for shelter when the bombs fell, for one who is
getting wealthy because of war. The connotation of a word may
not only indicate a special shade of meaning different from a near
synonym (such as "drunk" or "plastered") but also suggest attitudes,
such as approval or disapproval, ludicrous or serious.

> That poor shipping clerk needs somebody to *mother* him. (Ap-
> proval: to care for, give affection, comfort, and security)
>
> Janet is spoiled because the boss has been *mothering* her. (Dis-
> approval: overprotecting, catering to)

The adjectives "thin," "skinny," and "slender" all have the same
denotation in referring to below average weight for one's height.
But you may please a customer if you call her slender, displease
her if you call her *skinny*.

In using words with exact meaning, you must check both the
denotation and the connotation. Ask yourself two questions about
the word.

1 *Does the word have the meaning you give it?* Check the various
   definitions in the dictionary to see if the word has the meaning
   you are trying to give it. Are you confusing it with another
   word? For instance the word "infer" is occasionally misused
   as if it had the same meaning as "imply."

INCORRECT: He *inferred* by his smile that he had made a big
             sale.

EXACT: He *implied* by his smile that he had made a big sale.

EXACT: I *inferred* from his smile that he had made a big sale.

2 *Is the meaning of the word the meaning you want?* Check both the dictionary and your knowledge of human experience to see if the word has the proper shade of meaning to express your thought. Do you want to suggest approval or disapproval?

INEXACT: It certainly was an exhilarating experience to hear the president's after-dinner *spiel* about the future of the company.

EXACT: It certainly was an exhilarating experience to hear the president's after-dinner speech about the future of the company.

Here are some examples of words commonly confused in meaning.

all ready, already	"All ready" means entirely ready; "Already" means previously.
amount, number	Whenever you count the units, use "number." "Amount" refers to bulk, weight, or sums.
anxious, eager	"Anxious" implies worry, whereas "eager" conveys keen desire.
effect, affect	As a noun "effect" means result, condition or influence. "Affect" is not often used as a noun. Both words are verbs—to "effect" is to bring about, to "affect" is to influence.
fewer, less	If you can count the items, use "fewer"; "less" refers to amount or quantity.
personal, personnel	"Personal" relates to an individual; "personnel" refers to a group of people employed in the same work.
please, kindly	As a rule, use "please." "Kindly" means "in a kind manner." If you say, "kindly tell me," you are really asking someone to tell you something in a kind way.
principal, principle	"Principal" means "chief" or "main." Whenever you can substitute "rule," use "principle." In all other instances use "principal."
we, I	"We" means the organization; "I" refers to the individual.

| which, that, who | "That" refers to persons or things; "who" to people; "which" only to things. |

Part of the connotation of a word is the emotional tone it evokes. Besides its core idea, the word can suggest approval or disapproval, disgust or delight, dullness or alertness. Select the word or near synonym which suggests the desired emotional tone. For example, the following words have the same denotation, "never giving up in the face of difficulty": "persevering," "persistent," "obstinate," "stubborn," "pigheaded." If you want to describe Sam Cobbler, you will affect your reader's attitude according to whether you call Cobbler *persistent* or *pigheaded.* Likewise the tone is different if a person is designated as an "intellectual" or an "egghead," a "politician" or a "statesman," a "traveling salesman" or a "field representative." Select your words for the meaning (dictionary and emotional) you want. Bertrand Russell humorously illustrated the emotional meanings of words on a BBC radio program when he gave the following "conjugation" of an "irregular verb."

> I am firm.
> You are obstinate.
> He is a pigheaded fool.

Here are some others along the same line:

TABLE OF CONJUGATIONS

I am beautiful.
You have fairly good features.
She isn't bad-looking if you like that type.

I am rightfully indignant.
You are annoyed.
He is stirring up a lot of fuss over nothing.

I don't dance very well.
You ought to consider taking lessons.
He has the grace of a dilapidated camel.

I believe in being frank.
You sometimes speak too bluntly.

I am portly.
You are a trifle overweight.
He is a fat slob.

I am rather imaginative.
You are an escapist.
She ought to see a psychiatrist.

Of course I use a little makeup.
You really overdo it a little.

She is a painted clown.

I'm just an old-fashioned girl.
You're somewhat conservative.

He has as much tact as a moronic jackass.	She is living in the Dark Ages.
I collect rare, old objects of art.	I am careful.
You lucked into a thing or two that's worth looking at.	You are fussy.
She has a flair for surrounding herself with bric-a-brac.	He is a picky, old woman.

Another humorous way to illustrate words that show approval and disapproval is to compile what we could call "The Handbook of Duplicity." We pick one term to describe our friends and another to describe our enemies—although the core of meaning of both terms is the same.

THE HANDBOOK OF DUPLICITY

FOR ENEMIES	FOR FRIENDS
damned lie	white lie
bum	homeless unemployed
male chauvinist pig	forceful man
dog eat dog	free enterprise
freeloader	houseguest
pig	guardian of public safety
fuzz	guardian of public safety
goof-off	student working below capacity
brat	clever, active child
copping out through drugs	expanding one's consciousness
brainwashed	enlightened
flunk out	separate from college
dead drunk	unwinding
crackpot	original thinker
fanatic	person of conviction
loafer	temporarily unemployed
retreat	strategic withdrawal
prostitute	lady friend
garbage collector	sanitation engineer
communism	government of the people
shyster	lawyer
tyrant	father
alienated	doing your own thing
copping out	getting out of the rat race
lazy bums	poor and needy

ALIVE

For your message to be alive, your words must be *concrete* and *specific* rather than abstract and general, and they must be *fresh* rather than *worn-out*.

Concrete and Specific

Concrete words refer to things you can perceive through the five senses. They describe things that are tangible, things that you can point to—"dollar bill," "desk," "truck." Abstract words are conceptual. They refer only to general ideas in the mind—an abstraction of concrete things—such as "capital" (for "dollar bill") or "transportation" (for "truck").

A *general term* names a class or a group and stands for broad characteristics of things. A *specific term* names a member of a group and stands for more precise, definite things or characteristics. "Typewriter" is general; "IBM Selectric" is specific. "Vehicle" is general; "1977 Chevrolet ½ ton pickup" is more specific.

Using too many abstract and general terms makes writing vague and dull. You must use abstract words to state ideas of significance, but pin them down to tangible experience by using specific and concrete words.

VAGUE, GENERAL	CONCRETE, SPECIFIC
The new shipping clerk is a dedicated worker.	The new shipping clerk, Ted Alexander, worked two hours overtime without pay to get the Jenkins Corporation order off on schedule.
These tires provide the driver with miles of worry-free driving.	These Goodrich radial tires provide the driver with a 45,000-mile guarantee against blowouts.
A quick start	A three-second start.
Our company has won several prizes.	Jettison, Inc., has won first prize in four regional contests within the past three years.
This machine reproduces sales letters fast.	The IBM Model 1600 Jet types 2,000 personalized 125-word sales promotion letters in one hour.

A troublesome kind of general word is the *relative* word or *opinion* word, which probably has meanings different for the writer than it has for the reader. For instance, how expensive is expensive? An $8000-a-year man and a $75,000-a-year woman will have different opinions. How fast is fast? It's different if you're traveling by foot than by jet. If you ask the distributor to ship the goods fast, he may think you want them in two months for Christmas, when you really want them in two weeks for your special fall sale.

The following list suggests the kinds of words that can lead to vague, imprecise communication:

a few	more	slow
a small number	most	small
high	nice	soon
large	quick	tall
low	several	very
many	short	

Strategic Generalization

In some situations, of course, it is strategic to use general expressions. Although sometimes you may not have definite facts or figures, you need to get off your basic message. At other times you may want to be diplomatic, so you may use *strategic generalizations.* For instance, instead of writing, "We have sent you three notices about your delinquent account," you may strategically write to a prompt-paying customer, "We have sent you *several* reminders of this overdue payment." Or specific facts might be important, as in *"Many* people were waiting at the front door at opening time." Again, strategic generalization is preferred in some cases (as in refusing credit) when specific reasons might anger the potential customer.

Fresh

Use fresh expressions, not trite expressions. A trite expression is also called a *cliché* or a *stereotyped expression.* It is one that has become worn out through overuse, such as "straight from the shoulder," "burn the midnight oil," "last but not least."

Individual words themselves do not become trite. Words like "buy," "sell," "eat," "wise," "pay," "nose" can constantly be fresh. It is the phrase, perhaps once vivid and fresh, that has become commonplace and meaningless through overuse and lack of original thought. Consider the following sentence:

Bill Toler earns his *bread and butter* by the sweat of his *brow*.

We are not convinced of the genuineness of Bill Toler's industry or difficulty. Because of trite thinking the wording is trite and the experience is empty. The following simple sentence, although not worthy of Shakespearean tragedy, evokes our sympathy for Toler.

Bill Toler works 48 hours a week at hard labor in a machine shop.

You can hardly avoid trite expressions entirely. But you can do two things. First, you can do your own authentic, original thinking and use the best words to describe your actual thoughts. And second, you can become aware of current clichés and try to avoid them.

Here are a few examples of trite expressions. There are thousands more.

a long felt need	drastic action	nick of time
abreast of the times	financially embar-	slowly but surely
better late than	rassed	to the bitter end
never	heartfelt thanks	venture a sugges-
bring order out	last but not least	tion
of chaos	needless to say	white as snow
doomed to disap-		
pointment		

DIRECT

Good business writing should usually be natural, simple, and straightforward. The reader is likely to doubt your sincerity if you use pretentious, artificial direction. Such writing tends to emphasize words rather than ideas, usually not even interesting words, but vague, fuzzy, and abstract words. There are three main kinds of indirect diction that get in the way of effective communication: *jargon, exaggeration,* and *incorrect idiom*. There is one kind of indirect diction that is desirable in effective communication—the *calculated euphemism*.

Jargon

Jargon, in its best sense, is the technical or specialized vocabulary of a particular group, profession, or trade, such as legal jargon, educational jargon, medical jargon, real estate jargon, musicians' jargon. Such use of language is shoptalk and is quite appropriate if both reader and writer understand the terminology. But often specialists—insurance agents, lawyers, advertising executives, engineers, government bureaucrats, to list a few—forget that the outsider doesn't share their specialized language. Then we have cloud formations and private language.

For instance, somebody outside the real estate appraisal field might not understand such terms as "the residual techniques," "economic life," and "unit-in-place factors." Government bureaucrats may use the term "units of nutritional intake," but most readers would better understand the more direct word "food."

Jargon at its worst uses long, abstract words, elaborately constructed sentences, circumlocution, and technical language for its own sake.

The cure for most jargon is clear, direct thought and simple, straightforward language.

JARGON: It is my considered opinion that by examining Turner's thought processes, we shall be in a position to determine the real validity of his hypotheses and conclusions concerning the Hillsdale project.

NATURAL: I think we should examine Turner's theories about the Hillsdale project to see how valid they are.

If clear communication were not so important, the use of jargon could be considered ludicrous. We could construct a "jargon-making machine" to humorously illustrate the point that jargon just does not communicate sincere, serious ideas. The machine is made up of three columns of selected jargon words:

JARGON-MAKING MACHINE: CHECKLIST

Input A	Input B	Base
0. operational	0. input	0. concept
1. compatible	1. incremental	1. feedback
2. optional	2. reciprocal	2. capability
3. systematized	3. organizational	3. projection
4. finalized	4. interface	4. options
5. functional	5. policy	5. rationale
6. total	6. logistical	6. mobility
7. parallel	7. relevant	7. flexibility

| 8. responsive | 8. digital | 8. programming |
| 9. synchronized | 9. monitored | 9. contingency |

What you do as a writer to spare yourself the work of thinking up jargon is to chose a three-digit number. Then choose the corresponding word from each column. For example number 892 gives you "responsive monitored capability." Number 168 produces "compatible logistical programming." These phrases can be dropped into your reports at random to give them a tone of authoritative knowledge. Your reader won't have the slightest idea what you are talking about—and, of course, he won't ask you.

Exaggeration

Exaggerated expressions get in the way of direct communication. One kind of exaggeration makes use of extreme descriptions like "fabulous," "fantastic," "marvelous," "wonderful," and "miraculous." Another kind of exaggeration shows up in those intensifiers or superlatives that cover the universe like "very," "best," "must," "latest," "largest," "least," and "highest."

Such terms are obviously emotional, subjective, and inaccurate and so obscure or evade the basic information. The reader is disgruntled at the distortion or lack of information and also questions the writer's sincerity.

EXAGGERATED: This fantastic machine sells for $180.
    DIRECT: This machine sells for $180.

From other information given, the reader can draw his or her own conclusions as to the quality of the machine.

EXAGGERATED: The Full-Scan camera is *positively* the *best* money can buy, and our stores give the *largest* discount available *anywhere.*
    DIRECT: The Full-Scan Camera comes complete with high quality and low price. Compare.

It is a strain on communication to make the reader believe that the writer has such complete information and sound judgment about this and all other cameras.

Incorrect Idiom

Idioms are special word groups which have a total meaning not obviously suggested by the parts. The following idioms are ridiculous or nonsensical if analyzed literally:

board a train
look up an old friend
catch his eye
takes after her boss
strike a bargain

Prepositions especially get attached to certain words and natural usage demands accustomed combinations. We say "full of joy" not "full with joy," and "filled with joy" not "filled of joy." Likewise, you say "I differ *from* him" if you mean "unalike," and you say "I differ *with* him" if you mean "disagree."

Here are some examples of base words with their proper prepositions.

authority on (a subject)
authority over (a subordinate)
desirous of (doing something)
interest in
preparatory to
variance with (another)
vary from, in, with

Calculated Euphemism

Sometimes a business letter shouldn't be direct. The writer has to express an unpleasant idea, but doesn't want harsh words to produce a negative attitude toward the reader or the central message. The writer can ease around negative reactions by using euphemisms.

A euphemism is a word or phrase used instead of another word or phrase in order to avoid (or at least soften) a negative connotation. The substitute word is rarely as precise or as expressive as the original, but it is preferable because the reader understands it without reacting adversely to it. Instead of "die," you might use the less offensive term "pass on." Instead of "graveyard," you would use "memorial park." Through the process of euphemism, "toilets" become "rest rooms" or "powder rooms," "syphilis" becomes a "social disease," "old people" become "senior citizens," and "garbage" becomes "refuse."

As a business writer, you should become sensitive to the techniques of euphemism and to the need for it. You will have to, occasionally, search hard for euphemisms to avoid displeasing terms. A partial list of the hundreds of euphemisms presently in use appears in this checklist:

EUPHEMISMS: CHECKLIST

THE UNPLEASANT TERM	THE EUPHEMISM
toilet bowl	commode
toilet (room)	rest room, men's room, ladies' room
garbage	refuse
servants	household staff
social blunder	indiscretion, *faux pas*
false teeth	dentures
women's underwear	lingerie
bad breath	halitosis
to urinate or defecate	to void
to spit	to expectorate
to arrest	to detain
to spy	to do intelligence work
indoctrination	education, pacification
propaganda	information
blockade	quarantine
death blow	*coup de grace*
elderly people, old people	senior citizens
neurotic	sensitive, high strung
psychopathic	disturbed
homosexual	gay
a dying patient	a terminal patient
to die	to expire, pass on
corpse	body, remains
undertaker	mortician, funeral director, grief therapist
tombstone	monument
cemetery	memorial park
retarded child	special child
cheap	inexpensive
to steal	to lift
a lie	a fabrication
to kill (for punishment)	to execute
to kill (for mercy, an animal)	to put to sleep
to kill (for mercy, a person)	euthanasia
to disembowel	to eviscerate
beheaded	decapitated
rape	criminal assault
foul smell	odor
payments	premiums

EXERCISES AND PROBLEMS

1. Use each of the following words in a sentence to indicate the
   correct meaning.
a. advise	inform
b. enervate	invigorate
c. practical	practicable
d. disinterested	uninterested
e. immigrant	emigrant
f. receipt	recipe
g. climactic	climatic
h. acquiesce	consent
i. acknowledge	admit
j. opaque	translucent

2. Explain the differences in meaning among the following groups
   of words.
   a. outdo, surpass, excel, transcend, exceed
   b. fat, plump, obese, heavy, stout
   c. minimize, belittle, disparage, deprecate
   d. drunk, inebriated, plastered, intoxicated, stoned, potted
   e. dead, defunct, expired, deceased
   f. persistent, strong-willed, firm, stubborn, obstinate, pig-
      headed
   g. renown, fame, notoriety
   h. house, home, residence, dwelling, domicile, pad

3. Evaluate the word "old-fashioned" in the following sentences
   to see what meanings it has besides its denotation of referring
   to past time.
   a. The dress she was wearing was rather old-fashioned.
   b. He is decorating his living room in old-fashioned American.
   c. That idea is a little old-fashioned, isn't it?
   d. I'm just a simple, old-fashioned girl.
   e. I believe in the old-fashioned philosophy of no work, no
      eat.
   f. Stop in for some old-fashioned cooking.

4. Make a list of more specific words for the following general
   terms. For instance, for "say," you could list "mumble," "mut-
   ter," "whisper," "shout," "yell," "state," "utter," "drawl."
a. vehicle	f. bad
b. building	g. entertainment
c. goods	h. person
d. walk	i. landscaping
e. good	j. land

5. Rewrite the following sentences, making general words more specific.
   a. A man was looking into the store window.
   b. I did a lot of things during my vacation.
   c. Several aspects of the room made it unattractive.
   d. The injury that our best saleswoman had suffered was serious enough to keep her out for quite a while.
   e. After eating, we had some really good entertainment.
   f. One member of the group was irresponsible about some of his duties.
   g. During the last part of the project, we encountered several difficulties.
   h. Many items around the place needed to be repaired before the people could move in.
   i. It's an interesting machine.
   j. The actions of the people represented both a test of skill and an effort to gain prestige for the cause.
6. The following sentences lack vitality because of clichés. Rewrite them in fresh language.
   a. The manual is being sent under separate cover. Will you kindly acknowledge receipt of same?
   b. According to our records, the project is to be completed in the near future.
   c. Tilden is a borderline candidate for regional manager, but where there's a will there's a way.
   d. Mrs. Jones fought tooth and nail to get the new school bill passed.
   e. Mrs. Jenkins really burned the midnight oil; for seven straight days last week she worked until the wee small hours.
   f. I told Mayford what we needed, and it was no sooner said than done.
   g. He was up at the crack of dawn every morning because the early bird always gets the worm.
   h. Making ends meet is rough sledding in this day and age.
   i. For all intents and purposes, people who really care about their jobs are as scarce as hen's teeth.
   j. While some of the salesclerks were stealing to their heart's content, Mary Adams remained as honest as the day is long.
7. Eliminate jargon and hackneyed phrases from the following sentences, and write them in simple, straightforward diction.
   a. We may find it necessary to communicate with him tomorrow relative to the change in plans and ascertain what alternate arrangement he may consider feasible.

b. The last rays of the sun were sinking behind the western horizon, when I returned wearily to my domicile after my futile attempts to peddle my wares.

c. They did not find it practicable to make the journey to our place of business because of the inclement weather conditions.

d. They were holding an intense verbal contention as to whether canines or felines are the most desirable members of the animal kingdom.

e. We must be cognizant of the fact that although a substantial segment of the population occupies areas comprising numerous agricultural units, yet this same segment suffers a deficiency in units of nutritional intake.

8. These sentences use exaggerated terms. Tone them down, making them direct and believable.

a. We are positive that you will agree that this is a fantastic price for such a camera.

b. It's a marvelous time of the year to paint your house.

c. This vacuum sweeper is the most efficient on the market.

d. The fabulous increase in sales is attributed to the superb advertising campaign.

e. Supersell Outlets give the largest discount available anywhere.

9. Correct the unidiomatic use of prepositions.

a. We were quite desirous to arrive before the store closed.

b. Ever since Mrs. Buxton became angry at me, she has refused to buy here.

c. He would not admit to making the mistake, and his supervisor would not absolve him of the responsibility.

d. The usual customer seems oblivious to the feelings of the salesclerk.

e. His aims were identical to mine.

f. Your aims are different than mine.

g. The jury acquitted him from the crime of arson.

h. Three stenographers refuse to conform with the rule against smoking.

i. Everybody complied to his request to talk softly.

j. I am incompatible to his theories of let the buyer beware.

10. List several euphemisms for each of the following.

a. fire (as *The boss fired him.*)

b. dumb (not intelligent)

c. failure (as *His attempt ended in failure.*)

d. insane

e. Pay your bill.

11. The author of the following passage has a significant point to make about the relationship between business management and academic management. But the style is so involved and cumbersome that most readers will give up before they finish it. Rewrite the passage, stating the ideas clearly and directly.

> The salesmanlike abilities and the men of affairs that so are drawn into the academic personnel, are presumably, somewhat under grade in their kind; since the pecuniary inducement offered by the schools is rather low as compared with the remuneration for office work of a similar character in the common run of business occupations, and since businesslike employés of this kind may fairly be presumed to go unreservedly to the highest bidder. Yet these more unscholarly members of the staff will necessarily be assigned the more responsible and discretionary positions in the academic organization; since under such a scheme of standardization, accountancy, and control, the school becomes primarily a bureaucratic organization, and the first and unremitting duties of the staff are those of official management and accountancy. The further qualifications requisite in the members of the academic staff will be such as make for vendability,—volubility, tactful effrontery, conspicuous conformity to the popular taste in all matters of opinion, usage and conventions.
>
> The need of such a businesslike organization asserts itself in somewhat the same degree in which the academic policy is guided by considerations of magnitude and statistical renown; and this in turn is somewhat closely correlated with the extent of discretionary power exercised by the captain of erudition placed in control. At the same time, by provocation of the facilities which it offers for making an impressive demonstration, such bureaucratic organization will lead the university management to bend its energies with somewhat more singleness to the parade of magnitude and statistical gains. It also, and in the same connection, provokes to a persistent and detailed surveillance and direction of the work and manner of life of the academic staff, and so it acts to shut off initiative of any kind in the work done.
>
> (Thorstein Veblen, *The Higher Learning in America*, Huebsch, New York, 1918)

6

Sharpening Your Thought Processes

As you gather your report materials, you will naturally have to think about them, to think them through, to draw conclusions based on them. While this is partly a matter of organization and presentation, it also affects research. We will discuss some of these patterns of thought later, but they can also fix the pattern of your research. For this reason, your investigation will probably follow one of the standard methods by which the human mind thinks its way through facts, authority, evidence, opinions, and attitudes to come to a conclusion.

RULES OF EVIDENCE: INDUCTIVE REASONING

The thought process of examining evidence and forming a general rule to account for the separate pieces of evidence is called *inductive reasoning*. One begins with particulars and ends with a *generalization*. Note the following example.

Evidence: The ripe watermelon I tasted last week was sweet and juicy. This ripe watermelon I have here is sweet and juicy. All the ripe watermelons I have checked before, some 30 or 40, have been sweet and juicy.

Conclusion: Therefore, I can state as a general principle that ripe watermelons are sweet and juicy.

A generalization asserts that on the basis of evidence about some things in a class something is true of all or some or many in the class.

Induction is the process of arriving at a general conclusion on the basis of incomplete information; yet the conclusion may be quite valid. Almost everything a person knows, he knows by induction. A person believes, for example, that all tigers have stripes. But because he has not seen all tigers, his judgment is based on partial evidence. The two or three tigers he has seen at the zoo had stripes. Those he saw in *National Geographic* and in nature movies had stripes. Everyone he knows agrees they have stripes. From this information, he reasonably concludes that *all* tigers have stripes. This process is induction. One considers evidence he has seen or heard to draw a conclusion about things he has not seen or heard. The mental move from limited facts—called a *sample*—to a general conviction is called an inductive leap.

Most conclusions regarding past, present, and future events are based on this kind of leap. One believes that George Washington was the first president of the United States, that taking aspirin will ease a headache, that the Democrats will win the next presidential election. Because he can never secure all the evidence relating to these questions, he reasonably makes judgments from the facts he has.

A special kind of generalization is the *hypothesis*. A hypothesis is a conclusion or explanation to account for a number of related facts about a specific individual, event, or condition (as in a criminal trial).

> John and Mary were observed frequently in each other's company until last Saturday.
> Since last Saturday they have not been seen together.
> John is reported to have been very glum and irritable since last Saturday.
> Until last Saturday, Mary wore an engagement ring on her finger, but it has not been seen there since.
> When someone mentioned John's name to Mary yesterday, she quickly changed the subject.

Conclusion: John and Mary had a serious quarrel last Saturday.

The master thinker, Sherlock Holmes, illustrates the use of hypothesis to account for evidence.

> With a resigned air and a somewhat weary smile, Holmes begged the beautiful intruder to take a seat, and to inform us what it was that was troubling her.

"At least it cannot be your health," said he, as his keen eyes darted over her; "so ardent a bicyclist must be full of energy."

She glanced down in surprise at her own feet, and I observed the slight roughening of the side of the sole caused by the friction of the edge of the pedal.

"Yes, I bicycle a good deal, Mr. Holmes. . . ."

My friend took the lady's ungloved hand, and examined it with as close an attention and as little sentiment as a scientist would show to a specimen.

"You will excuse me, I am sure. It is my business," said he, as he dropped it. "I nearly fell into the error of supposing you were typewriting. Of course, it is obvious that it is music. You observe the spatulate finger-ends, Watson, which is common to both professions? There is a spirituality about the face, however"—she gently turned it towards the light—"which the typewriter does not generate. This lady is a musician."

"Yes, Mr. Holmes, I teach music."

"In the country, I presume, from your complexion."

"Yes sir, near Farnham, on the borders of Surrey."

(Arthur Conan Doyle, "The Adventure of The Solitary Cyclist," *The Return of Sherlock Holmes*, McClure, Phillips & Co., New York, 1905)

In using evidence reasonably, there are four main rules to follow:

1 Consider the actual evidence.
2 Take the simplest interpretation.
3 Consider likely alternatives.
4 Beware of drawing absolute conclusions.

Let's take a look at each of these principles in detail.

Consider the Evidence

You must actually look at the evidence itself. You must not begin with a ready-made conclusion or opinion and then select evidence and force it to fit. Start with the evidence and then follow it wherever it leads, guided by all the experience you have ever had with similar evidence.

To be reliable, a generalization must be based on a large number of verifiable and relevant facts, carefully interpreted. To be creditable, the evidence supporting a generalization must be (1) known or available, (2) sufficient, (3) relevant, and (4) representative. The following examples illustrate misuse of these principles:

Facts Completely Lacking or Unknown

UFO's are ships from outer space.
Ten out of fifteen businessmen use Rolaids.

One frequently meets statements which simply lack evidence. Advertisements announce that "Ban is preferred by 7 out of 10 American women," that "Eight out of ten Hollywood stars use Lux toilet soap." Rumor whispers that Viceroy filters are made of harmful fiberglass and that smoking Kents may cause sterility. Such claims can be safely ignored until evidence is offered to support them.

A variation popular with sensational writers is to make an extravagant claim and point to concrete evidence—which happens to be unavailable. They charge that Warren Harding was murdered by his wife and that Franklin Roosevelt was poisoned by the Russians at Teheran—then regret that evidence is lost in the past. They affirm the existence of abominable snowmen, Atlantis, and the Loch Ness monster—then lament that proof is out of reach. They know that UFO's are ships from outer space and that a massive conspiracy led to the assassination of President Kennedy— then insist that the U.S. Air Force, the FBI, and the CIA are withholding crucial evidence. These inductions are based on an absent sample; the facts are simply lacking or unknown.

Insufficient Evidence

A hasty interpreter concluded from the following evidence in the newspaper that crime and violence are taking over the city:

Last week the Denney murder case dominated the newspaper. Today the front page describes a murder and two car accidents. The inside pages report on three thefts, two muggings, a cafe brawl, and a non-casualty skirmish between policemen and strikers. The newspaper contains 24 pages.

The interpreter did not consider such other relevant evidence as the 500,000 population of the city; several other stories in the same paper describing happy social gatherings, entertainments, and charity drives; the abundance of evidence about city life from sources other than the newspaper. By comparison, the evidence used by the interpreter was insufficient to make his conclusion valid.

Induction with an insufficient sample is common. One regularly hears charges like these:

> Most labor leaders are crooks. Look at Dave Beck, Frank Brewster, and Jimmy Hoffa.
>
> College entrance examinations are unfair. Let me tell you what happened to my brother . . .
>
> Don't talk to me about Mexicans. I know all about them. I lived next to a Mexican family for two years.

Clearly the indicated samples—*three* labor leaders, *one* brother, *one* family—are not enough to justify a broad conclusion.

Spokesmen commonly try to broaden the effect of limited examples by declaring them "average" or "typical." They remain limited examples. In argument, the word "average" should be suspected immediately.

What is an adequate sample on which to base an induction? There is no easy answer. Quantity varies with the nature of the question and degree of probability one seeks. Remember, though, that a small sample—if genuinely representative—can support a broad conclusion. George Gallup assesses American political opinion by polling 1500 individuals. But because his sample is chosen so that every adult American has an equal chance of being interviewed, the Gallup poll (like similar polls) is a reliable source of information. The mathematical probability is that 95 times out of 100 a selection of 1500 anonymous people will give results no more than 3 percentage points off the figures which would be obtained by interviewing every voter.

In everyday experience, we commonly use very limited information to draw a tentative conclusion. Such a practice is not unreasonable. If we see an acquaintance not wearing her engagement ring and acting despondently, we may speculate that she has broken her engagement. The evidence is not sufficient for us to offer condolences, but it is enough to keep from making jokes about marriage. If we hear from a friend that a newly opened restaurant is disappointing, we will probably choose not to eat there—at least until we hear a contrary report. Our conclusion is based on a minute sample, but it is all the sample we have. As our sample grows, so will our degree of conviction.

Irrelevant Evidence

Beware of pleasant and otherwise interesting facts, examples, and associations that do not logically apply to the issue at hand.

> John Clammer is certainly the best candidate for Governor. He has been endorsed by Shirley Wyll, the popular movie star.

Shirley Wyll as a voter certainly has the value of her vote, but the evidence here of Clammer's suitability is Wyll's prestige as a movie star. The relevant point is this: What are her qualifications as an expert in politics? Does a movie star endorsement make for a good governor?

Non-typical Evidence

A sample is not valid when it is not typical of the whole class of things studied. It is easy to see that one cannot gauge his town's attitude toward liquor taxes by polling only the citizens at the corner bar or only the members of the local W.C.T.U. chapter.

Conclusions based on an unrepresentative sample can be quite deceptive at first glance: for example, "Women are better drivers than men; they have fewer accidents." Here the sample is large enough—a substantial body of accident statistics—but it is not broad enough to be meaningful. The conclusion concerns all drivers, but the sample group includes only drivers who have had accidents. To be representative (that is, typical of the whole area under investigation), the sample must include all four groups involved:

1 men
2 women
3 drivers who have had accidents
4 drivers who have had no accidents

With this broad sample one may see that there are fewer women in automobile accidents because there are fewer women driving. The isolated statistics are meaningless if not compared to those for all drivers.

Consider this misinterpretation in a report:

> A study of 2800 Chicago citizens who had recent heart attacks showed that 70% of them were 10 to 15 pounds overweight. Obviously, obesity is a cause of heart disease.

At first reading, you might think the report to be valid. But then you consider that 70% of all Chicago citizens might be overweight.

Any conclusion from inductive reasoning is open to question, then, if its sample is too small or if it is unreasonably weighted in some way. The Nielsen rating service claims to know the audience size for American television programs. But because its data comes from 1100 audiometers (one for every 50,000 homes), the sufficiency of the sample is doubtful. The Kinsey report was said to reveal the sexual habits of American women. But because the information came from 5940 women—most of whom were well-educated, white, non-Catholic, and Gentile, and all of whom were willing to describe their sex lives to interviewers—the representativeness of the sample is open to question. Any poll with a selective sample—that is, in which some choose to respond to it and others do not—is unrepresentative.

There is a special danger in the decimal point—like "95.3% of all doctors interviewed"—because figures seem like hard facts. To make reliable generalizations from statistical data, you must carefully process the kinds and sources of information. You must check kinds of samplings, numbers of samplings, breadth and relevance of coverage, and so on. Test this one.

A businessman accused of paying starvation wages replies that the average income of those working in his business is $10,000.

The statistics:	1 proprietor	$54,000
	1 office worker	6,000
	8 shop workers/ $5000 ea.	40,000
		$100,000
	(Average = $10,000)	

By selecting nontypical instances, we can prove almost anything. By interviewing only the malcontents among employees, we could "prove" that all American corporations are heartless, cold, and selfish. By talking only to housewives in an economically privileged group, we could greatly overestimate the potential sales of a new product. The report writer must rule out the possibilities of chance variations when he generalizes by insisting on a random sampling process or by being sure that his specific instances are representative.

Take the Simplest Interpretation

Following the second rule of evidence, you must not accept a complex interpretation until simpler ones will not fit. The simplest conclusion that accounts for the evidence is probably the best. This principle is called the Law of Occam's Razor. The simplest is likely the best because it is likely the interpretation that has before explained similar evidence. The odds favor it.

If, during a heavy rainstorm, you hear sharp clicks as if something were striking the window glass, they are probably caused by hail, not by somebody shooting buckshot. If all the lights suddenly go out in your house, one complex interpretation would be that an aircraft from outer space is hovering over your house and the magnetic field generated by the craft has set up a counterfield to blank out your house current. A simpler explanation, and most likely to be valid, is that an electrical overload has flipped the main fuse in the switch box.

A perfect illustration of the overcomplex interpretation occurred in 1967 when New Orleans district attorney James Garrison tried to prove that Clay Shaw was involved in the assassination of President Kennedy. He submitted that Shaw's address book carried the entry "Lee Odom, P.O. Box 19106, Dallas, Texas" and that the number "PO 19106," when properly decoded became "WH 15601," the unlisted phone number of Jack Ruby, the slayer of Lee Oswald. The process involved "unscrambling" the numerals and—since P and O equal 7 and 6 on a telephone dial—subtracting 1300. Thus, Garrison used the entry in Shaw's address book as inductive evidence leading to a sensational conclusion. But Occam's razor suggests a simpler conclusion, one which proved to be a fact: Shaw was acquainted with a businessman named Lee Odom, whose Dallas address was P.O. Box 19106.

Consider Likely Alternatives

Start with the simplest interpretation, as we have just said, but do not fix on it and refuse to consider others. All likely conclusions must be considered, for the best judgment requires comparison. Look at the following piece of evidence and the interpretation drawn from it.

> Mr. Jones has been taking the bus to work this week and his new Buick is not in his garage. Either he has sold his car or the loan company has foreclosed on him.

The two alternatives of selling and foreclosure are both simple and both common to experience. However, still another alternative to consider is that the car is in the repair shop having some major tune-up or adjustment made. There is no solid evidence for selling or foreclosure, and with a new car the third hypothesis seems most reasonable.

Consider these further examples:

> Jensen's worn appearance these days is a cause for concern. He certainly must be working too hard.

> Any applicant who writes like this must be lazy or stupid.

But Jensen in the first example might have sickness as a cause, and the applicant in the second example might be poorly trained or distracted. Can you think of other reasonable alternatives?

Beware of Absolutes

Don't claim more than the evidence allows. A generalization is a general rule and not an absolute. Don't let your statement say *all* when the evidence allows only for *some*. Instead of hundred-percenters like *all, never, always,* maybe you should use more exact terms like *many, sometimes, often,* and *probably*.

Absolute generalization:	The Scandinavians are exceptionally talented people.
The evidence:	1. Rölvaag's novel *Giants in the Earth*
	2. Lagerkvist's novel *The Dwarf*
	3. Music of Sibelius and Grieg
	4. Sculpture of Thorwaldsen
Qualified conclusion:	A number of Scandinavians have produced outstanding work in literature, music, and sculpture.

The joke about the logician and his friend is enlightening. The two were looking at the countryside from the window of a passing train. The friend said, "Look over these in the field. Those sheep have just been sheared."

"Well," commented the logician, "they seem to have been sheared, at least on this side."

RULES OF CONNECTION: DEDUCTIVE REASONING

Deductive reasoning is a companion to inductive reasoning. Deduction works with the generalizations arrived at by induction. Whereas induction moves from specific facts to a general conclusion, deduction applies a general principle, a background of knowledge, or a rule to a specific case. We deduce that since this company has a policy of hiring only college graduates, the new assistant to the president must be a college graduate. This is, of course, applying a generalization to a specific example. You put two related ideas together and draw a third idea or conclusion from the connection between the first two.

Very simply, the deductive process can be stated as a formula: $1 + 2 = 3$.

Idea 1:	This company hires only college graduates.
Idea 2:	This company has hired a new assistant to the president.

Idea 3 (Conclusion):   The new assistant to the president is a college graduate.

Or suppose you were asked to measure employees' attitudes towards the company's new lunch-break policy and to make recommendation on the basis of what you found. Let's assume that you learn through interrogation that employees don't really like the new policy but that it is not a major complaint of theirs. Having examined the various theories of personnel management, you also know that, as a general rule, most cases of employee discontent that don't involve wages or safety are best handled by letting the offending policy remain in force and making some other, unrelated good will gesture to the employees. Knowing what you do, then, you will put the two big ideas or generalizations together and reason deductively something like this.

> Some personnel problems, especially those not involving wages and safety, are best handled by making some unrelated good-will gesture.
> The problem of lunch breaks does not involve wages or safety.
> Therefore, I recommend that we leave the lunch-break policy unchanged but make some unrelated good-will gesture to our employees.

To be valid, a thought process must follow two principles.

Ideas Must Be True

An idea is true if the facts that support it are known, sufficient, relevant, and representative—as pointed out earlier in this chapter on "Consider the Evidence." Check the implications of the following typical propaganda:

> You should vote for Terry Wilson for governor. He's been a successful businessman in the city for 20 years.

The logical formula would run something like this:

> All successful businessmen make good governors.
> Terry Wilson is a successful businessman.
> Therefore, Terry Wilson would make a good governor.

We might grant that business sense can be helpful to a governor. But we would need a lot of evidence to accept as true the generalization that all successful businessmen make good governors.

You will find a similar lack of sound thinking in this statement.

Sure she can vote; she's an American citizen.

But there are other necessary conditions, such as being 18 years old and registered.

Ideas Must Have a Relevant Connection

Two ideas may be offered as having a strong logical connection when they have at most a weak connection or no connection at all. In an advertisement in which a baseball hero is used to sell razor blades, the apparent thought process we are asked to accept could be reduced to these straightforward terms:

Idea 1:   Tom Slaver has the highest RBI in the National League.
Idea 2:   Tom Slaver shaves with Slic blades.
Idea 3 (Conclusion): Therefore, all men should shave with Slic blades.

Ideas 1 and 2 may be accurate in themselves, but the thinker has not established a valid connection between these items:

Tom's hitting ability and shaving needs.

Tom's shaving needs and other men's shaving needs.

Tom's hitting ability and other men's shaving needs.

Slic blades and all of the first three ideas.

Besides having weak connection or no connection, the ideas themselves may be misleading. For instance, although Tom uses Slic blades, he may not like them, he may have used them only for the advertisement in question, and he may also use five other brands.

In evaluating the connection between two ideas, there are two kinds of poor connections to look out for: (a) the hidden connection and (b) the twisted connection.

The Hidden Connection

The process of following deductive arguments would be easier if premises were always clearly stated. But often as least one premise is omitted, either because a full statement would be clumsy and wordy or because the writer does not clearly realize what his premises are.

To evaluate your own thinking and that of others, be sure you understand the hidden assumptions. Trouble arises when you reason from an unstated assumption that your reader would be doubtful about if it were stated in bald terms. Check the unstated assumption in this line of reasoning:

> As a subsidiary of Continental Grain Company, Conti is able to provide the benefits of in-depth experience in hedging and the use of futures markets . . . experience that translates into knowing what to do, when to do it, and how to do it well.
>
> ("A Frequent Definition of Hedging,"
> ContiCommodity Services, Inc., *Wall Street Journal*, October 25, 1978, p. 5)

The hidden assumption is that a grain company is experienced in hedging because grains provide several major commodities for hedging—barley, corn, oats, rye, soybeans, wheat. The assumption is valid and the line of reasoning is valid.

But check the hidden assumption in this line of thought:

> Baker is obviously a new employee. Look at how fast he works.

The unstated premise is that only new employees work fast; a premise that many older employees would not accept.

The following statement has at least three hidden assumptions. You need to clarify them to evaluate the reliability of the deduction.

> One way to improve the reading habits of the youth of the nation would be to turn off all the television sets between 7 and 11 P.M. on every school night.

The statement assumes (1) that the youth of the nation watch television between 7 and 11 P.M., (2) that if they couldn't watch television, they would read, and (3) that if they did read, they would improve their reading habits. All three assumptions are doubtful.

The Twisted Connection

Here are some common kinds of twisted thinking in which the thinker fails to establish a strong connection between valid ideas and so does not draw a valid deductive conclusion.

a. Proof by repetition. Also called *begging the question* and *reasoning in a circle*. A synonym or repetition of the statement is offered as proof of that statement. The thing itself is offered as its own proof.

> His handwriting is hard to read because it is illegible.
> It is the beer beer drinkers drink.

b. Proof by false connection. Also called *post hoc, erqo propter hoc*. The event that happened first is presumed to be the cause and the event that follows, the result. Time sequence is confused with causal sequence.

All these improvements in the economy, and so on, occurred *because* I have been your Senator.

c. Proof by no connection. Also called *non sequitur* (it does not follow). A hasty or thinly connected inference is presented as a logical conclusion.

This is the best book I have read this year and should win the Pulitzer Prize (valid only if the reader is one of the judges for the Pulitzer).

d. Proof by comparison. Also called *false analogy.* One or a few similarities between two things (persons, ideas, events) are used to make the point that the two are entirely similar.

Don't change horses in the middle of a stream; don't change presidents during a crisis.

e. Proof by oversimplification. Also called *false dilemma, open-and-shut case, all-or-nothing fallacy, two-valued orientation, capsule thinking,* and *tabloid thinking.* Hasty or shallow thinking can leap over a very complex thought situation and come to large conclusions that are not contained in the basic generalizations and their connection. Oversimplification usually eliminates in-between relationships or degrees, or it claims absolute coverage for small premises.

Truth is sometimes an either–or sort of thing. A light is either on or it is off. You either went to St. Louis or you did not. You either passed the exam or you did not. But most things that we argue about are not so clear-cut. People, governments, business processes, actions are seldom either all good or all bad. It is a fallacy to argue as if there are only two possibilities when the evidence justifies several possibilities.

America—love it or leave it.

Whenever you find corruption in government, the people ought to vote another party into power.

This is the real issue: shall we put government into business, or shall we let initiative be free to create real wealth.

Look for the fallacy of oversimplification in your own writing and in others' when you come across phrases like these:

the simple, unvarnished truth
it all boils down to this

the issue is plain and clear
in a nutshell
good or bad
victory or defeat
militarism or pacifism
foreign aid or isolationism
true or false
right or wrong
on balance

f. Proof by evasion. This fallacy is the complete breakdown of
the principle of logical connection. The thinker either does not
connect the two premises or does not make the conclusion grow
out of the premises. He deviates from the subject or throws such
obstacles in the way that the real issue is lost track of. There are
many ways to evade the issue. Some of the common ones are called
*neglected aspect, ignoring the question, red herring, card stacking,
slanting, wrenching from context, obfuscation, equivocation, ambi-
guity,* and *tu toque* (you're another). Here are some examples.

Wrenching from context:	When Mr. Grant (who is married) was in New York last week, he was seen having dinner with a showgirl. . . . (*Context:* . . . and her husband and their two children.)
Equivocation (shift in meaning of terms):	If you work for a living, then you are in business. Therefore, what helps business helps you.
Tu toque (you too, or you're another):	*Charge:* "You are cheating on your expense account." *Defense:* "Well, others are too." (The issue, though, is the cheating of "you.")

g. Proof by nonsense. By nonsense here is meant no actual verifiable meaning or sense, although a sentence may *seem* to have
meaning. In looking for substantial meaning, keep in mind that
it takes two things to make responsible, substantial meaning. The
words must have definite meaning in our language, and a statement
sentence must be used. Groups of words without these two features
can only seem to have meaning.

Here are some kinds of outright nonsense.

Unfinished Comparisons

Add your own possible finish to unfinished comparisons to see what nonsense they actually can be.

Now in Ungentine TWO TIMES the pain-relieving medication for FASTER PAIN RELIEF.

("TWO TIMES" . . . the medication held by a container half the size of this one. "FASTER" . . . pain relief than you would get with a bed of spikes.)

Nonreferent Abstractions

These are abstract words that do not refer to any tangible thing in experience. Special device words, usually capitalized and often hyphenated, are concocted by the claimers and so have only their meaning; they are just *like* similar words. The *apparent* idea is not actual. To say "Swing-Out Shelves" is not the same as to say "shelves that swing out," which many refrigerators have.

Nonsense: Only Hotpoint Refrigerator-Freezers bring all these . . . Swing-Out Shelves . . . Reserve Cold Power and Frost-Away Automatic defrosting.

Reduced to Sense: The Hotpoint company makes a refrigerator just like many other brands, with shelves that swing out, capable of temperatures colder than needed, and with automatic defrosting. But only Hotpoint calls these features by these special names.

No-statement Claims

These are claims that are apparent rather than actual. The group of words may seem to make a statement or a claim that the speaker should stand behind, but actually makes no such claim.

Spray Contact nasal mist *to* stop nasal congestion.

This is almost complete nonsense. The word "to" indicates purpose, not effect. The words are a phrase, not a statement, and it normally takes a statement to make a claim. And, of course, the stuff may have no curative effect at all on the cold itself, since it is only for the congestion, not the cold. A blast of cold air could have the same effect.

Contradictions

This is the presentation of two ideas, one of which cancels out the other, since both cannot be true.

I never watch TV, but last night I was looking at this show, and . . .

I'd like to lend you $10, but . . .

Study the following piece of thinking by Sherlock Holmes as an example of logical connection and reliable conclusions.

Holmes had been seated for some hours in silence with his long, thin back curved over a chemical vessel in which he was brewing a particularly malodorous product. His head was sunk upon his breast, and he looked from my point of view like a strange, lank bird, with dull gray plumage and a black top-knot.

"So, Watson," said he, suddenly, "you do not propose to invest in South African securities?"

I gave a start of astonishment. Accustomed as I was to Holmes's curious faculties, this sudden intrusion into my most intimate thoughts was utterly inexplicable.

"How on earth do you know that?" I asked.

He wheeled round upon his stool, with a steaming test-tube in his hand, and a gleam of amusement in his deep-set eyes.

"Now, Watson, confess yourself utterly taken aback," said he.

"I am."

"I ought to make you sign a paper to that effect."

"Why?"

"Because in five minutes you will say that it is all so absurdly simple."

"I am sure that I shall say nothing of the kind."

"You see, my dear Watson"—he propped his test-tube in the rack, and began to lecture with the air of a professor addressing his class— "it is not really difficult to construct a series of inferences, each dependent upon its predecessor and each simple in itself. If, after doing so, one simply knocks out all the central inferences and presents one's audience with the starting-point and the conclusion, one may produce a startling, though possibly a meretricious, effect. Now, it was not really difficult, by an inspection of the groove between your left forefinger and thumb, to feel sure that you did *not* propose to invest your small capital in the gold fields."

"I see no connection."

"Very likely not; but I can quickly show you a close connection. Here are the missing links of the very simple chain: 1. You had chalk between your left finger and thumb when you returned from the club last night. 2. You put chalk there when you play billiards, to steady the cue. 3. You never play billiards except with Thurston. 4. You told me, four weeks ago, that Thurston had an option on some South African property which would expire in a month, and which he desired you to share with him. 5. Your check book is locked in my drawer, and you have not asked for the key. 6. You do not propose to invest your money in this manner."

"How absurdly simple!" I cried.

"Quite so!" said he, a little nettled. "Every problem becomes very childish when once it is explained to you.

(Arthur Conan Doyle, "The Adventures of the Dancing Men," *The Return of Sherlock Holmes*, McClure, Phillips, & Co., New York, 1905)

EMOTIONAL APPEALS

Some thoughts and actions should spring from emotion. Others should come from sound sense and logic. If your action, decision, or conclusion is to be logical, then you want the thought process to be logical and based on fact and analysis, rather than emotional and based on prejudiced interpretation. If your report has some persuasion in it, such as in suggestions and recommendations for an interpretive report or in public relations and promotional reports, then you may enlist the feelings in support of your appeal. Emotionally toned words, pleasant associations, and reference to basic human drives can favorably dispose the reader toward your thinking, even though there may be no rational connection.

The following examples in no way tangibly describe the product or offer verifiable facts or logical demonstration.

Carefree fun lovers can enjoy the glorious excitement of Arrowhead Beach.

For up-to-the-minute news reporting, all-round coverage, and the outspoken opinions that add zest to your own thinking— why not try *The New Reporter?*

Such appeals may create an emotional aura in hopes of captivating the reader. They appeal to basic human drives.

Basic Human Drives

The following list will give you ideas for appeals to use in various situations with all kinds of people.

BASIC HUMAN DESIRES AND MOTIVES: CHECKLIST

Making money
Success
Personal ambition
Protecting family and loved
     ones
Personal health and safety
Efficiency
Pride of possession
Attracting the opposite sex
Saving time
Saving money
Popularity
Desire to be stylish
Emulating others
Belonging to a club or society
Pride in accomplishment
Satisfying appetites (hunger,
     thirst)
Generosity
Individuality

Comfort
Leisure
Social approval
Education
Children's success
Making friends
Having a nice home
Curiosity
Romantic enchantment
Escape
Avoiding criticism
Protecting reputation
Exercising one's talent
Being well dressed
Travel
Being respected in the com-
     munity
Desire for knowledge and in-
     sight
Prestige
Beauty

Here are some examples of how these basic appeals may be used in business messages.

Appeal to making money:

> Dear Mr. Jensen:
> After carefully analyzing your primary market and your advertising program of the past year, we believe that Acme Advertising can offer you a plan that will bring you much more return for the same expenditure you are now making . . .

Appeal to efficiency (Note the tact in this memo in saying "we" instead of an accusing "you."):

> Mr. Turnbow, I think we have a bottleneck in the operation of the shipping department, a weak point that can be easily corrected if we do a little shifting . . .

Appeal to ease, escape, romantic enchantment:

> The single International Charge Card can take you anywhere you want to go . . .

Such appeals can be very helpful if used to support or color your use of tangible description, verifiable facts, and logical reasoning. An appeal based only on emotionalism, however, quickly drives off most readers, and all sophisticated ones.

Emotional Substitutes for Reasoning

Here are some common emotional appeals that deviate from a sensible thinking process. To find sense behind the nonsense, ask "Just what is the real issue?"

Personal Appeals

These exploit our being individual human beings. They work to discredit or praise the person connected with the issue, rather than dealing with the issue or idea itself. Common nicknames for the process are *name calling* and *appeals to pity.* Formal logic calls it *ad hominem,* or "appeal to the man." Such appeals seeks to praise or discredit the character, motive, family, associations, and so on, of a person. The person is called an atheist, leftist, hawk, dove, scab, pig, Commie, racist, or a family man, girl scout, Christian, good guy.

> "There sits the defendant. He is a good neighbor, a considerate husband, a kind father. He has never before been accused of a crime. He is an elder in the local church. Surely you don't think for a moment that such a man could commit murder." (But the one issue is this: *Did* he commit the murder?)

Popular Appeals

These exploit our urge to belong to groups. The appeals are based largely on a popular custom, belief, notion, figure, or symbol. Common nicknames for these appeals are *bandwagon, everybody's doing it,* and *appeal to the crowd.* Such appeals may refer to the flag, the church, mother, Uncle Sam, the gang, the Set, and so on.

> Joe Blow is a grass-roots candidate.
> I'd rather fight than switch.
> Four Roses for men of distinction.
> Mrs. Blount, a Kansas City housewife, says, "Use Tag in your washer."

Prejudiced Associations

These exploit the whole core of our emotional nature—desires, needs, urges, longings, and unfulfillments. This list is long. Compare also the list of "Basic Human Drives" given earlier in the chapter.

Check this list for emotional associations, pleasant or unpleasant, that come to your mind. Note how often logical thought turns off and emotion turns on.

sex	free prizes
ego	the free world
rich people	anybody over 30
establishment	anybody under 20
Commie	black
health	white
money	Formula X-9 with Celustan (or
silent majority	any scientific label)
computerize	middle class
modern	un-American
country club	migrant worker

Study the following excerpt as an example of the use of emotional appeals. The line of thinking is not intended to be serious, but it does illustrate how details selected for emotional value can affect an argument. Taken from Kenneth Vinson's *Prohibition's Last Stand*, it portrays a Mississippi judge's stand on Mississippi whiskey.

> If when you say whiskey you mean the devil's brew, the poison scourge, the bloody monster, that defiles innocence, dethrones reason, destroys the home, creates misery and poverty, yea, literally takes the bread from the mouths of little children; if you mean the evil drink that topples the Christian man and woman from the pinnacle of righteous, gracious living into the bottomless pit of degradation and despair, and shame, and helplessness, and hopelessness, then certainly I am against it.

But if when you say whiskey you mean the oil of conversation, the philosophic wine, the ale that puts a song in their hearts and laughter on their lips, and the warm glow of contentment in their eyes; if you mean Christmas cheer; if you mean the stimulating drink that puts the spring into the old gentleman's step on a frosty, crispy morning; if you mean the drink which enables a man to magnify his joy, and his happiness, and to forget, if only for a little while, life's great tragedies, and heartaches, and sorrows; if you mean that drink, the sale of which pours into our treasuries untold millions of dollars, which are used to provide tender care for our little crippled children, our blind, our deaf, our dumb, our pitiful aged and infirm; to build highways and hospitals and schools, then certainly I am for it.

This is my stand, I will not retreat from it. I will not compromise.

(Kenneth Vinson, "Prohibition's Last Stand," *The New Republic,* October 16, 1965, p. 11)

TRACING CAUSES AND EFFECTS

"Why?" we ask and "What brought this on?" and "What is going to come out of this?" In more specific terms, it is "Why did Ted Blake fall apart as manager of the West Branch?" "Why did sales fall off during the third quarter?" "What makes X-Tan sell better than our product?"

Whether you reason from a known cause to an effect or the other way around, the causal relationship is basically the same. You look out the window, for example, at an outdoor thermometer reading 15 degrees and reason that because of the freezing temperature your car radiator will be frozen (cause, freezing temperature; effect, frozen radiator). Or you may know the radiator is frozen and then reason back properly to the cause—freezing temperature. A business report forecasts trends, for instance, going from an analysis of today's basic conditions to the *effect* three months, a year, or five years from now. Reports analyzing decrease or increased sales or production, difficulty in hiring personnel, changes in price or quality of materials proceed from a known result (effect) back to cause or causes, just as a doctor reasons from your symptoms back to their basic cause. For either method, the tests are the same.

Tracing causes and effects may take any of several patterns. You may classify a list of causes or of effects. You may establish the cause and effect connection between two events, showing how one directly caused the other. Or you may trace a whole chain of events in which A is the cause of B, which is the cause of C, which is the cause of D, and so on. Or you may show how several otherwise unrelated events converge to cause something.

Analyzing causes and effects can be very complex. A given event, such as a young man's robbing a pharmacy, may have a chain of causes reaching back several generations and may have consequences reaching far into the future. Also, a given event may have several causes or consequences, not just one. What looks at first like a significant cause may be very minor or might not be a cause at all, such as the old medical belief that letting blood was a cause of a person's recovering health.

Check the following guides to help you think clearly about causes and effects.

Distinguish Immediate Cause from Remote Cause

What caused the death of Tim Johnson, who died in an automobile accident? The most immediate cause was brain concussion. A less immediate cause was the oil slick on the road that caused the car to slide out of control. Another less immediate cause was his heavy drinking, which led to an argument with his wife, which shook him up so much that he could not control the car. An even more remote cause was the pampering he received as a child from his mother, which made it difficult for him to cope with the problems of adult living, including his wife, and so on. A written analysis might logically stop at any point, of course, depending entirely on your purpose.

Look for Several Causes

As you analyze causes and effects, don't fasten immediately on the first one that comes to mind and decide there is only one cause or one effect. There are probably several, all at once or in sequence. It is likely hasty thinking to conclude that a young man took up hard drugs for one reason—to gain acceptance with the group. It is likewise shallow thinking to say that a divorce was caused by the wife's heavy drinking.

Don't Leave Out Any Links in a Sequence

If you leave only one link out of a chain of causes, the reader may be lost. For example, a cause and effect series could run something like this.

Business losses depress the boss; boss nags secretary; secretary nags husband; ugly scene drives son to gang; gang tests son; son robs pharmacy; police catch son; son ends up in jail.

If we leave out one link, such as "ugly scene drives son to gang," we could not get a true account of the important events and conditions that led to the boy's ending up in jail.

Don't Confuse Causal Relationship with Time Relationship

In logic, this error is called the *post hoc, ergo propter hoc* fallacy ("after this, therefore because of this"). Just because one event happened at the same time or just after another event does not necessarily mean that the one caused the other. Your losing your wallet just after a black cat crossed your path was not likely caused by the black cat. Many an incumbent politician campaigns by saying, "These glorious things happend *because* I was in office." The truth of the matter is often that those things happened not because but *while* he was in office, and he himself had little or no causal connection in producing them.

Analyze the following account as a practice in discerning causes. What brought about Mr. Mead's death? Who is responsible? Consider immediate, remote, and multiple causes. Where would the emphasis be if you were a safety inspector, a medical examiner, a represenative from the child welfare agency, or a political reformer?

Mr. Alford owns an old apartment building which does not conform to the safety regulations of the city. Because of Mr. Alford's political connections, the fire inspection of the building is superficial.

In one of the apartments of the building lives a family by the name of Gordon, composed of Mr. and Mrs. Gordon, their son Jimmy, and Mrs. Gordon's mother. Mr. Gordon has managed to get the apartment by means of business pressure put upon Mr. Alford.

Mrs. Gordon is a rather careless housekeeper and allows trash to accumulate in closets and pantries. Mrs. Gordon's

mother, an impatient and irritable woman, one day locks
Jimmy in the pantry because of some piece of misbehavior.
In his bad temper Jimmy kicks the brooms and mops about.
A metal mop head falls against a piece of exposed electrical
wiring and the short circuit ignites some old papers and rags
which Mrs. Gordon has left in the pantry.

Jimmy's screams warn the family, who escape from the burning building, but Mr. Mead, asleep in an apartment above, is
burned to death.

PREDICTING CONSEQUENCES

Predicting consequences is a special form of cause and effect analysis. We often try to look into the future and foresee the effects
or outcome of a certain situation or course of action. An important
factor in making present decisions or promoting changes is trying
to foresee consequences. We plan to market a new product, we
ponder firing somebody, we consider relocating an assembly plant,
or we worry about a growing surliness in the sales manager. To
predict wisely and then follow up with a course of action can certainly affect our future success. Wise predictions observe three
main principles.

Use Available Evidence

Predictions must be based on evidence and expectation, not on
hope, desire, or emotionalism. The better the evidence, the better
the prediction. A racing fan may bet on a particular horse because
of its name or its color or because he hopes it will win and pay
25 to 1. But a safer prediction of the outcome of the race would
be based on expectation derived from past performance of the
horse reckoned against present racing conditions. You may hope
your team wins, and you may be loyal to your school, but a safer
prediction of the outcome of the game will be made by comparing
the evidence of the abilities of the two teams.

Compare with Similar Situations

Much of what we call wisdom is learning by what the past
teaches. Sound prediction applies human experience to the future.
The more situations studied, the better the prediction. A doctor

predicts the course and outcome of a particular streptococcus infection on the basis of all other strep cases he or she has had experience with.

Beware of Over-Prediction and Over-Simplification

While weighing evidence and reckoning your situation against other similar situations, you must go beyond the evidence you have collected and must allow for any factors that make the new situation different. This means you must be careful not to predict too large a consequence or future direction for the facts observed.

The *Population Reference Bureau* of 1955 showed that the percentage of Americans 65 years of age and over had doubled since 1900. It also showed an increase in the proportion of older women. At the time, somebody predicted that "in terms of voting power, ownership of land and common stocks, the U.S. can be seen on the road to a gerontomatriarchy—control by aging females." Time has shown the view to have been an overprediction.

Here is another example of predicting beyond evidence and reason. "The life expectancy in the country has been practically doubled in the past century (from about 35 to about 70). It is likely; therefore, that within another century most people will live to be a hundred and forty."

The following paragraph traces the consequences of a poor condition of soil—from the first stage of exposed soil to the final consequence of a poor economy in which industry and commerce stop.

If the soil is exposed, unprotected from the rains by cover and by roots, the people will be poor and the river will be muddy, heavy with the best soil of the fields. And as a consequence each year the farmers will be forced more and more to use their land in ways that speed up this cycle of ruin, until the cover and then the top soil itself are wholly gone. When that day comes, as it has in the great reaches of China's sorrowful Yellow River Valley, or in once flourishing Mesopotamia, now gaunt and desolate, then the rains run off the land almost as rapidly as water runs from a pavement. Even a moderate rainfall forces the river from its banks, and every downpour brings disastrous floods, destroying crops and homes and bridges and highways, not only where the land is poor, but down the river's length, down in the areas where people are more prosperous, where the soil is still protected and factories have been built at the river's bend. Industries and railroads will be interrupted, farms flooded out, towns and villages destroyed, while heavy silt deposits fill the power reservoirs and stop up the channels of navigation.

(David E. Lilienthal, *TVA: Democracy on the March*, Harper & Bros., New York, 1944)

Note that Lilienthal's predictions are taken from general experience and knowledge. Has he made any statement that you would dispute? What specific examples or comparative situations does he cite?

COMPARISON AND CONTRAST

We compare or contrast two items for three basic reasons. (1) We clarify something familiar, such as comparing the factory system in Russia with that of the United States. Here one term is used to shed light on the other. (2) We may want to explain both items in terms of similarities and differences, such as the blue-collar and the white-collar worker. Here we want to give information about both terms. (3) We may want to show that one thing is superior to another, such as one of two sites for a proposed factory location. Establishing values and making decisions require comparing and contrasting. We use these methods when we decide which job to take, which person to hire, which product to manufacture.

Pro and con thinking necessarily uses comparative methods. All decision making involves pro and con thinking. You weigh two or more sides of a question and make a judgment as to which is the better. There are two related types of thought patterns. You choose one thing over two or more alternatives, or you rank several items in order of worth or preference.

You decide to watch TV rather than to study. You decide to push sports outfits rather than business suits. You form an opinion that the advantages of getting a college degree outweigh the luxuries you will give up in the process.

You judge items in order of worth or preference when you decide in which order to begin manufacturing the five new products, when you choose sides for a team, or when you have four examinations coming up with barely enough time to study for two.

With both kinds of judging processes, the thought pattern follows three main principles. (1) You weigh the pros and cons, the advantages and the disadvantages, and the strong points and weak points of two or more things. (2) You try not to overlook any significant item. (3) You try to forecast the consequences, good and bad, of possible courses of action. If all sides balance, or rate the same, then you must treat them the same and can make no deliberate choice. If a quarterback can't decide whether to hand off, pass, or run, he will be sacked. A girl who can't weigh the pros and cons of three men in order of value is likely to have three men or none. Usually, though, one side of an issue weighs more heavily than another. Then you can make a decision, form an opinion, or move in a definite direction.

Analogy is a special form of comparison used to clarify something unfamiliar. Analogy takes one instance and by comparing it with another instance attempts to conclude that what happened in the one instance will also happen in the other. By analogy, we might reason that since last year we had increased prices on our products with a resulting loss in sales, and since all conditions are the same this year, the same result will occur if we raise prices. This form of analogy, used for reasoning, is generally called a *logical analogy.* It should be clearly distinguished from what is called *figurative analogy,* which is a method of explanation using an apparent similarity between two things. For example, our comparison in Chapter 2 between a report design and a road map is a figurative analogy, used to explain but not to draw any logical conclusions.

In general, the logical analogy can best be used in reports which draw conclusions by comparing business conditions at one time and another. By analogy, you might report that since business conditions in 1971 and 1980 are basically the same and since sales increased in the last six months of 1971, it would follow that sales will increase in the latter half of 1980. Or your report might follow an analogy between your stenographic staff, which was centralized and effected certain economies, and your purchasing function, which you now advocate centralizing for economy. There is one test for a logical analogy, and it must be applied rigorously: *Are the two things being compared fundamentally similar in the essential characteristics relating to the conclusion?*

If there is only an apparent similarity, you may find that you have a useful method of explanation but not a method of reasoning. Analogies involving human beings can especially be dangerous. Should you report that because you hired Jim Bell with certain grades, activities, and personal qualities last year from Ohio University and had to terminate his employment, you shouldn't hire Tom Ball this year with just about the same grades, activities, and personal qualities and from the same institution? Perhaps, but you'll be on safer ground if you can apply a larger statistical yardstick to Tom Ball, such as experience over 15 years shows that four out of five Ohio University graduates who are in the upper third of their class have had successful careers with your company.

PROBLEM SOLVING

You can be sure that as long as you have life you will have problems to solve by thinking. The car won't start; you're getting low grades in psychology; your boy friend or girl friend seems too interested in others; you need more money for clothes and pizza; or you're losing sleep at night because of the neighbor's loud radio. In solving problems we must keep in mind five important principles.

Clarify the Problem

The first thing to do is to make sure that you have a real problem and that you identify just what the real problem is. For example, your car is running rough. You tell the mechanic that the carburetor is out of adjustment and the engine needs new plugs. He looks at you and grunts and then checks many things besides the plugs and carburetor. He runs the motor and listens. He pulls plug wires off one at a time. He watches the exhaust coming out of the tailpipe. He tests each cylinder with a compression gauge. He finally clarifies your problem as not carburetor maladjustment at all, but as faulty valves. The problem clarified, you can then work out a solution— repair the valves, get a new car, etc.

Consider Alternatives

Don't be prepared to settle for the first apparent solution that comes to mind. In order to arrive at the best solution consider all possibilities. For instance, suppose your girl friend is showing interest in another person. If you think the solution to that problem is to keep her away from the competition, you probably should consider other alternatives. Likely alternatives might be to change some of your own unattractive characteristics, to do more things specifically to please your friend, to get a new friend who is more compatible, etc.

Forecast Consequences

The possible consequences of a given solution must be considered in order not to create new conditions worse than the original problem. A solution to the neighbor's noisy radio would be to cut the power lines. A solution to the high price of food would be to rob a supermarket. These solutions would indeed solve their respective problems for a time, but the consequences of such solutions would likely create new and worse problems.

Make Sure the Solution Is Real

It is not a real solution to say that the problem of alcoholism would be solved if people just wouldn't drink so much. Drinking so much is what alcoholism means, and you just hide the problem by stating it in other words. You would still have to work at the problem of what drives people to drinking so much alcohol. It is not a real solution to say that so many young people would not be driven to alienation and delinquency if their parents just loved them and controlled them more. You have identified one aspect of the problem, but, again, you would have to work at what it is that causes parents not to love or to control their children.

Know You Can Make the Solution Work

A solution to your not being able to get your car to run right would be to buy a new car. That would solve the problem. But if you do not have the money to buy a new car, you will have to consider more practical alternatives. Here is an incident from the life of that practical and enterprising American, Ben Franklin, showing how he solved a problem. The incident is an illustration of the kind of common problem solving that frequently confronts us all. We meet an obstruction in getting along with other people or in achieving our goals; then we have to find some way to remove or get around the obstruction.

> I therefore did not like the opposition of this new member, who was a gentleman of fortune and education with talents that were likely to give him in time great influence in the House, which, indeed, afterwards happened. I did not, however, aim at gaining his favour by paying any servile respect to him, but after some time took this other method. Having heard that he had in his library a certain very scarce and curious book, I wrote a note to him expressing my desire of perusing that book and requesting he would do me the favour of lending it to me for a few days. He sent it immediately; and I returned it in about a week with another note expressing strongly my sense of the favour. When we next met in the House, he spoke to me (which he had never done before), and with great

civility. And he ever afterwards manifested a readiness to serve me on all occasions, so that we became great friends, and our friendship continued to his death. This is another instance of the truth of an old maxim I had learned, which says, "He that has once done you a kindness will be more ready to do you another than he whom you yourself have obliged." And it shows how much more profitable it is prudently to remove, than to resent, return and continue inimical proceedings.

(Benjamin Franklin, *Autobiography*,
Collier, New York, 1909)

Point out specifically how the thought process involves all five of the principles of problem solving. (1) The problem is clarified. (2) A possible solution is arrived at, but (3) rejected for a better alternative because of undesirable consequences. (4) The real solution is arrived at. (5) There is evidence of the solution's workability.

EXERCISES AND PROBLEMS

1. Evaluate the reliability of the generalizations from the evidence given.
   a. Though she has made some mistakes, her record as a political prognosticator is quite good. At least three-quarters of her predictions have been borne out by subsequent events. I should think she would be a reasonable guide to follow in the future.
   b. It is quite certain that Chapman wrote the letter. It is in his handwriting, on his personal stationery, and his fingerprints and no one else's are on it. Moreover, two reliable witnesses have testified under oath that they saw him writing it at his desk.
   c. I have looked everywhere for my watch. It is not in any of my clothes or in any likely place around the house. I have checked with the lost and found departments of the stores and buses I have been in during the week. I have even looked around outside the house. The only thing I can think of is that it has been stolen.
   d. Joe Barcerini, who arrived five months ago from Italy, is sure to make a poor record in all of his college work. He has already received five low grades on examinations.
   e. Nine out of ten people interviewed said they preferred Sani-Cool cigarettes. Sani-Cool is the favorite of American smokers.

2. Evaluate these pieces of evidence, determine which generalizations, if any, are reliable, and circle the letters.
   a. Of hundreds of references to college students in the *Washington Post* between June and September 1979, a majority of students mentioned were involved in car accidents that were partly caused by carelessness on their part. This evidence shows that
      (1) most college students are reckless drivers who become involved in car accidents;
      (2) car accidents are the most newsworthy item about college students during the summer;
      (3) most car accidents are caused by careless young people.
   b. During the month of July, about 10,000 people were interviewed on their way into Athletic Stadium, and 8581 said they opposed the Athletics moving to another city. This evidence shows that
      (1) the city enthusiastically supports the ball club;
      (2) about 85.8% of the people of the city are opposed to the Athletics moving to another city;
      (3) people who go to see the Athletics play like to see the Athletics play.
   c. A Dodge won the Annual Marathon Race from Los Angeles to La Paz. Dodge cars are commonly used by the highway patrolmen in our state. Fifteen garagemen selected at random report that Dodge cars need less repair than four other common brands. This evidence shows that
      (1) Dodge cars are the most durable cars;
      (2) many Dodge cars are rugged cars;
      (3) you should buy a Dodge car.
3. Which hypothesis better accounts for the evidence?
   a. *Evidence:* This light doesn't go on, but the bulb is all right.
      Hypothesis A: Two of the workmen at the power plant got into an argument and accidentally threw a switch that cut off the electric power from this neighborhood.
      Hypothesis B: The plug is loose in the wall outlet.
   b. *Evidence:* Three people assert that they saw Mr. X fire a gun at Mr. Y at 1:00 A.M. in the garden behind Shilly's roadhouse. Mr. X claims he went home at 12:00, but none of the employees recall seeing him leave or seeing him present after midnight.
      Hypothesis A: Mr. X fired the gun at Mr. Y.
      Hypothesis B: Mr. X was home in bed, but the three witnesses invented the story in order to give Mr. X some bad

publicity to lessen his chances of winning the forthcoming election against Mr. Y.

c. *Evidence:*   Three people assert that they saw Mr. X fire a gun at Mr. Y at 1:00 A.M. in the garden behind Shilly's roadhouse. Mr. X claims he went home at 12:00, but none of the employees recalls seeing him leave or seeing him present after midnight. The night was very dark. The three witnesses are well-known gamblers from out of town who are contributing to Mr. Y's campaign because Mr. Y is strongly in favor of legalizing gambling in the state. A policeman says he saw Mr. X entering his apartment in town at 10 minutes to 1:00.

Hypothesis A: Mr. X fired the gun at Mr. Y.

Hypothesis: B: Mr. X was home in bed, but the three witnesses invented the story in order to give Mr. X some bad publicity to lessen his chances of winning the forthcoming election against Mr. Y.

4. Suggest one or more probably hypotheses to explain each of the following situations.

   a. "Different cats were trained to come for their food in reponse to signals of each of six different colors. But the cats always confused their particular color with one of a number of shades of grey, when these were offered at the same time as the color." (H. Munro Fox)

   b. A traveler in the Highlands of Scotland was entertained in a castle on the seacoast and was lodged in a chamber supposed to be haunted. During the night a ghostly figure appeared and for an hour watched him and refused to allow him to leave his bed. The traveler was a revenue officer; the district was notorious for smuggling. (After Sir Walter Scott.)

   c. An instructor meets his eight o'clock class as usual but fails to appear for his nine o'clock class. His lecture notes for his nine o'clock class are lying on his desk. His office door is open. His car is gone from the parking lot.

   d. A student has been assigned a term paper on a certain topic; he is expected to submit an outline and note cards in advance. He submits neither outline nor note cards. At the last possible minute he produces an excellent paper which does not fit the assignment. (If he wrote an excellent final examination, how would this fact affect your hypothesis?)

5. Spot the kinds of twisted thinking in each of these reasoning processes.
   a. Houses with shallow foundations should be avoided at all costs, but since this house has an unusually deep, reinforced foundation, you can have no reason for rejecting it.
   b. Early to bed and early to rise makes a man healthy, wealthy, and wise.
   c. Use Q-Tips because they are safer.
   d. A good school does not limit its efforts to preparation for life, since it is life itself.
   e. If politicians can hire ghost writers, students ought to be able to do the same thing.
   f. There have been fewer strikes since Steve Martin has been your Senator. You can see that he is the man to keep peace between capital and labor.
   g. If everyone on the sales force would do his best, we would outsell our competition.
   h. It's time we stopped throwing our money away on foreign aid. We have problems of our own: unemployment, race relations, education, juvenile delinquency, and we'd better be spending our time and money on them.
   i. No race is inferior; in fact, some are superior.
   j. The State will prove, ladies and gentlemen of the jury, that this criminal sitting before you, this ruthless enemy of society, shot Lily Miller in cold blood, with malice aforethought, and should be punished to the fullest extent of the law.
   k. Science is the servant of peace and will eventually outlaw war. Every day the radio, television, telephone, fast ships and planes, and so on, are bringing nations closer together. Once we were weeks and months apart. Now we are separated literally only by seconds. The day will come when we will speak one language and think similar thoughts. Then war will be impossible because we will be one people.
   l. I know a man who had seven year's bad luck because he broke a mirror.
   m. Ann is a happy woman because she is not troubled by inhibitions.
   n. He is a poor speaker. I can barely hear what he is saying.
6. Find the hidden assumptions in the excerpts below. Then evaluate the thought process.
   a. You can't expect the custodians to do a very good job—after all, they're among our lowest paid employees.

b. Soil that is loosened by a disk harrow holds moisture better than soil that is turned over by a plow; so it must give a better yield in crops.

c. Every intelligent businessman should prefer to have his son major in economics in college.

d. Most American communities are badly in need of qualified automobile mechanics; so the high school should provide such training for anyone who demands it.

e. History has proved that you can't abolish war.

f. Because business students have to write reports when they get out of college, report writing should be a required course for all business students.

g. College education is not as important for a woman as for a man unless she is going to be the breadwinner of the family.

h. It is not worthwhile to send aid to Insomnia because the Insomnian government refuses to support our resolutions in the United Nations.

i. The marked improvement in admissions standards over the past decade has resulted in an equally remarkable increase in the number of football games lost.

j. There must be unhappy people, for there are certainly wicked ones.

7. Analyze the following report as a model of valid thought processes. Here are some suggestions to help you in your analysis.

a. Find instances in which the writer avoids absolute statements, such as "probably" in paragraph 1.

b. How effective is the definition of the term in paragraph 1?

c. Trace the various parts of the reasoning process in paragraph 2.

d. Check the validity and relevance of the examples given in paragraph 3.

e. What contrasts are brought out in paragraph 3?

f. Find the hidden assumptions in paragraph 4.

g. Analyze the emotional value and logical implications of "total attraction" and "flourishing diversity."

1 Cities need old buildings so badly it is probably impossible for vigorous streets and districts to grow without them. By old buildings I mean not museum-piece old buildings, not old buildings in an excellent and expensive state of rehabilitation—although these make fine ingredients—but also a good lot of plain, ordinary, low-value old buildings, including some rundown old buildings.

2   If a city area has only new buildings, the enterprises that can exist there are automatically limited to those that can support the high costs of new construction. These high costs of occupying new buildings may be levied in the form of rent, or they may be levied in the form of an owner's interest and amortization payments on the capital costs of the construction. However the costs are paid off, they have to be paid off. And for this reason, enterprises that support the cost of new construction must be capable of paying a relatively high overhead high in comparison to that necessarily required by old buildings. To support such high overheads, the enterprises must be either (a) high profit or (b) well subsidized.

3   If you look about, you will see that only operations that are well established, high-turnover, standardized or heavily subsidized can afford, commonly, to carry the costs of new construction. Chain stores, chain restaurants and banks go into new construction. But neighborhood bars, foreign restaurants and pawn shops go into older buildings. Supermarkets and shoe stores often go into new buildings; good bookstores and antique dealers seldom do. Well-subsidized opera and art museums often go into new buildings. But the unformalized feeders of the arts—studios, galleries, stores for musical instruments and art supplies, backrooms where the low earning power of a seat and a table can absorb uneconomic discussions—these go into old buildings. Perhaps more significant, hundreds of ordinary enterprises, necessary to the safety and public life of streets and neighborhoods, and appreciated for their convenience and personal quality, can make out successfully in old buildings, but are inexorably slain by the high overhead of new construction.

4   As for really new ideas of any kind—no matter how ultimately profitable or otherwise successful some of them might prove to be—there is no leeway for such chancy trial, error and experimentation in the high-overhead economy of new construction. Old ideas can sometimes use new buildings. New ideas must use old buildings.

5   Even the enterprises that can support new construction in cities need old construction in their immediate vicinity. Otherwise they are part of a total attraction and total environment that is economically too limited—and therefore functionally too limited to be lively, interesting and convenient. Flourishing diversity anywhere in a city means the mingling of high-yield, middling-yield, low-yield and no-yield enterprises.

8. Evaluate the following leaflet as an example of unworthy emotional appeals and twisted logic.

HELP!

Our American Birthright,
Christian Heritage and our American
Way of Life need your active DEFENSE.

USE AND DISTRIBUTE

"FIGHT COMMUNISM"

Stamps
200 for $1; 1000 for $2

The use of these stamps is an easy and inexpensive way to STAND UP AND BE COUNTED. Their use injures or embarrasses no one other than tools of those of evil influence, communists, anti-anti-communists, traitors, dual loyalists, fellow travelers, one-worlders, gullible stooges (including educators and churchmen, male and female), "experts" (?), and professional do-gooders. . . .

GET THE U.S. OUT OF THE U.N. AND THE U.N. OUT OF THE U.S.

(Leaflet of the American Birthright
Committee, Los Angeles, California)

9. Find a printed advertisement that you consider especially effective. Point out the devices and appeals used in the ad, such as language, construction and design, graphic appeals, emotional appeals, and informative and emotional content.

10. Prepare a report to the advertising department, analyzing and recommending a set of appeals and devices for a company ad. Compare the ads from four or five different companies promoting a competitive product.

7
Using Graphic Messages

The picture that is worth a thousand words can certainly help make your report clear, interesting, and significant. Preparation for writing may have taken several months, but your aim when writing is to communicate your material completely and quickly. When you can report material in a graph, a chart, or a table, do so. Give the reader the best help you can.

In some kinds of reports, graphics are almost indispensable. Think of the difficulty of using only words to describe how to tie a simple slip knot.

Imagine trying to report in sentence form all the detail that is included in a balance sheet or a profit and loss statement. Or imagine the problems of a designer in using only words to describe a new line of dresses or a new emission control system. Graphs, tables, charts, photographs, sketches, drawings, diagrams, and maps can all serve to illustrate a report or present essential information in compressed form. Even when graphics are not absolutely necessary, they add variety and interest to your report. They support, clarify, and expand the points. They can snap a wandering reader to attention. They increase the reader's understanding and retention of your information. They give both clarity and impact.

TABLES

A table is a display of numerical data in rows and columns. Using tables saves words. They present simply and clearly large blocks of information without all the connective devices needed in sentence style. A table can be very effective in laying before the reader a frequency distribution or a statistical comparison. The table in Figure 7.1 illustrates effective layout, appropriate title, and clearly labeled headings for the vertical columns and the horizontal rows of items. Unless you gathered the data yourself, a source note may be put at the bottom of the table showing who deserves credit for gathering the data.

Guidelines for Setting Up Tables

1 Set up the table so that it can be typed on the page in normal fashion, if at all possible. Center it between the left and right margins.
2 Make each ruled column or row the same width, whenever possible.
3 Label each column and row to identify the data. If a column shows amounts, state the units in which the amounts are given, using standard symbols and abbreviations to save space. Center a column heading above the column.
4 If the space between columns is wide, use spaced dots or dashes as leaders.
5 If columns are long, double space every fifth entry.
6 If column entries are of uneven length, center the longest one and align the rest, using the expressed or implied decimal points as a guide.
7 If the table is a word table or a phrase table, align entries on an imaginary left margin in each column.
8 If a particular column or row lacks data, use three periods or dashes in each space lacking data.
9 If they improve legibility, use vertical lines to separate columns. See Figure 7.2 for an example.

GRAPHS

Graphs are the presentation of data in diagram form. They can give the reader sharp pictures of significant statistical relationships and comparative values. The *bar graph, pie graph,* and *line graph* are the most common types of graphs.

TABLE 8

A Comparison of Annual Cost per Employee of Medical Insurance Policies
Submitted by Seven Companies May 1, 1978

Company	Plan 1 $10,000 Maximum Annual Coverage	Plan 2 $15,000 Maximum Annual Coverage
Allegheny	$325.00	$450.00
ATA Life	350.00	475.00
Cleveland Mutual	375.00	492.50
Great Lakes General	315.50	445.50
Midwest Life	380.50	480.60
National Security	415.00	503.00
Surety, Inc.	308.40	403.28

Figure 7.1 Sample table

Bar graphs

Bar graphs, as shown in Figures 7.3 and 7.4, usually compare
relationships and show trends. Many laymen find bar graphs easier
to understand than line graphs. Each bar represents a quantity.

Table B: Projected Population, Employment, and Dwelling Unit Characteristics

	Study Area			Lincoln County			5-County metro area		
	population	employment	dwelling units	population	employment	dwelling units	population	employment	dwelling units
1960	27,960	5,209	7,385	52,431	8,640	13,716	1,523,956	607,032	451,974
1970	40,462	8,647	10,699	82,890	16,001	21,258	1,874,093	853,138	573,265
1980	60,600	15,700	18,558	118,800	29,200	34,765	2,230,100	1,106,600	702,629
1990	99,000	28,700	31,799	185,800	49,300	55,633	2,687,000	1,330,800	871,601
2000	144,100	54,400	48,263	267,500	90,300	83,981	3,176,300	1,610,250	1,029,955

Source: Chamber of Commerce

Figure 7.2   Table using vertical lines to separate columns

The height or length of the bar indicates the amount of the quantity. It makes little difference whether the bar runs horizontially or vertically, but horizontal bar graphs are often used to report quantities of time, length, and distance; vertical bar graphs to report heights, depths, etc.

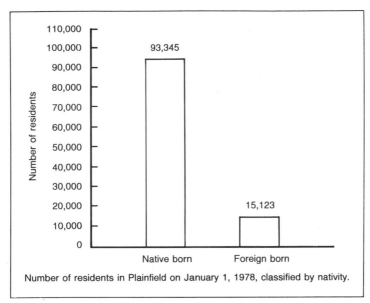

Figure 7.3 Vertical bar graph

Divided-bar Graphs

These can be used to show fractions or percentages of a total. The bar is divided into segments, and the entire field of the bar represents the total amount. Figure 7.5 shows a one-column graph. Figure 7.6 shows a multiple-column graph with comparative statistics.

Guidelines for Setting Up a Bar Graph

1 Determine whether horizontal or vertical style is better for your data.
2 Choose a scale for determining bar length (for instance, having 1 inch represent every $10,000 of sales).
3 Measure off lengths of each bar.
4 Draw the line to make each bar. Make all bars the same width. Separate each bar an equal space.
5 Shade the bars to make them show up, if necessary.
6 Label each bar (what it represents) and each scale (what the quantities and units of measure are). If desired, indicate the exact value at the end of each bar.
7 If desired, rule a border around the chart.

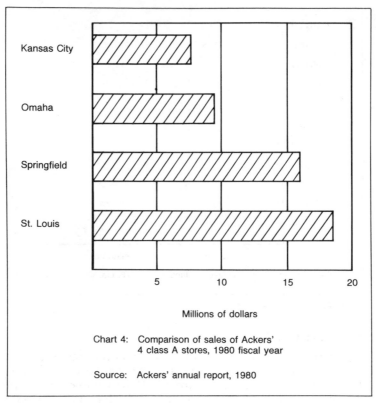

Figure 7.4   Horizontal bar graph with parts labeled

Pie Graphs

Pie graphs are used to display the distribution of parts of a whole. Like divided-bar charts, these show and compare percentages of a whole. Each slice of the pie constitutes a percentage or a part. As in Figure 7.7, the pie must total 100% of something, and the caption tells what that something is. The first slice of the pie usually starts at 12:00 o'clock, and the graph is read clockwise. The first slice is the largest slice, the second is second largest, and so on.

Guidelines for Setting Up a Pie Graph

1 Draw the circle.
2 Beginning at the 12 o'clock position and moving clockwise, slice the pie into appropriate wedges.

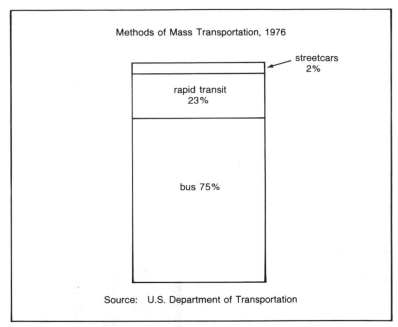

Methods of Mass Transportation, 1976

streetcars
2%

rapid transit
23%

bus 75%

Source: U.S. Department of Transportation

Figure 7.5   One-column divided-bar graph

3 Make the slices in descending order.
4 Group extremely small percentages (less than 2%) into one segment. The grouped segment may be labeled *miscellaneous* or *other* with the individual groups or percentages given in parentheses or in a footnote.
5 Label slices to identify items and percentages.

Line graphs

Line graphs are especially useful in representing changes over a series of short time intervals (such as monthly sales figures for a year or turnover in personnel over several years). The line graph in Figure 7.8 shows the fluctuations in the Consumer Price Index from January 1977 to January 1978. The January 1978 figure of 187.2 means that the products that consumers bought for $100 in 1967 cost $187.20 in 1978.

Guidelines for Setting Up a Line Graph

1 Determine the scale for variables.
2 Rule horizontal and vertical lines.

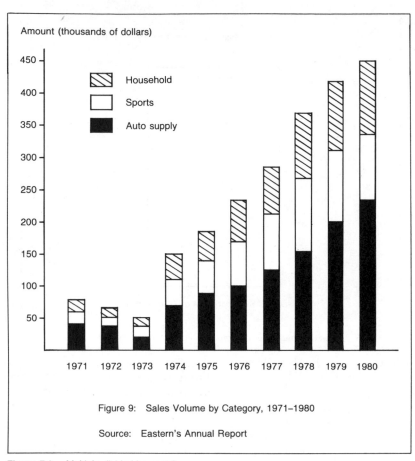

Figure 9:   Sales Volume by Category, 1971–1980

Source: Eastern's Annual Report

Figure 7.6   Multiple divided-bar graph

3 Mark off points of measurement.
4 Label variables, units of measurement, and so on.
5 If desired, rule a border around the chart.

Pictographs

These graphs are pictorial symbols drawn in appropriate proportion and number (such as a little house to represent new housing units, a human figure to indicate every 1000 workers, or little oil derricks to represent each ten thousand barrels of oil produced). Figure 7.9 illustrates a pictograph, using a number of similar pictures. Figure 7.10 uses pictures of different sizes to show relative amounts.

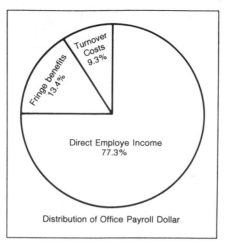

Figure 7.7   Sample pie graph

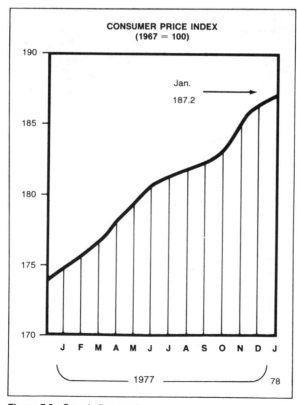

Figure 7.8   Sample line graph

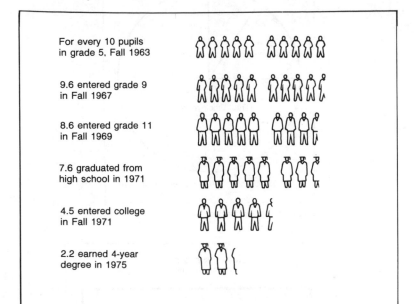

For every 10 pupils
in grade 5, Fall 1963

9.6 entered grade 9
in Fall 1967

8.6 entered grade 11
in Fall 1969

7.6 graduated from
high school in 1971

4.5 entered college
in Fall 1971

2.2 earned 4-year
degree in 1975

Figure 8.   Educational retention rate, 5th grade through college graduation, United States, 1963–75. (Source: U.S. Department of Health, Education, and Welfare.)

Figure 7.9   Sample pictograph

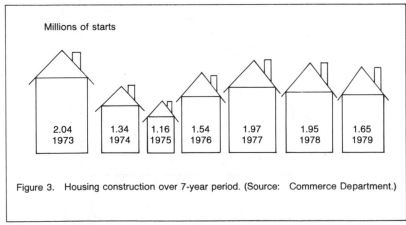

Millions of starts

| 2.04 | 1.34 | 1.16 | 1.54 | 1.97 | 1.95 | 1.65 |
| 1973 | 1974 | 1975 | 1976 | 1977 | 1978 | 1979 |

Figure 3.   Housing construction over 7-year period. (Source: Commerce Department.)

Figure 7.10   Sample pictograph with pictures of proportionate size

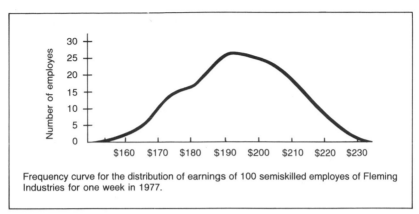

Frequency curve for the distribution of earnings of 100 semiskilled employes of Fleming Industries for one week in 1977.

Figure 7.11   Line graph

Many variations of graphs are possible. For instance, a frequency curve of weekly earnings is illustrated by a line graph in Figure 7.11. In Figure 7.12 the same frequency distribution is shown by a bar graph. The line graph in Figure 7.13 includes a trend line with a comparison of output of services over a ten-year period. The bilateral bar graph in Figure 7.14 shows a minus deviation.

CHARTS

Charts can be used to show relationships between nonquantitative items. The *organization chart* and the *flow chart* are the two most

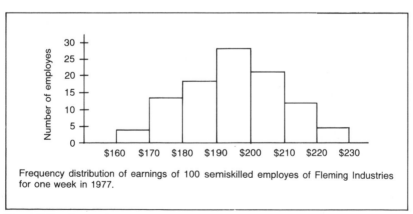

Frequency distribution of earnings of 100 semiskilled employes of Fleming Industries for one week in 1977.

Figure 7.12   Bar graph

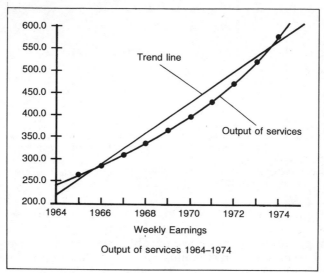

Figure 7.13   Line graph with trend line

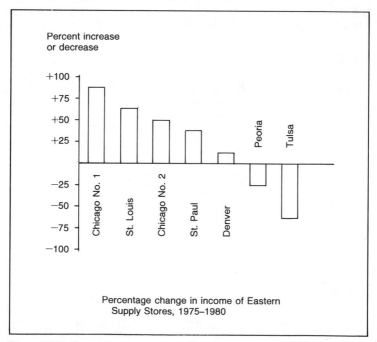

Figure 7.14   Bar graph with minus deviation

common kinds. A typical organization chart is the diagram of labeled boxes with connecting lines to show the hierarchy of authority within a company, as in Figure 7.15. When completed, an organization chart looks like a pyramid, with the top executive or office at the top.

A flow chart gives an overview of the activity of a process. A typical flow chart would trace a piece of raw material through a manufacturing process—from chunk of metal through milling, trepanning, lathing, and drilling to hydraulic landing gear tube. The block diagram, the simplest form of flow chart, shows the steps of a process by means of labeled blocks connected by arrows. The arrows indicate the direction of the activity flow.

Most flow charts are designed to be read from left to right and, if more space is needed, from first row to second row to third. If you were to describe a manufacturing process, your flow chart might look like this.

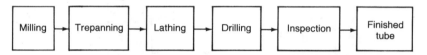

If the flow chart illustrates a cyclical process, it is very often a circle, designed to be read clockwise. If you were to explain the operation of a four-stroke gasoline engine, your flow chart might look like this.

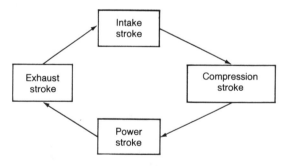

Flow charts used in computer programming almost always go from top to bottom.

Some flow charts use pictorial or schematic symbols to indicate activity at specific points in the process. A pictorial flow chart is an interesting way to provide a broad overview of a process. But flow charts consisting of schematic symbols and formulas should

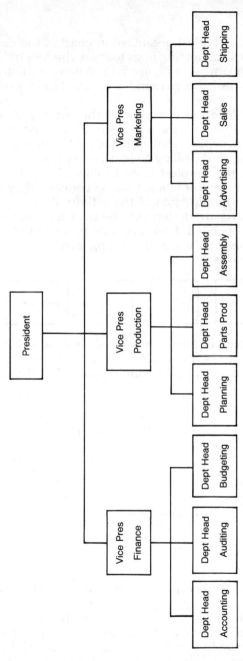

Figure 7.15   Sample organization chart

be used only if your readers can understand them. For example, $2H_2 + O_2 \rightarrow 2H_2O$ may be an efficient way of summarizing a chemical process. But if your readers can't read the formula, you will have to use language that they understand, such as, "When two molecules of hydrogen are reacted with one molecule of oxygen, two molecules of water are formed."

Maps are simply geographical diagrams. They make useful illustrations for just about anything that has geographical implications: geographical distributions, distances, and movement between places. The map in Figure 7.16 shows quantitative differences by geographical areas. Figure 7.17 shows proposed sites for a new distribution center.

PHOTOGRAPHS, DRAWINGS, SKETCHES

Photographs provide the most realistic kind of illustration. Consider using a photograph when you want to illustrate the external appearance of an object and want to make the surface detail stand out. Drawings and line sketches are sometimes better than photographs because they omit extraneous detail and shadows. A dia-

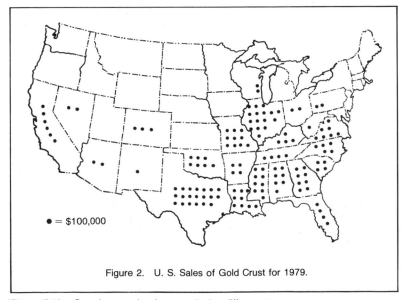

● = $100,000

Figure 2.   U. S. Sales of Gold Crust for 1979.

Figure 7.16   Sample map showing quantitative differences

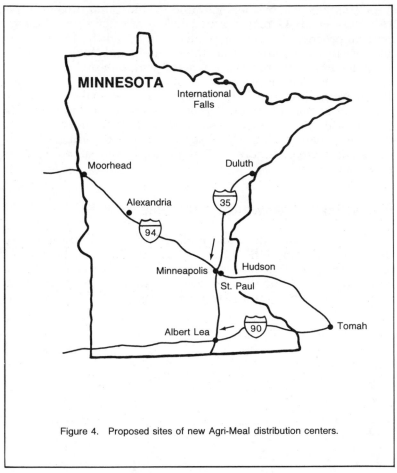

Figure 4.   Proposed sites of new Agri-Meal distribution centers.

Figure 7.17   Sample map showing site locations

gram or a sketch can also be used to provide a look inside of an object. With sketches, for instance, you can show how heat circulates in a house, or illustrate the cooling system in a car, or describe a highway interchange.

By means of a sketch and a photograph, as in Figures 7.18 and 7.19, a report writer shows a costume in two stages of production—the original concept and the finished garment.

"A MAN FOR
ALL SEASONS"
Duke of Norfolk
Earl Marshal
of England

Figure 7.18   Sample sketch

Guidelines for Setting Up Graphics

Some report writers have problems using graphics. Here are six suggestions that will help you handle them. If you follow these suggestions, you will also make your readers' task easier when they come to the graphics in your reports.

1 Don't use an illustration for its own sake; its purpose is to clarify and emphasize.
2 Make any illustration as simple as it can be and still serve the purpose.

Figure 7.19   Sample photograph

3 Make your graphics large enough to be read easily. If possible, keep them of a size to fit sheets of paper with the same dimensions as your report. If you can fit them on a sheet with some text of your report, fine. Separate them from the text above and below with adequate white space—triple space on a typed page should do it.

When your graphics are too large to fit on a page with text, put them on a page by themselves immediately following or facing the page on which you analyze the contents. When they are too large to fit on a page, they may be folded or photographically reduced. The latter is preferable if the reduction doesn't make them too small to read without a magnifying glass.

4 Place your graphics where they will help readers most. Lists are part of the natural sequence of information in your reports, and their placement is no problem. But graphics require your reader to read both them and the text, sometimes jumping back and forth from text to graphic. If you don't place them near the text they illustrate, you can make readers do a lot of flipping around through your report, rereading text and reexamining the graphic. Place the graphic at or very near your discussion of it.

5 Label everything clearly and carefully so that your readers know exactly what they are looking at. If possible, arrange all lettering to be read from left to right. Identify graphics by letters or numbers and by descriptive titles. Often a separate numbering system is used to distinguish tables from other kinds of graphics. Usually, capital letters or capital Roman numerals are used for tables; Arabic numerals are used for all other figures. The most important rule, though, is to be consistent and distinctive.

Figure 2. Weekly earnings.

Table II
A Comparison of Annual Insurance Costs per Employee

The title and number of a table is usually placed at the top of the table with the number of the table centered above the title. The number and title of other figures are usually placed on the same line below the figure.

Label by name or symbol the parts of objects and components of diagrams that you want your reader to pay attention to. If you use letters to identify parts, identify the letters in an explanatory legend below the figure.

Label every column, row, axis, bar, and line in charts and tables. If you borrow or adapt a graphic from other sources, give credit following the title.

6 Introduce graphics before readers get to them. They are introduced or referred to by call-outs, which are references in the text of your report to direct readers to your graphics. They are referred to like this:

> Figure 1 shows . . .
> . . . as shown in Figure 1 . . .
> . . . (see Figure 1) . . .
> . . . (Figure 1) . . .
> Table A shows . . .
> . . . as shown in Table A . . .
> . . . (see Table A) . . .
> . . . (Table A) . . .

If the graphic is not on the same page as the call-out, include its location in the call-out, as in this example:

> Recommended storage tanks (see Figure 3 on p. 7) can be either buried or above ground.

Check to make sure that your graphics are numbered or lettered consecutively, that they appear in the order you want them to, and that they are referred to by call-outs.

EXERCISES AND PROBLEMS

1. In a survey of 2700 holders of savings accounts, a bank asked the question "Why do you save?" and received these replies:

	Percent	Total
Security	51	1377
Retirement	15	405
Vacation	4	108
Investment	7	189
Education of children	17	459
Rainy day	27	729
Buy things later	9	243

Present the numerical information in a table, then in a pie graph, and then in a bar graph.

2. Itemize the major steps in some business process. Submit to your instructor (1) a sentence listing the major steps and (2) a flow chart depicting the major steps.

   Suggestions: A credit rating is checked; a letter is written and goes through the mails; a mail order purchase is made and delivered; an organization hires an employee.

3. Analyze the visual aids in an article selected from a business journal such as *U.S. News and World Report, Business Week,* or *Industry Week.*

4. Analyze the graphics in a corporation's annual report for content and appropriateness to the text of the report.

5. Prepare a line graph of your annual income over the past five years with a projection over the next five years.

6. Get cost estimates of the same item or service from at least three different companies and present the data in a simple graph.

   Suggestions: Car insurance; a set of four-ply auto tires; a television set of similar specifications; college expenses.

7. Analyze the following percentages of the total dollar spent on advertising in the United States in the last several decades. Note the shifts in trends.

	1950	1960	1970	1980
Newspapers	36.3%	31.0%	29.9%	27.7%
TV	3.0	13.3	18.3	22.4
D. Mail	14.1	15.3	13.7	12.2
Magazines	9.4	8.2	7.2	6.1
Radio	10.6	5.8	6.5	6.9
Business papers	4.4	5.1	3.7	3.8
Outdoor	2.5	1.7	1.0	1.1
Misc.	19.7	19.6	19.7	19.8
	100.0%	100.0%	100.0%	100.0%

From the information given, prepare the following graphics:

a. Indicate the data on a bar graph.
b. Indicate the data on a pie graph.

c. From what you know about the trends in American society and from the patterns suggested by the table, make a reasonable projection of trends in newspaper and TV advertising in 1990. Use a double line graph.

III
WRITING REPORTS

8

Defining and Analyzing the Report Problem

Now as you get ready to write a full-fledged report, the job may seem overwhelming. After all, a 30 page, a 10 page, or a 3 page report involves a lot of time, work, and responsibility. There is a huge mass of material to bring together and present. Even the single page report may represent the condensed final stage of an extensive project.

But the most complex matter looked at piece by piece becomes simple, and proper method makes any job easy. You can bring your report project under easy control if you can get perspective on it—see it as a step by step process that moves through several definite stages from beginning to end.

It is a matter of thinking skills—of seeing the problem clearly, of gathering the right materials, of analyzing and evaluating information, and of organizing. Every report except the briefest and most routine of messages requires a series of steps. Follow these steps to a successful report.

1 Define and analyze the report problem and prepare a plan of operation.
2 Gather the data and organize it.
3 Present the findings in proper format. This stage includes the substeps of writing the rough draft, revising and working up graphics, and preparing the parts of the final report package.

We will consider each of these broad steps through successive chapters. In the present chapter, we will look in detail at Step 1, defining and analyzing the report problem.

DEFINE THE PROBLEM

Definition of the problem is usually begun for you by the one who requested the report. Except for reports you initiate yourself, every report begins with an authorization. Either you are asked by the person in charge to write a report on a certain subject, or the responsibilities of your job require that you report on certain things. If a superior has requested the report, he or she, no doubt, has specified the purpose. If your superior did not make clear what was expected, ask for a clarification of the request. If you initiate the report, you have a reason for developing it. Whatever the situation, you should write down, clearly and accurately, the purpose of the report.

Three kinds of tests can especially help you define the problem. Ask the 5 w's and one h, formulate a meaningful title, and identify the readers.

Five W's and One H

Ask "who, what, when, where, why, and how." This kind of pinpointing will help you to break a large problem into smaller ones and to see them all clearly. Studying the parts leads to studying the whole.

Usually not all of these six questions will apply to a specific problem, but asking them helps to clarify the problem. For example, suppose your boss asks you to write a report to "find out what our people think about our new system of short lunch period and early checkout." Ask the five w's and one h.

Who? The memo says "our people," but whom does "our people" include? Whom does it rule out? Does it include executives or only nonexecutive staff? Does it include part-time employees and seasonal help or only permanent full-time employees? Does the boss want the opinions of the people in the suburban branch, or only those in the home office? All these questions need to be answered if the report is to be researched effectively.

What? The boss wants opinions: "what our people think about the new system." Does this statement include opinions only of the new system or opinions comparing the old system with the new? Does it also include suggestions for changes in the lunch-break system?

When? This question isn't central to the definition of this particular problem, except that your report should state how long after the policy revision the opinions were measured.

Where? The answer is self-evident.

Why? This question raises the issue of whether your report need concern itself with the reasons for the opinions you elicit. If the memo isn't clear on this point, you had better consult the boss. Also, ask why the boss wants the report. The answer may affect any recommendations you make.

How? This question is obviously not relevant to the present problem, though asking it of yourself might suggest a later study on how best to comply with employees' wishes and company requirements about short lunch period and early checkout if the new policy proves unsatisfactory.

Asking the five w's and one helps you to define the problem and then to gather information for your report.

Meaningful Title

A report title should clearly indicate what is covered. To determine how well you recognize the problem, write a title for the report. Remember that you can't say enough in a word or two to cover the scope of the report. This brief title, for example, gives no definition or sense of direction, but indicates only a broad area of interest:

The New Lunch Break and Checkout System

You need more definition. A better title would read:

Attitudes of Nonexecutive Employees toward the New System of Short Lunch Break and Early Checkout

If you have clearly defined the problem, you will be able to write a clear indication of the direction of your report.

Keep in mind at this early stage of the writing project that the title is tentative. Don't try at this stage to make a final, formal title. What you need now is to indicate for yourself the direction and scope of your problem.

Your Reader

Identify the reader or readers who are to be your primary audience. How deeply should you go into your subject to satisfy that audience? How technical or nontechnical should you be? What attitudes towards your subject does the audience have? Just what do your readers expect? These considerations are important because the purpose of the report is to help the reader make decisions.

FACTORING THE REPORT PROBLEM

Once you have defined the problem, you must analyze it. Problem analysis consists of breaking down your well-defined problem into its logical subdivisions, or factors. Then you break these subdivisions down into their component parts, and so on, until you have identified the elements of the problem and their relationships. Here your study of the thought process of classification and division should be helpful. What you end up with in analyzing your problem is a tentative working outline.

These factors, usually, are of three types. First, they may be merely *subtopics* of the broader topics that the report deals with. Second, they may be *hypotheses* that are to be tested by investigation and review. Third, they may be *bases of comparison* in problems that involve comparison and evaluation. Obviously, the process is a mental one, and you can begin by applying your best logic and comprehensive abilities to the problem.

Subtopics

Break the subject into its component parts or subtopics. If the problem is mainly one of presenting information, then you should come up with the main areas about which information is needed. For instance, your job might be to give a review of the company's activities during the past quarter. Clearly, this is a routine and informational type of problem; that is, it requires no analysis, no conclusions, no recommendations. It requires only that information be presented. The mental process is concerned with determining what subdivisions of the overall subject to cover. After thoroughly evaluating the possibilities, you might come up with the following factor analysis:

Problem statement: To review operations of Eastern Supply from
                      April 1 through June 30.
Factors: 1. Production
                      2. Sales and promotion
                      3. Plant and equipment
                      4. Research and development

5. Personnel
6. Financial status

An informative report on company attitudes towards the company policy of short lunch break and early checkout would likely break down into categories of employees:

1 Shop workers
2 Shop supervisors
3 Clerical staff
4 Clerical staff supervisors
5 Skilled technicians
6 Maintenance crew
7 Executives

Problems of quantitative valuation, such as a report estimating the cost of a proposed construction project, usually break down into logical categories.

Cost-Estimate on Proposed New Office Addition
1. Architect's fees
2. Contractor's fees
3. Building permits
4. Construction materials
5. Labor

Hypotheses

Problems by their very nature seek a solution. There may be a situation that has to be explained or a condition that needs to be corrected. Such explanations or solutions are called *hypotheses.* After you formulate a hypothesis, you test it to see how well it applies to the problem. For instance, a home and auto supply chain wants to find out why sales at one of its stores are dropping. In preparing to investigate, the report writer would logically think of all possible explanations, or hypotheses, for the decline in sales. Since he would likely think of more explanations than would fit, his task would be one of studying, weighing, and selecting. After analysis, he might come up with such explanations as these:

Problem statement: Why have sales declined at the Springfield store?
Factors: 1. Unusual changes in the economy of the area.
2. Change in competition in the area.
3. Merchandising deficiencies.

Logically, in his investigation the researcher would test each of his hypotheses. He might find that one, two, or all apply. He might find that none fit, and then he would have to come up with additional hypotheses for investigation.

Bases of Comparison

When your problem deals with a qualitative evaluation, your best plan is to determine the bases for the evaluation. Specifically, determine *what characteristics* you will evaluate and the *criteria* to be used in evaluating each characteristic. For instance, comparison is involved when the company wants to build a new factory—where should they locate it? The factors here will be the criteria used to make the ultimate choice.

Where to Locate Agri-Tech's New Assembly Plant
1. Accessibility to suppliers
2. Proximity to major markets
3. Availability of labor force
4. Local tax requirements
5. Initial cost of building site
6. Desirability to members of top management

When the first logical factoring is done by criteria, the second breakdown will likely be a logical listing of alternative ends.

Accessibility to Suppliers

1. Site 1
2. Site 2
3. Site 3

Each of the factors selected for investigation could have subfactors of their own. With each of the three sites under "Accessibility to Suppliers," for example, it might be necessary to look at shipping companies, freight costs, and traffic patterns. Other subfactors could exist for these. You could continue the breakdown process as far as it would be helpful to you.

DETERMINE THE OUTLINE STRUCTURE

Now with the problem clarified and factored, you are ready to make a tentative outline of your report. The outline is simply the plan you will use in the writing task which follows. It is your blueprint or roadmap. In addition to guiding your work efforts, the outline compels you to think before you write. And when you think, your material is likely to be right and your writing clear.

You should be able to break your well-defined subject into natural subdivisions. You may not know all the parts of the problem until you've actually done some research, but you should be able to write down several related areas that you will need to investigate in gathering material for the report. Write them down. You will adjust your working outline some as you go along.

The most commonly used system is the one you probably used throughout your school days. Called the conventional form, this system is the alternating number–letter system.

    I. First degree of division
        A. Second degree of division
           1. Third degree of division
              a. Fourth degree of division
                (1) Fifth degree of division
                    (a) Sixth degree of division

Examples of outlines carried through with full degree breakdown can be found in the following places: p. 248, "Checklist: Parts and Guidelines for Reports"; p. 253, report for the Agri-Tech Company; and p. 279, proposal for pyrolysis.

A second system of symbols is the numerical or decimal form. This system makes use of whole numbers to designate the major sections of a paper. Whole numbers followed by decimals and additional digits indicate subsections of the major sections. That is, an additional digit to the right of the decimal designates each successive step in the subdivision.

    1. First degree of division
        1.1 Second degree of division
           1.11 Third degree of division
              1.111 Fourth degree of division
    2. First degree of division
        2.1 Second degree of division
           2.11 Third degree of division (first item)
           2.12 Third degree of division (second item)
              2.121 Fourth degree of division (first item)
              2.122 Fourth degree of division (second item)

Be careful with numbers over 10. For example, 1.19 shows that this is item 9 of the third degree of division, not the 19th item of the second degree, which would be written 1.(19).

An easier and clear decimal outline system is to place a decimal after each numeral representing an item of information at a particular degree of division.

   1.
      1.1
         1.1.1
         1.1.2

If parts of your working outline do not give you sufficient directions for beginning systematic research, go back and clarify the request and the problem.

EXERCISES AND PROBLEMS

1. Clearly define, then analyze each of the following generally stated report problems. For each, formulate a tentative title for the report and a detailed working outline. Determine which kind of factors are involved in each problem—subtopics, hypotheses, or bases of comparison.
   a. The washing machine that will give us the most serious competition.
   b. Services performed by travel agents.
   c. Who patronizes motels?
   d. Entertainment tastes of American teenagers.
   e. Should our company make an individual effort at community charity?
   f. Illegal uses of CB radios.
   g. Should our company institute incentive pay?
   h. Low morale in the steno pool.
   i. Bad attitudes towards supervisors.
   j. Which machine to buy?
2. As an exercise in clear, complete, informative writing, categorize and describe the layout and equipment of your classroom. Evaluate how effectively functional the facility is.

9
Gathering and Organizing the Data

GATHERING THE DATA

Once you have defined the purpose of the report, the readers, and the scope or exact coverage of the problem, you are ready to begin gathering data. Much of the information needed will probably already be available in books, pamphlets, magazines, and other pieces of writing. Much will likely be in the company files.

Uncovering this recorded material is called *secondary research* (or *library research,* since much of this investigation is done in the library). For many reports, however, secondary research will not be enough. For current or local situations never before examined, you may have to do your own *primary research* (or *first-hand research*). Primary research includes observation, experimentation, and interviewing. Let's look in detail at these two methods of research.

Secondary Research—Read

The first step is to read up on your subject. Most businesses keep a shelf of handy reference books containing information likely to be needed on the job. If the information you need isn't close at hand, you have to turn to the library.

USING THE LIBRARY

The search for information—such as books, articles, bulletins—usually begins in the library. There you are most likely to use three main guides or indexes to basic materials: (1) The card catalog, (2) indexes to periodicals and (3) reference books.

The Card Catalog

The card catalog lists all books and bound magazines held by the library. For most books you will find at least three cards: an *author* card, a *title* card, and at least one *subject* card. Cards may give leads to other books by listing bibliographies or other subject areas.

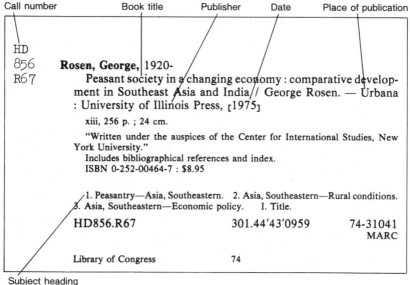

Call number   Book title   Publisher   Date   Place of publication

HD
856   **Rosen, George,** 1920-
R67   Peasant society in a changing economy : comparative development in Southeast Asia and India // George Rosen. — Urbana : University of Illinois Press, [1975]
        xiii, 256 p. ; 24 cm.

        "Written under the auspices of the Center for International Studies, New York University."
        Includes bibliographical references and index.
        ISBN 0-252-00464-7 : $8.95

        1. Peasantry—Asia, Southeastern.   2. Asia, Southeastern—Rural conditions.
        3. Asia, Southeastern—Economic policy.   I. Title.
        HD856.R67   301.44'43'0959   74-31041
                                                                 MARC

        Library of Congress   74

Subject heading

Reference Books

Bodies of statistics, trends and developments, guides to markets, changing methods, administrative practices—all are available in libraries. Much of this type of information is contained in handbooks, encyclopedias, yearbooks, almanacs, dictionaries, directo-

HD   Peasant society in a changing economy.
856   **Rosen, George,** 1920-
R67   Peasant society in a changing economy : comparative develop-
       ment in Southeast Asia and India / George Rosen. — Urbana
       : University of Illinois Press, [1975]
            xiii, 256 p. ; 24 cm.
            "Written under the auspices of the Center for International Studies, New
            York University."
            Includes bibliographical references and index.
            ISBN 0-252-00464-7 : $8.95

            1. Peasantry—Asia, Southeastern.   2. Asia, Southeastern—Rural conditions.
            3. Asia, Southeastern—Economic policy.   I. Title.
            HD856.R67   301.44′43′0959   74-31041
                                                                 MARC

            Library of Congress   74

HD   ASIA, SOUTHEASTERN - ECONOMIC POLICY.
856   **Rosen, George,** 1920-
R67   Peasant society in a changing economy : comparative develop-
       ment in Southeast Asia and India / George Rosen. — Urbana
       : University of Illinois Press, [1975]
            xiii, 256 p. ; 24 cm.
            "Written under the auspices of the Center for International Studies, New
            York University."
            Includes bibliographical references and index.
            ISBN 0-252-00464-7 : $8.95

            1. Peasantry—Asia, Southeastern.   2. Asia, Southeastern—Rural conditions.
            3. Asia, Southeastern—Economic policy.   I. Title.
            HD856.R67   301.44′43′0959   74-31041
                                                                 MARC

            Library of Congress   74

ries, and other compilations. Some of these are general reference; others are highly specialized.

Handbooks

Business handbooks contain the condensed picture of an entire field of business. They are highly factual. Some are revised annually, keeping the information up to date. Most libraries have the following handbooks for reference. The titles indicate the field of coverage.

Business Executive's Handbook
Corporate Treasurer's and Controller's Handbook
Sales Promotion Handbook
Personnel Handbook
Foreman's Handbook
Handbook of Industrial Relations
Accountants' Handbook
Handbook of Auditing Methods
Industrial Accountant's Handbook
Handbook of Business Administration
Corporate Secretaries' Manual and Guide
Handbook of Insurance
Handbook of International Organizations in the Americas
Financial Handbook
An Estate Planner's Handbook
Handbook of Labor Unions
Management's Handbook
Marketing Handbook
Production Handbook
Sales Executives' Handbook
Printing and Promotion Handbook
Sales Manager's Handbook
The Real Estate Handbook
Current Abbreviations
The United States Government Organization Manual
United States Postal Manual
Public Relations Handbook
Guide to Women's Organizations
Corporate Treasurer's and Controller's Handbook
Coffin's Interest Tables
Handbook of Foreign Currencies

Yearbooks and Almanacs

Yearbooks, published annually, give the year's summary of facts and data in specialized categories.

The United States in World Affairs surveys U.S. involvement in international affairs during the preceding year.

Sales Management Survey of Buying Power is an annual supplement to *Sales Management Magazine.*

World Almanac and Book of Facts (general)

Whitaker's Almanac (British publication strong on Commonwealth organizations and institutions).

Economic Almanac

U.S. Census Report (decennial)

The Management Almanac

The Statistical Abstract of the United States presents summary statistics in industrial, social, political, and economic fields and covers statistics on such topics as population, education, employment, military affairs, social security, manufacturing, commerce, and vital statistics.

The Commerce Yearbook provides information on commerce, trade, and industry.

The Shipping World Yearbook gives shipping data for the year.

The Spectator Insurance Yearbook presents pertinent facts on insurance companies such as history, administration, policy types, officers, and firms.

Encyclopedias and Dictionaries

Encyclopedia Americana

Encyclopedia Britannica

Encyclopedia Canadiana

New International Encyclopedia

The Accountant's Encyclopedia

The Encyclopedia of Banking and Finance

The Encyclopedia of the Social Sciences

The Exporters' Encyclopedia

Prentice-Hall's *Encyclopedic Dictionary of Business*

Crowell's *Dictionary of Business and Finance*

The Government Printing Office's *Dictionary of Occupational Titles*

E. L. Kohler's *Dictionary for Accountants*

Frank Henius' *Dictionary of Foreign Trade*

Marquis' *Who's Who in America*

Marquis' *Who's Who in Commerce and Industry*
Marquis' *Who's Who in the Midwest, In the Southwest, etc.*
M. G. Kendall and W. R. Buckland's *Dictionary of Statistical Terms*

Government Publications

The Monthly Catalog of U.S. Government Publications lists publications issued by the various government agencies and departments. Includes prices, catalog numbers, and annotations.

The Congressional Record gives the proceedings and debates of Congress.

The Congressional Digest contains digests and summaries of the bills in Congress.

The Congressional Directory gives names and sketches of Senators and Representatives. Lists committees, agencies, commissions, and their memberships.

The Occupational Outlook Handbook gives salary scales, opportunities, and trends pertaining to all occupations.

The World Trade Information Series is useful in studying the economy and development of any country.

The Small Business Management Series is helpful to anyone owning or managing a small business.

Directories

A directory provides a handy reference for specific facts and listings in particular fields. These consist of alphabetized names and addresses, professional organizations, geographic locations, product listings, and such. Some directories give general information; others give specialized information. Telephone and city directories are among the common general directories. Here are some of the more popular specialized directories.

Moody's Manual of Industrials (annually). Separate volumes deal with public utilities, railroads, government and municipals, together with banks, insurance, real estate, and investment firms. The volume on corporations includes U.S., Canadian, and foreign corporations. It contains information on company history, organization, operation, and financial condition. It includes financial statements from reports submitted to the Securities and Exchange Commission. It is indispensable to sellers of securities and to the banking community generally, and is useful in market research, sales, credit reference, production, planning, financing, and investment analysis work. The material is cumulated and issued in annual volumes.

Standard's Corporation Manual (monthly). Similar to Moody's but lists corporations only. It is also issued cumulatively so that current information is always available.

Poor's Register of Directors and Executives (annually). About 90,000 names of executives and directors of manufacturing and mining concerns, utilities, railroads, banks, and insurance companies, as well as partners of financial and investment institutions and of law firms are listed. It is divided into six main sections, each alphabetically arranged: product index, classified index, corporation directory, register of directors, obituary, and new names. Cumulative supplements are issued in May, August, and November.

Thomas' Register of American Manufacturers (annually). A full and informative buying guide for people in purchasing activities. It is divided into alphabetically arranged lists of manufacturers, trade names, international trade sections, commercial organizations, and trade papers.

Mac Rae's Blue Book. Not as voluminous as *Thomas' Register* but a good purchasing guide. Its information is arranged under product headings.

Directory of House Organs (annually). It lists both internal and external publications as well as employee and sales magazines and gives the name, editor, and company.

Ayer's Directory of Newspapers and Periodicals (annually). It gives name of newspaper, editor, publisher, and circulation.

The Congressional Directory. Published annually by the U.S. Government Printing Office: gives alphabetical lists and short sketches of United States senators and representatives; lists committees and outlines special agencies and commissions and main departments of government.

National Organizations of the U.S. Lists associations, societies, federations, chambers of commerce, unions, etc. Gives name, headquarters, number of members, staff, chapters, committees, publications, dates and places of conventions. Associations classified as business, education, and agriculture.

Trade Names Index. Lists trade names, definitions and uses, name and address of firms, etc.

Guide to American Directories. Alphabetically lists United States and foreign directories.

American Architects Directory

*Kelley's Directory of Merchants
Manufacturers and Shippers of the World*

Atlases and Gazeteers

Atlases contain maps and accompanying information. Gazeteers offer data on places around the world.

> *Columbia Gazeteer of the World*
> *Webster's Geographical Dictionary*
> *Rand McNally Commercial Atlas* (Maps and data are updated each year)
> *N. W. Ayer & Sons Directory of Newspapers and Periodicals* (Provides information on every city and town in the U.S. in which a newspaper is published)

Periodicals, Pamphlets, and Bulletins

Here are some indexes for finding articles, pamphlets, bulletins, and newspaper accounts.

General Indexes

Reader's Guide to Periodical Literature indexes articles of a popular nature from over 100 magazines. Monthly supplements issued and cumulated semiannually and annually. Author, title, and subject.

Social Sciences and Humanities Index. Emphasizes humanities and scholarly articles. Cumulative like the *Reader's Guide.*

Indexes to Pamphlets and Bulletins

The Monthly Catalog of U.S. Government Publications
Public Affairs Information Service
Vertical File Index: Subject and Title Index to Selected Pamphlet Material. 1935–present

Specialized Indexes

The Industrial Arts Index for articles pertaining to business, industry, and commerce. First published in 1913, issued monthly, and cumulated quarterly and annually until 1958. All subjects covered; over 200 specialized technical and business magazines indexed, including publications of a number of technical societies and associations in Great Britain, Canada, France, Germany, and the United States, as well as publications of the U.S. Bureau of Foreign and Domestic Commerce.

Business Periodical Index for articles pertaining to fields of business. Accounting, advertising, banking and finance, general business, insurance, labor and management, marketing and purchasing, office management, public administration, taxation, and specific businesses, industries, and trades. Succeeded *The Industrial Arts Index.* First published in 1958. Issued monthly and in a bound cumulation annually.

The Applied Science and Technology Index for articles pertaining to the sciences, industry, and technical fields. Likewise succeeded *The Industrial Arts Index* in 1958. Together with the *Business Periodical Index* provides a wider coverage of subjects and an index of more magazines than were formerly found in *The Industrial Arts Index.*

Applied Arts Index for articles on architecture, engineering, and applied sciences. Issued monthly, cumulated annually since 1957.

The Accountants Index
Agriculture Index
Engineering Index
Index to Legal Periodicals
The Management Index
New York Times Index for newspaper items. Gives a complete coverage, is published semimonthly, and is cumulated annually.

In addition to general libraries there are many special libraries maintained by trade associations, professional schools, chambers of commerce, foundations, labor unions, and companies themselves. Access to these libraries is not always general, but permission to use these special collections can often be obtained upon request. The better special libraries around the country are listed in the guidebook *Special Library Resources.*

Once you have found a source of information you need, you must extract and record that information for use in your report. As you gather your information, keep two principles in mind: evaluate your sources and take careful notes.

You must evaluate your source of information as you prepare a bibliography and as you take notes. Early evaluation may lead you to reject a source without wasting the time of taking notes on it. Or you may find yourself taking notes with reservations. You must evaluate continuously as you gather, sift, and organize your material. But even casual consideration in some specific areas may lead you either to suspect or to reject a source.

a. Author. Is the author an authority in the field? Ask yourself whether the author has sufficient experience or is a casual observer. The economic situation in the Mid-East can probably be better assessed by a known economist whose speciality is the Mid-East than by a state governor who toured there or a TV commentator who passed through. Consider what other books and articles the authors have written, what institutions they are affiliated with, what their records are. Some information could be found in a biographical dictionary.

b. Publisher. Is the publisher known, with a tradition of sound publications and a reputation to maintain? Does the material come from a professional journal or from a magazine circulated for the masses, from a university press or from a popular book club? You might suspect a book written by James Dawson and published by the Dawson press. An article on "Employee Profit-Sharing" is probably better if taken from *Industrial Relations Magazine* than from a Sunday supplement or the *Reader's Digest.*

c. Date of publication. Is the work recent enough to reflect new developments? An article about the character of the executive published in 1945 could be quite valid. An article published five years ago on investment possibilities in Columbian oil might be antiquated.

d. Nature of the study. Does it give valid information? Are opinions and generalizations supported by evidence and sound judgment? Does it seem one-sided, incomplete? Are alternatives considered, other authorities? Has the author sifted evidence and thought as carefully and objectively as you are supposed to be doing now?

Once you have found a source of information you need, you must extract and record that information for use in your report. As you gather your information, keep the following guidelines in mind.

GUIDELINES—NOTETAKING

1. Try to divide the subject into main headings. Investigate these main headings first.
2. When you locate a promising source, search out the information you need by consulting the table of contents and then the index. If the source has neither, you must skim it very carefully.
3. Take notes on material you need. The following tips are useful in taking notes.
    a. *Follow major topics.* Take only notes that come under one

of your major topics. You may, of course, decide that you
need to add one or two topics to your list, but don't let your
list get too long. Avoid irrelevant and unreliable information.
b. *Use note cards.* Take notes on cards (usually 4 × 6) labeled
with the major topic at the top of each card. By using note
cards, you can easily add new material, throw out useless
material, and reorganize what you have collected.
c. *List the source.* At the bottom of a note card identify the
source from which the notes are taken. This can be done
by a number system or by writing the name of the author.
d. *Give page number.* If there is material on the card—quotations, exact figures, or information or ideas not widely known
among educated people—that will require a footnote, be sure
to write the page number where this material is found. You
will need the page number or numbers for writing the footnotes.
e. *Separate your topics.* Notes for different major topics should
always be put on different cards.
f. *Separate your sources.* Notes from different sources should
always be put on different cards.
g. *Identify the kind of note.* Distinguish on the card just what
kind of note it is—how close it is to a complete passage or
an exact quotation. You will need to know this when you
work the note into the paper. Usually there are four kinds
of notes:
(1) Direct quotation (must be exact)—use quotation marks.
(2) Paraphrase—can be labeled "par."
(3) Summary—can be labeled "sum."
(4) Your own comment—brackets are useful.

Notes on the following passage illustrate different kinds of note
cards. Each card has sufficient identification of four items:

1 the topic,
2 the source (author, book or article, page number),
3 the note itself,
4 the kind of note (direct quotation, paraphrase, summary, or
personal comment).

Up to 50,000 Americans weren't so fortunate last year. They took
their own lives, according to estimates by several experts on suicide.
While many organic diseases yield to medical science, self-destruc-
tion is steadily rising as a cause of death—and as a cause of concern
to psychiatrists and other medical authorities.

In eight industrialized nations studied, suicide now is the third most frequent cause of death. In the U.S. it is fourth. There is an alarming increase in suicide among young Americans. For college students, suicide now is the second most frequent cause of death, after accidental fatalities. . . .

About twice as many men as women commit suicide, partly because they choose more violent and lethal means. Women, who favor sleeping pills or barbiturates, often become afraid after taking a few pills. Or they are largely concerned with evoking a sympathetic response from someone close to them, so the dose isn't lethal.

> (W. Stewart Pinkerton, "The
> Lethal Impulse, *Wall Street
> Journal,* March 6, 1969, p. 10)

Direct quotation, with personal comment

men and women

women are often "largely concerned with evoking a sympathetic response from someone close to them, so the dose isn't lethal."

— Pinkerton, p. 1

[By contrast, men choose violent means, like guns, which give no second thoughts.]

Primary Research—Observe, Experiment, Interrogate

In *observational research* you systematically observe a situation and record the significant facts about it. It might be noting what effects the noise in a shop has on the attitudes and efficiency of workers. It might be studying the workmen assembling an automobile or watching a woman buy a bottle of perfume. It may involve any of the senses—not just the eyes. You may be listening to the

Summary

Number of suicides

    50,000 in 1968, estimates of some
      experts.

   In 8 industrialized nations:
     - 3rd most frequent cause of death
     - 4th in U.S.
     - 2nd among college students

          - Pinkerton, p.1
              (sum.)

Paraphrase

Men and Women

   Half as many women as men
commit suicide!

    Some reasons:

     1. Because they usually take the
less sudden means like pills and can
change their mind in the process.
     2. Women may not be seeking
death, but sympathy.
         - Pinkerton, p.1
           (Par.)

noise in an office, tasting wines, sniffing for gases, or fingering fine cloth.

You may use other instruments besides pad and pencil. There are cameras, tape recorders, microscopes, micrometers, tachometers, thermometers, traffic counters, and many other devices to help you in speedy and systematic research.

Observational research has its special strengths and limitations. Its greatest strength is probably its reliability, if done right. Secondary sources can be unreliable, experiments can be distorted by variables you do not even know exist, and respondents in interviews may be untrustworthy and prejudiced. But with observation, it's all up to you. Your findings are as reliable as you are.

The main weakness of observational research is that you cannot probe beyond what the senses perceive. Observation cannot, for example, determine attitudes and motives. You can observe that two out of five women at the supermarket buy Flair over other brands, but you cannot observe why they buy it.

Another difficulty with observational research is that of achieving significance. You must design your observational materials carefully—*when* to observe your subject, *how long* to observe, and from what location or vantage point. For example, December 26 is not the best time of the year to observe "typical shopping patterns." One week would not be enough time to observe a trend in the demand for citrus substitutes. Los Angeles would not be sufficient as a location for observing nationwide trends in women's fashions. You must be sure that your observations are typical of the situation you are investigating.

In *experimental research* you set up test cases under uniform conditions, add a variable, and note the results. Any change is assumed to be due to the new factor. If your project is to study the effects of incentive pay on clerk-typists, you may wish to set up an experiment. You separate the clerk-typists into two groups that are about equal in experience, skill, and production rates. Then you place one group on an incentive-pay basis for a time and note the difference in production of the two groups. If the incentive pay is the only variable, it has caused the difference.

Experimentation, if well controlled, produces highly accurate and reliable results. The method is useful, however, only where the object or the condition under study is susceptible to manipulation and control by the researcher. Such conditions do not often prevail in business-report problems.

In *interrogational research* you ask people questions. In method, interrogational research can range from an informal chat over coffee to the formal interviewing of a department store manager, to a survey of 10,000 car drivers. Basically, there are three different ways of delivering your questions to the ones you want to interrogate: *questionnaires,* the *telephone,* and *face-to-face interviews.* Each has its advantages and its drawbacks.

1. *Questionnaires.* Questionnaires save time and money. You can distribute 500 questionnaires much more quickly than you can do 500 interviews face-to-face or over the telephone. Mailed questionnaires also give you wide geographic coverage at relatively lost cost. Furthermore, a questionnaire in the hands of a respondent allows time to think out the answers and to look up forgotten data. Also in the hands of a team of interviewers (who will ask its questions face-to-face), questionnaires can assure that your questions will be consistently posed.

For disadvantages, it is easy to ignore questionnaires since there is no interviewer waiting for an answer. They can also be poor tools for obtaining highly personal information. A highly skilled interviewer can often bring out the information. Unless interest in your questions is very high, many of your questionnaires will not be returned. And this is not merely a problem of numbers. If only those who feel strongly about your questions respond to them, your answers will not be representative of the random sample to whom you aimed those questions.

2. *The Telephone.* The main advantages of the telephone are its speed in reaching people and its relatively low cost. Also, direct voice contact (as compared to a distributed questionnaire) makes it harder for respondents to ignore your questions.

The longer the questioning, however, the less effective the telephone is. Furthermore, people will not supply much personal information over the telephone unless they know you. You are also unable to observe your respondents as they make their answers and to note the implications of body language. Because so many deceptive sales appeals are made over the phone, the public has a distrust of telephone interviews and so hamper the honest telephone researcher.

3. *Face-to-Face Interviews.* The face-to-face interview is the most personal way to ask questions. If you are tactful, you can ask longer, more detailed, and more personal questions face-to-face than by any other means. You can also, as over the phone, revise your line of questioning as need arises, and you can clear up any confusion that occurs.

The main drawbacks of face-to-face interviewing are its cost and its consumption of time. If you have many respondents or if they are geographically widespread, the cost of face-to-face questioning can be prohibitive.

Whichever technique of questioning you use, the preparation for questioning remains much the same.

First, you should determine that interrogation will be an effective way to get the information you need. The complexities of the inter-rogational process make it, on the whole, the least reliable kind of research. While it is not unreliable, it is more susceptible to error and distortion. Usually, however, interrogation is the necessary method for ascertaining motives, intentions, preferences, and reasons. Report writers in search of this kind of information, therefore, sharpen their interrogational techniques and avoid pitfalls.

Before asking questions, you must carefully determine *whom* to ask and *how* to phrase your questions.

Whom to Interview

If you need only one person's answers, or those of a small group, whom to ask becomes obvious. You can interview the shop foreman or the sales staff. But if you want to measure the buying motives of 50,000 consumers, whom to ask becomes a complex problem. Because you can't ask them all, you have to take a sample that will still speak for all.

How can you be sure of getting representative answers? You can't be sure, but you can come very close if you make your random sample. A sample is random if every member of the total possible group had an equal chance of being selected. Theoretically, drawing a sample random is as easy as drawing names out of a hat or putting checkmarks on a list of names. But you must be sure the list is a cross section. Beware, for instance, of lists like the telephone directory and automobile registration lists. People on a lower socioeconomic level are likely to have fewer phones and cars per person than those higher up. All types of people do not have an equal chance to be selected from such lists. The famous Kinsey report that purported to reveal the sexual habits of American women is unreliable, because the sample was not random. The 5940 women interviewed were all well-educated, white, non-Catholic, and Gentile and all were willing to describe their sex lives to interviewers. In a random sampling, all members of the total group concerned must have an equal chance of being chosen.

What Questions to Ask

The kind of questions you ask can determine how reliable your information will be and how easily you can organize your findings. There are three main kinds of questions you can ask:

1. *Either–or* questions, which must be answered by one of two possibilities.

	Yes	No
a. Are you employed?		

	Red	Green
b. Is the light red or green?		

A serious hazard of the either–or question is that it eliminates degrees or alternative possibilities.

2. *Multiple-choice* questions, which give the respondent a large number of possible answers.
   a. Do you approve of solar heating for homes?
   ____ Yes
   ____ No
   ____ Am not sure
   ____ Don't know about it
   ____ Don't care

3. *Discussion* questions, which allow the respondent to answer in any way.
   a. What do you like about living in Mason County?
   b. How can we market a better-selling tennis racket?

Discussion questions can be quite effective when you are asking only one or a few people. But if you are conducting a survey of many people, you must have answers that are definite, consistent, and easy to tabulate. Surveys, consequently, must often use either–or and multiple-choice questions.

Phrase your questions with great care. Your questions must be easy to answer or your respondent just won't answer or will give you a confused answer. Your questions must yield answers that are accurate, definite, and consistent or you won't be able to draw any significant conclusions.

The following section from a questionaire illustrates some of the qualities of effectively framed questions. They are taken from a 16-item questionaire used by Standard Oil of California to determine communication effectiveness between company and employees. They yield a range of fact, opinion, and preferences. They can be checked quickly and objectively by the respondent and can be tabulated easily by the questioner.

12. How well do you feel your Company keeps you informed about the Company's activities?

☐ 1. Always keeps me informed
☐ 2. Usually keeps me informed
☐ 3. Sometimes keeps me informed
☐ 4. Seldom keeps me informed

13. I get *most* of my information about our Company from: (Please check *one* only.)
    ☐ 1. Notices on bulletin boards
    ☐ 2. Articles in *The Standard Oiler*
    ☐ 3. Letters to me at home
    ☐ 4. Talks with my supervisor
    ☐ 5. Employee handbook ("You and Your Company")
    ☐ 6. Group meetings
    ☐ 7. Newspapers
    ☐ 8. Fellow employees
    ☐ 9. Other (Please specify) _____

14. I would *prefer* to get most of my information about our Company from: (Please check *one* only.)
    ☐ 1. Notices on bulletin boards
    ☐ 2. Articles in *The Standard Oiler*
    ☐ 3. Letters to me at home
    ☐ 4. Talks with my supervisor
    ☐ 5. Employee handbook ("You and Your Company")
    ☐ 6. Group meetings
    ☐ 7. Newspapers
    ☐ 8. Fellow employees
    ☐ 9. Other (Please specify) _____

15. Your Company is interested in knowing how you feel about your opportunities for expressing your ideas and obtaining answers to your questions. Do you feel free to go to your immediate supervisor and discuss: (Please check *one* answer to *each* part.)

	Always	Usually	Some-times	Sel-dom
a. Questions about your job	☐ 1.	☐ 2.	☐ 3.	☐ 4.
b. Ideas and suggestions	☐ 1.	☐ 2.	☐ 3.	☐ 4.
c. Personnel practices	☐ 1.	☐ 2.	☐ 3.	☐ 4.
d. Complaints	☐ 1.	☐ 2.	☐ 3.	☐ 4.
e. Personal problems	☐ 1.	☐ 2.	☐ 3.	☐ 4.

16. How do you feel about the amount of information your Company gives you on: (Please check *one* answer to *each* part.)

	Not Enough	About Right	Too Much	No Opinion
a. Company's expansion plans	□ 1.	□ 2.	□ 3.	□ 4.
b. Company's financial problems—income, expenses, and profit	□ 1.	□ 2.	□ 3.	□ 4.
k. Information on employee benefit plans	□ 1.	□ 2.	□ 3.	□ 4.
l. The American business system in general—how it operates	□ 1.	□ 2.	□ 3.	□ 4.

As you carry out your research, regardless of the research techniques you use, keep complete and accurate reference notations. If you use printed materials, keep a bibliography. If you conduct interviews, be sure to be consistent and careful in identifying who said what. Even though careful documentation may seem to take extra time, it will save time in the long run. Since the report must include any sources used in its preparation, an accurate list is essential.

ORGANIZING THE DATA

You have collected the information you expect to use in your report. You have a small stack of cards on which you have made notes from your reading, a stack on which you jotted down notes from interviews, and perhaps a batch of questionnaires that were completed by interviewees. Now there are five immediate steps ahead of you.

1 Analyze the information.
2 Decide on a pattern of organization.
3 Prepare an outline to write from.
4 Determine graphics.
5 Draw conclusions and make recommendations.

Analyze the Information

Which parts of the information are most significant to developing the stated purpose of the report? How are these parts significant? Select only the information pertinent to the specific purpose under consideration. Eliminate any information that is, upon closer analysis, clearly irrelevant. You might file less significant information for future reference. The selected information will compose the body of the report, and the other parts will be taken from the body of the report.

Decide on a Pattern of Organization

Before you put your tentative outline into final form and begin to write, you will need to decide on which pattern, or writing sequence, to use in the report. There are many variations, but two basic patterns exist. One is the indirect, also called the logical and inductive. The other is the direct, also called psychological and deductive.

In the indirect arrangement, you put your findings in inductive order, moving from the known to the unknown. Preceding the report findings are whatever introductory materials that are necessary to orient the reader to the problem. Then come the facts, possibly with their analysis. And from these facts you draw your conclusions or summary statements. In some reports, you may also include recommendations. Thus in report form, this arrangement puts the sections in this order: Introductory section, report body (which usually includes several parts), and the terminal section (which includes summary, conclusions, and recommendations).

For illustration of the indirect arrangement, let's look at the structure of a brief report dealing with a certain employee problem. Only the key parts of the structure are given.

> Several incidents during the past three months indicate that an investigation should be made of the work record of Michael Dawson, field representative in the Northwest District. . .
>
> The investigation of his work record for the past two months reveals the following:
>
> 1. He has failed to check in on six occasions.
> 2. His sales volume has fallen below normal.
> 3. On two occasions he appeared at the main office in a drunken and disorderly condition.
> 4. Three complaints from customers.
> 5. Etc.
>
> The evidence presented leads to one conclusion. Michael Dawson should be fired.

In contrast to the logical sequence is the direct arrangement. This sequence presents the subject matter in deductive method. Conclusions, summaries, or recommendations come first, and are followed by the facts and analyses they are drawn from. A typical report following such an order would begin with a presentation of summary, conclusions, and recommendations. Then come findings and the analysis from which the beginning section is derived—the body of the report.

Michael Dawson, field representative in the Northwest District, should be fired. This conclusion is reached after a thorough investigation made because of numerous incidents during the past three months.

The recommended action is supported by this information from this work record for the past three months:

1. He has failed to check in on six occasions.
2. His sales volume has fallen below normal.
3. On two occasions he appeared at the main office in a drunken and disorderly condition.
4. Three complaints from customers.
5. Etc.

The direct sequence is used largely with shorter, day-to-day types of reports. It is used especially when conclusions are the main points of emphasis and the supporting facts and analyses on secondary. On the other hand, the indirect pattern is most useful in longer types of problems requiring a careful build up, thorough analysis, and conclusion. But exceptions exist to this general observation, and you should use the one order that is best for your particular case.

Obviously, as you decide on a pattern of organization for your report, you will determine some of the structure of the outline. You will decide whether to use and where to place such parts as introduction, conclusion, summary, and recommendation. With these decisions behind you, your concern is now with arranging the findings and analyses (the body) of your report. This means preparing a writing outline.

Prepare an Outline to Write From

For this, you have to rethink your original outline. Adjust the outline you developed in analyzing the problem prior to research. Each of the questions raised in that outline has been answered now. You may find that your outline, as you fit your findings into it, needs some revision to allow those findings to relate more logically to one another. This is nothing to be concerned about; a working outline should not be rigid. During research you may have found information you didn't anticipate earlier; it must now be worked into an outline. Perhaps some information you anticipated and found proves to be unnecessary; it must be trimmed. The process of fitting your findings into the working outline will also reveal any contradictions or inconsistencies that need to be resolved. Gaps in your information may also be revealed, pointing to the need for further research.

Determine Graphics

Consider here if any of your materials should be presented in graphic form. What numerical data should be put into tables? What trends or changes can best be shown by graphs? Can objects or facilities be illustrated by simple sketches, maps, or diagrams? Review the chapter on graphics.

Draw Conclusions and Make Recommendations

Often a report requires conclusions and recommendations. On the basis of the information collected, the writer draws conclusions and formulates recommendations. Generally any investigation will result in a conclusion, which may be nothing more than the recognition of a need for further investigation. Conclusions reached should be arranged in order from the most important to the least important. If an investigation reveals a need for recommendations, the writer formulates these recommendations and includes them within the report. Conclusions and recommendations should be presented at the same point within a report and identified by a heading: "Conclusions" or "Recommendations." For an example, see the report on p. 30 to Thomas Munson of the Ohio Department of Highways. Any conclusion reached and any recommendation suggested should be based solely on the evidence offered in the report.

EXERCISES AND PROBLEMS

1. Do the preliminary work for interrogational research on each of the following topics. State whom you would interview and how you would select them. Prepare the questions you would ask, giving special attention to the wording of each question and the form of the answer.
   a. The public's attitude towards used car dealers
   b. What local employers think about trade unions

   c. The career aims of today's college student

   d. The job outlook for majors in marketing/sales

   e. How workers in a local factory feel about their management

   f. The feasibility of installing a cafeteria for use by company workers

   g. Liquor purchase patterns by age groups

   h. Community acceptance of a proposed new bank

2. You are to recommend a retail outlet for Ace jogging equipment. Ace, Inc. is looking for an outlet for its jogging equipment in the Springfield area. There are three sporting goods stores in the area, and Ace wants to select the best store for its products. Ace has an image of quality goods at a reasonable price. The line of jogging equipment is complete, with such basic items as shoes, shorts, shirts, warm-up suits, and jackets. There are attractive accessories such as the pedometer and the belt wallet.

   Determine what kind of information you will need to make your analysis and how you would go about gathering that information. Give your instructor a memo on your preliminary plan.

3. The Business and Industry Council of your city has asked you to conduct a survey of students in an attempt to learn why fewer and fewer students seem interested in careers in marketing. It is your job to specifically define and analyze the problem and to prepare the questioning procedure.

   In a memo to your instructor indicate how you have defined and analyzed the problem and submit a list of the questions you plan to ask.

4. Assume you are working for the Gerald D. Hines Interests, which is an investment building/development firm with international enterprises. Your immediate supervisor plans to leave soon on a business trip to South America. He will visit Brazil, Argentina, Chile, Columbia, and Venezuela. As part of his preparation, he wants information on the general economic conditions of these countries. Investigate conditions in one of these countries and prepare a letter report. Your supervisor is specifically interested in developing building programs for industry, commerce, and residences.

   Address your letter to Michael Topham, Vice President, Gerald D. Hines Interests, 2100 Post Oak Tower, Houston, Texas, 77056.

5. Prepare an experiment to determine the effect on sales of giveaway samples. As advertising manager of National Pharmaceuticals, you want to determine how effective giveaway sam-

ples are in selling the company's mouthwash, Fresh. Design your experiment, using one of two comparable cities as a control city, keeping records in all stores, etc. The samples will be 2-ounce replicas of the large 8-ounce bottle. They will be distributed to area retail stores and mailed to residents in the test area.

Describe as specifically as possible all the control factors you would set up to conduct a reliable experiment.

6. Prepare to write a report on "Frustration Patterns at Check-Out Stands," a study of what it takes to be a good check-out clerk at a supermarket or department store. A major part of your research will be observational. You will have to make both quantitative observations (how much time the cashier takes) and qualitative observations (what manner and method the cashier uses in both checking and dealing with customer attitudes).

Plan just how you would go about this observational research and write a memo to your instructor describing your plan. Remember that if the subjects know they are being observed, their behavior will be affected.

On a second level of research, support your study by interrogational research, submitting details to your instructor.

7. Prepare a bibliography for each of the following topics, or those selected by your instructor.
   a. Patterns of child abuse
   b. The future of passenger train travel
   c. The present state of domestic oil production
   d. The incidence of lung cancer in the United States
   e. Professional sports as big business
   f. The boom in condominiums
   g. U.S. economic interests in the Mid-East
   h. Trends in advertising media during the last 10 or 20 years
   i. Industry and public relations
   j. The movement of business to the Southwest
   k. The growth of cable TV
   l. The battle between car manufacturers and federal pollution controls

8. Plan how you would conduct a business experiment on some problem that interests you. Assume that you have enough funds and time that you do not have to skimp. Define and analyze your problem carefully, and indicate clearly the details of just how you would conduct the experiment.

9. Assume that a business man is considering extending opera-

tions to another city of medium size. He has asked you to write a report of about two pages, a concise summary of the city's economic life, along with population, industries, recreational facilities, transportation, climate, communications, natural resources, and other pertinent material.

For your report choose a city with a population of ¼ to ¾ million people. List sources of information at the end of your report.

10. Select a local specialty shop that you know fairly well and write a report to the manager on one of the following subjects:
    a. Techniques for developing telephone and mail-order business
    b. The use of letters to increase sales to present customers
    c. Methods of preparing a selected mailing list of prospective customers

10
Writing the Report

The actual writing of the report can be seen in three large stages: writing the rough draft, revising and working up graphics, and preparing the parts of the final report package.

WRITING THE FIRST DRAFT

The first draft of your report is divided into these steps:

1 Getting ideas down on paper
2 Writing headings
3 Writing introductory material
4 Writing a title
5 Supplying identifying information

Get Your Ideas Down on Paper

In writing the report, get your notes handy and follow the writing outline you just made. Write as rapidly as possible. Put your ideas on paper; a blank sheet of paper is frustrating. At this stage don't worry too much about spelling a certain word correctly, writing each sentence perfectly, punctuation, mechanics, or organizing the material in final order. All these things can be corrected during revision. Right now the big issue is to get your idea continuity on paper.

However, from the beginning you will have to give attention to two aspects of writing: the style level and the paragraph structure. These are important early since they are built organically into your whole subject and its treatment.

Style

You must determine whether your style should be formal or informal and also whether it should be personal or impersonal. Formal and informal styles of writing do not mean exactly the same thing to all writers. Just as in the choice of clothing, what seems informal to one person may seem too formal to another. But there are several features standard to the different levels of style.

Formal writing will not include contractions, slang, abbreviated sentences, or sentence fragments. It is likely to be written in the impersonal tone, with no first- or second-person pronouns. The informal style will most likely use the personal tone. It may include contractions and casual conversational phrases or modes of expressions.

The informal style may occasionally make use of some kinds of slang. Slang, however, should be used with the utmost discretion, for several reasons. First, slang is often not nationwide, and so may not be understood by the reader. Second, even the mildest slang offends some people; or, if it doesn't offend, it is considered of questionable taste and unbusinesslike. Third, slang becomes quickly dated, and what seems fresh and new to the writer may already have been discarded by the reader. Fourth, the use of unconventional or startling words or phrases may be distracting and thus delay the reception of the message.

Here is an example of formal writing:

> Research is also continuing on some substances that may prove useful in the future. Medical institutes soon will begin tests in cancer patients of interferon, a natural body substance that seems to protect cells from viruses. And a Brown University researcher recently reported that in a laboratory test a chemical called DMF seemed to convert human cancer cells into noncancerous cells. It probably will be years before scientists can fully gauge the usefulness of such substances for people, however.
>
> (Rich Jaroslovsky, "Elusive Quest," *Wall Street Journal*, October 24, 1978, p. 1)

A sample of informal style can use the "you" viewpoint, contractions, conversational tone, and short sentences.

Did you ever try cleaning around the bolts on a toilet seat? It's darn near impossible. So instead of scrubbing and scrubbing, we just take all the old seats off, scrub up the bowls and put on new seats. They're all small things, but they make all the difference in the world to prospective buyers.

> (Robert Bidwell, "Condo Conversion:
> No Business for Amateurs," *Journal*
> *of Property Management,*
> July/August, 1978, p. 191)

No matter how formal or informal the situation, the writing should not sound unnatural, stilted, or pretentious. No matter what the style level, you should use standard English and arrange your words and sentences with your reader in mind.

The personal tone uses the pronouns "I," "we," "our," or any other first-person pronouns, and the second-person pronouns of "you," "your," and "yourself." Material written strictly in the impersonal tone does not include any first- or second-person pronouns. The impersonal tone is used for newspaper writing, many magazine articles, and some textbooks and business reports.

Which style is better? It depends on your subject and your reader. Both the personal and the impersonal tones have their advantages and disadvantages. The personal is more natural, more vivid, more forceful—and easier to write. The "you" makes the writing seem more directly related to the reader. The personal tone is used in almost all business letters and memorandums, and in many business reports and business magazine articles. The personal tone is not best for some business reports because the report should emphasize, not the person, but the facts and other information reported.

The writer may express opinions, but emphasis should be upon conclusions based upon the findings of the report, not upon the unsupported beliefs of the researcher. The use of "I" and "we" in a formal report may lead readers' thoughts away from the information being reported to the person who did the reporting. This undue emphasis is often reason enough for wording some types of writing in the impersonal tone.

Another objection to the personal tone is that it seems to be more biased than the impersonal tone. This description is not necessarily true, for pronouns alone do not make the information true or untrue; and the use of the impersonal tone does not prevent slanting or interpreting the information in the light of the reporter's desires or beliefs. However, when it is essential that the writing convey the impression of objectivity and unbiased research, the impersonal tone is perhaps the better choice. Opinions can be stated impersonally without the use of "I." Here is an example.

PERSONAL: I believe more cotton shirts could be sold if they were produced in a wider range of colors.

IMPERSONAL: The results of the study indicate that more cotton shirts could be sold if they were produced in a wider range of colors.

IMPERSONAL: The study indicates that the company should manufacture cotton shirts in a wider range of colors.

It is apparent in most cases that it is the report writer who is recommending the increase in color selection, since he or she has done the research and has written the report.

The same recommendations or conclusions can be written in the personal tone and still keep their objectivity.

I believe that the results of the study show that we should include more colors in our line of cotton shirts.

The results of the study indicate that we should include more colors in our line of cotton shirts.

The personal tone makes for a more natural and informal approach, but in the first example the words "I believe" (especially since they are in the emphatic first position) emphasize the writer of the report and not the recommendation. The second version uses "we" and "our," but uses the important first position of the sentence for the results.

Even with the personal tone, don't use "I," "we," or other personal pronouns unnecessarily. Too many "I's" and "we's" will weaken the you-approach, as well as take emphasis away from the meaning of the message itself.

You are likely to do more writing in the personal tone than in the impersonal. However, the skilled writer can write well in either style and can choose wisely between the two according to the particular material and business situation.

If your style is to be formal, you often do well to match it with the impersonal tone; with the informal style, the personal tone should be used. These combinations are not always necessary, however, or even desirable. Try to judge each bit of writing according to what you have to say and according to who will read it.

Paragraph Structure

As you put your material down on paper, follow the points of your outline. Normally each subdivision of your outline should use at least a paragraph to put across the idea. Here's where you think back through the chapter on paragraph development. What kind of idea does the point represent? And what principles of structure and support should it take? Is it a method, a process, a trend? Then define and describe each step in proper sequence. Is it a breakdown into component parts or categories? Then classify and analyze consistently, completely, and meaningfully. Are you tracing causes? Check the rules of causal analysis. Are you drawing a conclusion or making general statements? Then supply evidence, data, explanation. Are there special terms that need definition? If so, make their meaning clear to the reader. If your report calls for recommendations, you must give sufficient justification for any conclusions and recommendations you make. The writer who has a reputation for knowledge in a certain field may not need to include as much supporting material as the unknown writer. It is a good idea, however, to give adequate support for conclusions and recommendations, regardless of your status.

Include only material relevant to the specific subject of the report. Sometimes you may be tempted to bring in side issues discovered during investigation and research. Put the temptation aside. If you have uncovered some information of value to your employer or the company, present it in a separate report.

Write Headings

Once the body of the report is written, you can analyze the content and write final headings to identify various parts of the material. If you divided the report subject into headings during research you may use these headings, or a modification of them, in the final report. The outline, whether formal or informal, should also aid you to determine headings for parts of the report.

Headings are perhaps the major difference between reports and other compositions. They help to subdivide the material for a comprehensive listing in the table of contents and thus provide a quick reference to specific sections of the report. A reader interested in only one or two sections of the report can rapidly locate these sections.

Write Introductory Material

After writing the body of the report, you will be thoroughly familiar with its actual content and better able to write an adequate introductory section. Include a brief statement of the main purpose, the main points of the body of the report, and conclusions and recommendations. In a longer report the conclusions and recommendations may also make up the final portion of the report.

Write a Final Title

You probably wrote a tentative title at an earlier stage to keep yourself on the subject as you collected data and wrote the first draft. Evaluate that title carefully in view of what the report actually says. If necessary, change the title so that it clearly identifies the report and makes it easy to retrieve the report at a later date from files. Most reports are kept on file, by title, for future reference; thus it is essential that the title clearly identify the report.

Supply Identifying Information

Any report should include identifying information. While there is no standard list of needed identification, there are identifying facts that should always be included, such as the name of the person or persons writing the report and the date. Often the name of the person or group to whom the report is directed are included. You should supply any identifying information you think is necessary, depending on the purpose of the report.

REVISE THE REPORT

The report should be revised. Read it through several times, looking each time for specific needed corrections. For example, read the report one time to check the correctness of technical data. Then read it to check organization and development. Read it again to check mechanics (spelling, punctuation, grammar). Conciseness is important but meaning should not be clouded. Eliminate all irrelevant data. Use graphs, charts, and tables, whenever possible, to replace or to clarify words. The report may grow shorter as it is revised, but length is less important than that the report includes all information necessary for complete understanding. Meaning must not be sacrificed for brevity.

In writing all reports, use what is generally identified as "formal language." Use complete sentences, good grammar, correct spelling, correct punctuation, and effective word choice. Avoid the use of slang, contractions, clipped terms *(auto, phone, TV)*, and colloquial words and phrases.

Put the report aside for a while; then reread it. Ask someone to read it and comment on its effectiveness. Read the report aloud or ask someone else to do so. These techniques may reveal additional needed revisions.

Make a final check of organization, sentence structure, development of ideas, spelling, mechanics—any area of the report that might possibly have a flaw that would reduce clearness.

PUT THE REPORT INTO PROPER FORMAT

Write the final draft of the report. All technical reports should be typewritten. Be sure to proofread the copy that is to be submitted to an instructor or employer to catch any typographical or other errors you might have overlooked. Correct any errors and, if necessary, retype the report; the final draft should contain no errors.

You have probably already been writing some reports based on the three-part "Structural Patterns" delineated in Chapter 2: preliminary material, the text (details and findings), and final matter (such as conclusions and recommendations). There you were given a framework to get you underway. It is now time to look more extensively at standard parts and structure of the full report.

Numerous forms may be used to organize and present the information in a report. Some companies require certain forms for reports and an employee of that company would be expected to use the appropriate form. If no form is specified, choose the one that seems best suited to a clear presentation of the material in a given report. Any report must have a logical organization if it is to achieve its basic reason for being: to communicate.

Parts of the Report

The basic plan of a report will usually include the following parts in the order listed. The short informal report will seldom have all of these parts explicitly labeled, but the kind of material they indicate will usually be present. Letter reports and memo reports, for instance, usually absorb the title into the subject line, and introductory matters such as purpose and problem are normally stated in the first paragraph.

Title or subject
Summary—gives the main points of the report
Introduction or background—explains briefly any information needed to understand the report
Body—presents all the facts of the report in detail
Conclusions
Recommendations
Appendix—when applicable
Bibliography—when applicable

Let's look at each of these parts in more detail.

Title

The title of a report must give an accurate and comprehensive identification of the subject or content of the report. A word or a short phrase is usually not enough for a title. Make sure your title indicates the coverage of the report. An inadequate report might run like this:

Wild Cat Oil in Texas

The title does not indicate what is in the report, just its area of interest. Here is a better title:

The Attempt-Success Ratio of Wild Cat Oil Wells in Texas in 1978

Since the title is the first thing a reader sees and it is a clue to finding a specific report after it has been filed, great care should be taken in titling a report. Usually the title is the last step in writing the report.

Summary

The summary is a concise presentation of the main points of the report, conclusions, and recommendations. If the information is not included elsewhere, the summary may include the date when the information of the report was requested and the name of the person requesting the report, although this material usually appears on a page with the report title.

Introduction

The introduction usually tells who requested the report (especially if the letter of transmittal has not included this information) and clearly presents the purpose of the report. It then goes on to state the main points included and gives reasons why certain points have not been included, or simply lists these points. The introduction explains something of the procedure followed in gathering the information and mentions any persons who may have helped with the investigation and preparation of the report. Also, this section includes the significant findings, major conclusions, and recommendations. Detailed explanation of results, conclusions, and recommendations will be given in the body of the report.

Body

The body of the report contains the complete, detailed discussion of the report. It develops the main points mentioned in the summary or introduction. It provides evidence or support for conclusions and recommendations. No specific listing of parts of the body will be usable in all types of report.

The body may give historical background needed for complete understanding of the report. It may describe the procedure used in carrying out the study; for example, in an experimental report the body might include a description of the devices and techniques used in the experiment. The body may explain what the writer did in carrying out the experiment. The explanation of procedure leads directly into a detailed discussion of the results mentioned briefly in the summary. Then follows a detailed presentation of conclusions and recommendations, also included briefly in the summary. The presentation of conclusions and recommendations should be clear and logical because they are the parts that are of major significance to the reader.

Since footnoted material must be used properly and put into proper form, special attention is given here to footnoting.

Footnotes

Footnotes are used in business reports for either of two reasons: (1) to elaborate on something in the text if that elaboration in the text would be digressive, or (2) to give the source of a piece of information in the text.

Beginning report writers sometimes have trouble determining what kinds of information require footnoting and what kinds do not. It is clear that direct quotations, charts, diagrams, tables, discussions that summarize ideas and opinions of others in your own words, and the like all require acknowledgment in footnotes. Difficulties arise principally in acknowledging opinion which the writer has paraphrased from others rather than reached independently, and in determining what is "common knowledge" and therefore does not require acknowledgment. With respect to the first, the student writer should be very careful to distinguish clearly between those opinions which he has actually arrived at independently in the course of his reading on the subject, and which therefore need no acknowledgment, and those which in fact he has paraphrased more or less wholly from a particular source and which therefore must be acknowledged. The writer should be careful to remember that ideas, interpretations, opinions, and conclusions reached by another writer are in many ways more important contributions on his part than bald facts, and therefore even more deserving of acknowledgment.

What constitutes "common knowledge" is really less difficult to determine than some students seem to feel. Any writer who reads in his subject to some depth will quickly come to see that certain kinds of facts are taken for granted by nearly all writers discussing the subject, while others are matters of dispute, or the result of special investigation.

Specialized facts—such as the number of Minolta cameras sold in 1978, the estimated population of Kuwait in 1970, the highest recorded tide in Galveston Bay, or the number of earthquakes in Central America in the 20th century—are not likely to be common knowledge. In contrast, the precise date of the Santa Barbara oil spill, the birth and death dates of Henry Ford, or the latitude and longitude of Chicago are considered common knowledge, even though they may not be held very sharply in the memory at the moment. When common sense, supported by the knowledge you have gained from your reading in a subject, still leaves you in doubt, footnote the information.

Here are some tips for working quoted material into your writing.

1. *Quote exactly.* Quotations must be exact down to the last comma, hyphen, capital letter, or abbreviation. Be careful at the note-taking stage and check your paper against your notecard to insure against error.

2. *Use ellipses for omissions.* If you omit material from a quoted sentence, use an ellipsis mark of three spaced periods (. . .). If you omit from the end of a quoted sentence but the part quoted makes a complete sentence in your text, use a period followed by three spaced dots, even if you go on to continue quoting from a following sentence.

Note various ways to use quoted matter from this excerpt:

Up to 50,000 Americans weren't so fortunate last year. They took their own lives, according to estimates by several experts on suicide.

(W. Stewart, Pinkerton, "The Lethal Dose," *Wall Street Journal,* March 6, 1969, p. 10)

Ellipsis within sentence: "Up to 50,000 . . . weren't so fortunate last year."
Ellipsis and end of sentence: "Up to 50,00 Americans weren't so fortunate. . . ."
Ellipsis overlapping two or more sentences: "Up to 50,000 Americans weren't so fortunate . . . . They took their own lives, according to estimates by several experts on suicide."
3. *Use brackets for your own insertions.*

"Up to 50,000 Americans weren't so fortunate last year [1968]."

4. *Make the quotation a piece with your sentence.* The quotation is part of your style and sentence structure. Use word order, punctuation, and capitalization to fit.

Pinkerton says that 50,000 "took their own lives, according to estimates by several experts on suicide."
Pinkerton has this to say about the suicide motives of women: "They are largely concerned with evoking a sympathetic response from someone close to them."

Make small quotations a part of your paragraph. Set off and indent long quotations. When you indent, do not use quotation marks.
5. *Avoid long quotations.* Chunks of quotations much longer than six to ten lines put the burden of interpretation on the reader. It is not the quotation that is important, but your use of it in your report.
Footnotes should be numbered consecutively throughout the paper and placed at the bottom of the page on which the cited material occurs (or, if your reader prefers, in one list at the end of the paper). The first footnote for a source must be complete with author, title, and all facts of publication. Later references to that footnote can be abbreviated. Follow these rules for the format of footnotes:

FOOTNOTES—GUIDELINES

1 Set the footnotes off from the rest of the page by typing a 1½-inch dash at the left margin, single spaced after the last line on the page. Double-space after typing this line.
2 Indent five spaces, and number each footnote consecutively by typing a superior figure at the beginning of the footnote.
3 Single-space each footnote, but double-space between footnotes.
4 Type the name of the author, if any, in a first name, last name sequence.
5 Indicate the complete title of the cited reference. Put quotation marks around the titles of magazine articles, sections of books, and newspaper columns. Underline the titles of books, magazines, and newspapers.
6 After the complete title of the book, put the city where it was published, the name of the publisher, and the date of publication. Indicate the edition, if other than the first.
7 After the complete title of magazines and newspapers, put the date of publication.
8 End each footnote with the page number of the cited material.

The following sample footnotes illustrate common forms.

Book with one author:

[1] Charles P. Blankenship, *History of Industry in Kentucky* (Chicago: Palmer Publishers, 1974), p. 78.

Book with more than one author:

[2] E. Bryant Phillips and Sylvia Lane, *Personal Finance*, 2nd ed. (New York: John Wiley & Sons, Inc., 1969), p. 234.

Magazine or periodical:

[3] Henry Roberts, "Univac Flies with United," *Business Week*, December 25, 1970, p. 34.
[4] Carol J. Loomis, "For the Utilities, It's a Fight for Survival," *Fortune*, Vol. XCI, No. 3 (March, 1975), p. 98.

Newspaper:

[5] Dana L. Spitzer, "Negro Teachers Tell of Job Losses," St. Louis *Post-Dispatch*, July 1, 1970, Sec. D, p. 1.
[6] "Wall Street Slippage," *Christian Science Monitor*, April 28, 1978, p. 2.

Explanatory material:

⁷ You can place the credit terms either before or after the resale or promotion. If before, the reader is more likely to notice them; if after, you seem to be stressing the you attitude rather than "what's in it for me."

Bulletin, Pamphlet:

⁸ U.S. Bureau of the Census. *Statistical Abstract of the United States,* 1975, 96th ed. (Washington, D.C., U.S. Government Printing Office, 1975), p. 345.

Interview:

⁹ John Jeffries, Executive of Regional Division of Continental Hotels, November 2, 1977.

Second References: Use a shortened form, usually the author's last name and the page number.

¹⁰ Roberts, p. 35.

Conclusions and Recommendations

In a brief report the conclusions and the recommendations, if any, are given in the summary only. In a longer report the main conclusions and the recommendations are given in the summary, and the detailed explanation of conclusions and recommendations is given as the last section of the report.

Appendix

Often even a relatively brief report will include an appendix and a bibliography. The appendix includes items such as detailed graphs, charts, or maps that are necessary for a complete understanding of a report. The information from these items may be summarized within the body of the report. Generally, all illustrative material is placed in the appendix except for material needed to make a point immediately clear, which should be placed within the body of the report.

Bibliography

If a report includes many references to sources, a bibliographical list of these references is usually included as a separate part of the report. If a report includes only a few references, these can be identified in a footnote or within the text of the report. In a single report the method used should be consistent. If a footnote is used for the first reference, use footnotes for all references in the report. A list of sources, such as the one shown in Figure 10.7, should be added as a back section to any report for which you needed to consult at least several published sources. Your reader will probably be interested in these sources too. The following rules and examples should be followed in preparing a report bibliography.

BIBLIOGRAPHY—GUIDELINES

1 List the items in the bibliography alphabetically by the author's last name.
2 Type the heading "Bibliography" or "List of Sources."
3 Triple-space between the heading and the first reference. Single-space each reference, and double-space between references. If a reference requires more than one line, indent the second line (and each succeeding line) five spaces.
4 If an author has written more than one of your sources, type a five-space line in place of his or her name for each item after the first.
5 When the author is unknown, alphabetize the reference by its title.
6 End each reference to a magazine, journal, or other multi-articled source with page indicators.

The parts of this basic plan can be adapted to most reports— whether the brief informal report or the longer formal report. The longer report will usually require additional parts to the basic plan. We will describe these later when we get to the long formal report.

Typical Reports

Short Informal Reports

Most of the business reports you are called upon to write will probably be short informal reports. There is almost a constant need for organized data and recommendations from which decisions can be made—from day to day and week to week. A short informal report usually deals with a limited subject. It is generally written to a specific request. Some typical short informal reports are field reports, periodic reports, credit reports, progress reports, personnel reports, cost reports, sales reports, and committee reports. Any of these could, of course, be long formal reports, depending on such things as complexity and extent of subject, purpose of report, permanent or temporary value, and formal relationship of reader and writer.

Short informal reports usually range from one to ten pages. They have neither a cover page nor a table of contents, and the pages are paper-clipped or stapled. Typically, they take one of two forms: letter form or interoffice memorandum.

Letter form. An informal report in letter form is addressed to a specific person, who usually is not a part of the writer's own company. (See Figure 10.1.) The letter includes the standard parts of a business letter: heading, date, inside address, salutation, body, complimentary close, and signature. The letter also may include

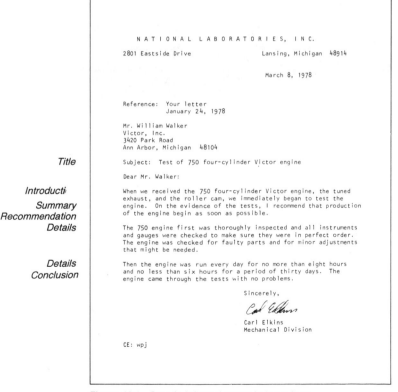

Figure 10.1   Sample informal report in letter form

an attention line, a reference line, a subject line, typist's initials, and notice of enclosures and carbon copies mailed to others. The body of the letter includes the content of the report, and it follows the basic plan outlined.

Summary
Introduction
Details of the investigation
Conclusions
Recommendations

It may also include an appendix and a list of references.

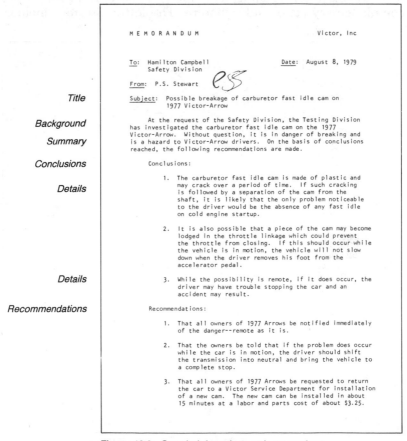

Figure 10.2 Sample informal report in memo form

Interoffice memorandum. The brief informal report may also be presented in the form of a memorandum. (See Figure 10.2.) The report memo includes the standard parts of a memo plus the elements in the basic plan for a report. You will use a heading for "To," "From," "Subject," "Date," possibly the "Name of the Company," and perhaps "Reference."

The body of the memo contains the details of the report and adapts the parts of the basic plan:

> Summary
> Introduction
> Details of the investigation
> Conclusion
> Recommendations

An appendix and list of references may be included.

Longer Formal Reports

With a complex subject the reports becomes longer and more formal. It may range in length from several pages to several volumes. It may present materials on which a decision will be made to open a branch store, to launch a new product on the market, to change the system of paying employees. It may deal with the development of new products or techniques that may involve huge sums of money. Any large-scale investigation of any problem, situation, or condition provides material for a formal report. Listed below are the items included in the longer formal report. Again, these parts are adapted to a specific report depending on its purpose. Only a very long, elaborate report would include all these items.

> Cover
> Title page
> Letter of transmittal
> Table of contents
> Abstract
> Introduction
>> Background
>> Results
>> Conclusions
>> Recommendations
> Body
>> History of subject
>> Explanation of study

Results
Conclusions (with detailed discussion)
Recommendations
Appendix
Bibliography
Supplemental material
Index

Let's describe the major parts of the formal report which have not been detailed earlier in the chapter under "Parts of the Report."

Title page. The title page includes the following information, usually the same as the headings for a memo: the subject of the report; the name of the person, company, or organization to whom the report is submitted; the name of the person, company, or organization submitting the report; and the date. A sample title page is shown in Figure 10.3.

Letter of transmittal. A transmittal is used to forward the report to a person, a company, or an organization. It actually introduces the report and can take the place of the summary (see Figure 10.4). Most often it simply introduces the report, sometimes saying little more than "Attached is the report you asked for about customer complaints at the Southland Store."

Table of contents. The table of contents lists the divisions of the report and the page on which each division begins. If a report uses several graphs, charts, pictures, or other illustrations, there is a separate list of these. The table of contents helps the reader to select and locate parts of the report he or she may want to read (see Figure 10.5).

Abstract. The abstract may be the most important part of the report. It provides a concise synopsis of the main points of the report. The abstract may well be the only part of the report read by busy executives, board members, or engineers. The summary should include a statement of the main purpose of the report, the main points of the investigation, and the main conclusions and recommendations (see Figure 10.6). It is a separate and complete part of the whole, depending on no other parts for meaning.

Its aim is to distill the substance without changing idea, point of view, or attitude. If the original is written in first person, for instance, the abstract should be written in first person. It should not use phrases like "The author says that." The abstract *is*, in condensed form, what the author says. Preserving the style of the original is not important unless style is a key to sense. If, for exam-

INDUSTRY AND THE ECONOMIC FUTURE

A Study of the Potential for Industrial

Growth in Springfield, Kentucky

presented to

The Springfield Chamber of Commerce

by

Perkins-Jones and Associates

Cincinnati, Ohio

May 18, 1978

Figure 10.3 Sample title page from a business report

PERKINS-JONES AND ASSOCIATES

Industrial Consultants

298 Lakewood Blvd.

Cincinnati, Ohio

Milton Thomas, Director

May 18, 1978

The Chamber of Commerce
Springfield, Kentucky   40208

Gentlemen:

We are pleased to submit to the Chamber of Commerce this
report on "Industry and the Economic Future of Springfield."

Perkins-Jones and Associates has analyzed the factors it
believes pertinent to the potential for industrial expansion
in the city. Definite conclusions came from this study,
conclusions that we believe speak well for the future of
Springfield.

Please call upon us for any further service we can give you
on this matter.

Sincerely,

Milton Thomas

Milton Thomas

MT:lg

Figure 10.4   Sample transmittal letter for a business report

Table of Contents

Figure 10.5 Sample table of contents for a business report

Abstract

After careful analysis of pertinent factors, Perkins-Jones and Associates conclude (1) that Springfield's most likely sources of industrial growth are (a) diversification of present industries to open new markets and (b) attraction of new industry; (2) that the industries most likely to be attracted are certain light industries not requiring huge movements of heavy materials; and (3) that as a result of diversification and new industry the economic conditions in Springfield will improve greatly.

We recommend (1) that the data and conclusions of this report on diversification be made available to appropriate area industries and (2) that a public relations firm, one specializing in industrial relocations, be retained by the Chamber of Commerce to devise plans for attracting new industries.

Figure 10.6   Sample abstract for a business report

Bibliography

Blankenship, Charles P. History of Industry in Kentucky. Chicago:
Palmer Publishers, 1974.

Dalton, Paul. Midwest Markets. New York: Hutton and Co., 1976.

Hempleman, Gerald. Guide to City and State Taxes. Louisville,
Kentucky: Hill Press, 1974.

Roberts, Henry. "Univac Flies with United." Business Week,
December 25, 1970, pp. 33-39.

U.S. Bureau of the Census. Statistical Abstract of the United
States. 1975. 96th ed. Washington, D.C.: U.S. Government
Printing Office, 1975.

Figure 10.7   Sample bibliography for a business report

ple, a sarcastic tone is part of the sense of the original, the abstract would have to make clear the author's intent.

Besides the abstract—an important part of a report—an executive might occasionally ask an assistant to abstract books and articles that have information of importance. The techniques used are the same as those for the abstract of a report. At the beginning of the abstract, identify fully the book or article you are summarizing.

PARTS AND GUIDELINES FOR REPORTS: CHECKLIST

I. *Letter of Transmittal*
   A. Let the letter of transmittal carry your cordial greeting to the reader.
   B. Open quickly with a "Here is the report you requested" tone.
   C. Establish the subject in the first sentence.
   D. Follow the opening with a brief summary of the study. Expand the discussion if a separate summary is not to be included in the report.
   E. Acknowledge the assistance of those who helped with the study.
   F. Close the letter with a "thank you" and a forward look.
II. *Title Page*
   A. Include the following on the title page:
      1. The title of the report.
      2. Full identification of the authority for the report (the party for whom the report is prepared).
      3. Full identification of the one who prepared the report.
      4. The date of completion of the report.
   B. Use attractive layout. If the items are to be centered, leave an extra ½ inch on the left for binding.
III. *Contents Page*
   A. Use either "Contents" or "Table of Contents" as the title.
   B. Use a tabular arrangement to indicate the heading degrees used in the report.
   C. All headings used in the report should be included in the content outline.
   D. If many graphs or tables are used, list them in a separate "List of Figures." Otherwise, the graphs or tables should not be listed, because they are not separate sections of your outline but only supporting data within a section of the report.

    E. Center the content outline horizontally and vertically on the page.

IV. *Abstract*
    A. Center the word "Abstract" at the top of the page, or use some other one-word title such as "synopsis," "summary," "brief," or "précis."
    B. Prepare the synopsis from condensed statements of your purpose, methods, findings, and conclusions sections of the report body.
    C. Concentrate on writing effective, generalized statements that avoid detail available in the report itself.

V. *The Body of the Report*
    A. Physical layout
       1. Use headings to assist the reader by making them descriptive of the contents of the section. Verbal headings are preferred.
       2. Maintain consistency in the mechanical placement of headings of the same degree.
       3. Use parallel construction in headings of the same degree in the same section of the report.
       4. Use the picture-frame layout for all pages. The margins should be: top—1 inch, right—1 inch, bottom—1½ inches, left—1½ inches. (the extra ½ inch is for binding.)
       5. Number all pages, with the first page of the body of the report being page one. For pages such as page one, having a major title at the top, omit the number or place it in the center of a line a double space below the last line on the page. For all other pages place the number in the center of the line or in the upper-right corner a double space above the first line on the page, or center the number a double space below the last line on the page.
    B. Graphics or tabular data:
       1. Number consecutively the graphs and tables used in the report.
       2. Give each graph or table a descriptive title.
       3. Refer to the graph or table within the text discussion.
       4. Place the graph or table as close to the textual reference as possible.
       5. Use effective layout, appropriate captions and legends, and realistic vertical and horizontal scales that help the table or graph stand clearly by itself.
    C. Reporting your analysis:

    1. Question each statement for its contributior. to the solution of the problem. Is each statement either descriptive or evaluative?

    2. Reduce large, unwieldy numbers to understandable ones through a common language, such as units of production, percentage, or ratios.

    3. Use an objective reporting style rather than persuasive language; avoid emotional terms. Identify assumptions and opinions. Avoid unwarranted judgments and inferences.

    4. Document your report wherever necessary.

    5. Tabulate or enumerate items when it will simplify the reading.

  D. Drawing conclusions:

    1. State the conclusions carefully and clearly, and make sure they grow out of your findings.

    2. If you believe it necessary, repeat the major supporting findings for each conclusion.

    3. If recommendations are called for, make them grow naturally from the conclusions.

VI. *The Addenda*

  A. Prepare the bibliography in alphabetic sequence by author from index cards.

  B. If the bibliography is lengthy, include separate sections for books, articles, governmental publications, and unpublished references.

  C. Use an alphabetic sequence, such as *A, B, C,* and so on, for each exhibit in the appendix.

The following sample report written by Bender-Oakes and Associates for the Agri-Tech Company illustrates several elements of a complete formal report. As an outside report, it is accompanied by a transmittal letter. The report itself contains title page, table of contents, abstract or summary, and the text itself.

May 15, 1979

Mr. James Clemson, President
Agri-Tech Company
4438 Southwest Drive
Dallas, Texas   75211

Dear Mr. Clemson:

The attached report presents our analysis of the three
proposed sites for the new Agri-Tech Company.

Data gathered from interviews with business sources and
civic leaders in the three communities revealed almost
identical cost considerations between Irving and
Lewisville. Because Irving offers you the greatest
employee availability advantages of the three locations,
it is recommended as the most favorable site.

We've enjoyed making this study for you. We wish you
the best of success and look forward to helping you again.

Sincerely yours,

BENDER-OAKES and ASSOCIATES

Thomas R Bender

TRB: ld   Thomas R. Bender, President

RECOMMENDATION OF IRVING AS THE LOCATION FOR THE

NEW AGRI-TECH COMPANY PLANT

Presented to

Mr. James Clemson

President

Agri-Tech Company, Southwest Division

By

Bender-Oakes and Associates

Ft. Worth, Texas

May 15, 1979

CONTENTS

ii

SUMMARY

The Irving building site on Interstate 35 near
Interstate 20 is recommended as the location for the
future home of the Southwest Division of the Agri-Tech
Company.

Three sites--Irving, Lewisville, and Arlington--
were selected by the Company for consideration as
possible locations for the construction of a seventy-
acre assembly plant. To evaluate the sites, the following
criteria were established:

1. Availability of the sites to the market area.
2. Cost of site acquisition and development.
3. Cost of taxes.
4. Availability of employees.

Interviews with property owners, county and city
civic officials, real estate appraisers, trucking and
railroad operators, and Agri-Tech employees revealed
that:

1. Lewisville and Irving offered cost advantages
    of about $8000 a year over Arlington.

2. The Irving site required the least capital
    outlay during the first year.

3. Future employee recruitment would be convenient
    at all three locations, but Irving was
    considered most convenient by the present Agri-
    Tech employees, most of whom live in the North
    Dallas area.

Therefore, Irving offers definite advantages over
the other sites for the proposed relocation of the
Southwest Division of the Agri-Tech Company.

RECOMMENDATION OF IRVING, TEXAS, AS THE LOCATION

FOR A NEW AGRI-TECH COMPANY PLANT

Background of This Report

Purpose. This report presents the analysis of three sites--
Irving, Lewisville, and Arlington--as the future home of the
Southwest Division of the Agri-Tech Company.

Present Situation and Future Plans of the Company. The
following information, well-known to Agri-Tech's management, simply
provides background for the problem serving as the basis for this
report. The Agri-Tech Company of Dallas, Texas, manufactures and
markets agricultural machinery and implements. Its distribution
area consists of the five-state territory of Texas and adjoining
states--Texas, Oklahoma, Louisiana, Arkansas, and New Mexico.
Dallas is near the center of the region.

Because of the increasingly competitive market, the Company
has decided to establish a local assembly plant to save on
transportation costs. Machinery is now shipped into Dallas from
factories in Indianapolis and Des Moines as complete units, ready
for sale except for minor last-minute conditioning.

After construction of a new plant, the Company will ship parts
from Company factories and other suppliers and assemble complete
farm machines.

About 50 employees now work at the limited facility in North
Dallas. The Company plans to strengthen its competitive position
by engaging in light manufacturing in addition to assembling and
marketing its agricultural equipment. Eventually about 200
employees will be required. To avoid tying up expansion capital
in land purchase, the Company plans to lease 70 acres of land
necessary for effective plant development. The estimated building
program will require a capital outlay of about $1,800,000.

Method of Procedure and Sources of Data. This study was made
through direct first-hand investigation of the three sites. Data
for analysis was obtained from interviews with the following groups:

1

1. Owners of the three property sites.
2. Three real estate appraisers, each holding the M.A.I.
   designation.
3. Chamber of Commerce representatives of the three
   communities.
4. Business offices of Dallas County, Tarrant County, and the
   City of Lewisville.
5. Representatives of the T&P (Texas & Pacific) and the MKT
   (Missouri-Kansas-Texas) railroads.
6. Representatives of three trucking companies in the Dallas
   area.
7. Representative employees of the Agri-Tech Company, SW.

The data has been analyzed on both a yearly and a thirty-year
basis as requested.

Criteria Used and Organization of the Report.   As requested,
the criteria used in evaluating the three sites were as follows:

1. Availability of the three sites to the receiving and
   marketing areas.
2. Cost of site acquisition and development.
3. Cost of taxes.
4. Availability of employees.

These criteria serve as the basis for the organization of the
remainder of the report.   No attempt has been made to foresee the
future of the agricultural equipment business.

Irving Nearest to the Market Area

The Irving site, lying 12 1/2 miles from the center of Dallas
as shown on the map on page 3, is centrally located within the market
area.   It has the best access to the receiving and shipping lanes.
The Irving location is on I-35, the region's major north-south
freeway.   It is six miles north of I-20, the region's major east-west
freeway.   It is also on a spur of the MKT railroad.

The Arlington site is on the I-20 east-west freeway and a spur
of the T&P railroad.   But it is 25 miles west of the center of
Dallas and the I-35 north-south freeway.

The Lewisville site is on I-35 and the MKT railroad, but it is
25 miles north of central Dallas and I-20.

All three sites have easy access to the freeway and the
railroad systems, but Irving best meets the criterion of availability
to the market.

2

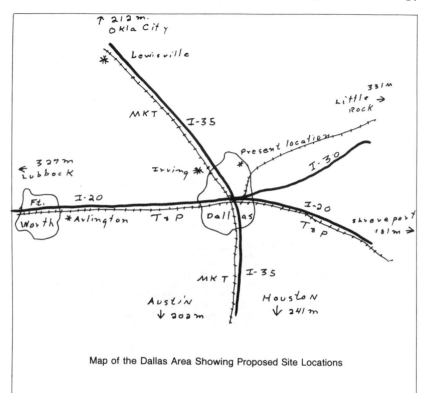

Map of the Dallas Area Showing Proposed Site Locations

3

Site Acquisition and Development Favor

Irving and Arlington

A yearly-lease cost for each 70-acre site and the initial
costs of grading and of developing access roads were computed
to evaluate the locations for site acquisition and development
criterion.

Lease Costs Favor Irving. Seventy acres of land, established
as necessary for the site, are available at all three locations.
Because of the capital necessary to purchase sufficient land, a
lease basis was used in determining cost. The Irving yearly lease
of $1500 an acre was less than either the $1600 at Arlington or
the $1650 at Lewisville. On a 70-acre basis, the $105,000 yearly
cost of the Irving site is 90 percent of the $115,500 lease cost
of the Lewisville site. The yearly cost at Irving is 93 percent
of the $112,000 lease cost of the Arlington site.

Arlington Has the Highest Site-Development Costs. Because of
the level land available at both Lewisville and Irving, the only
site development of those locations is the construction of access
roads on the property. According to the real estate appraisers
consulted, the access roads would cost about $40,000 at either
location. Building access roads and grading the rough terrain
at the Arlington location would cost about $55,000. Even though
there is little value in prorating these first-year costs over the
30-year period, the prorata figure does point to the significance
of these costs--$1333 a year at Irving and Lewisville and $1833
at Arlington. Combining the yearly-lease cost rates and the site
development costs for each location, as shown in Table 1, shows
the advantage of Irving on this criterion.

Table 1

Summary of Site Acquisition and Development Costs

Site	First-Year Cost	30-Year Cost
Lewisville	$116,833	$3,504,990
Arlington	113,833	3,414,990
Irving	106,333	3,189,990

4

Although site acquisition and development costs represent substantial fixed amounts, so do tax expenses.

Yearly Property Tax Costs Favor Lewisville

Although the site acquisition and development costs would remain fixed over the 30-year lease period, there is no assurance that cost of property taxes would remain constant. The best approach to the analysis of these costs is to assume that any change occurring would be proportionate to current costs.

Lewisville Offers a Tax Advantage. The Lewisville site, which is outside both Tarrant County and Dallas County, offers a yearly tax advantage of $9000 over either Irving or Arlington. Taxes would be $24,000 a year on the property and improvements at both Arlington and Irving, but only $15,000 at Lewisville. Yearly and 30-year tax costs are shown in Table 2.

Table 2

Property Tax

Site	Yearly Taxes	30-Year Total
Lewisville	$15,000	$450,000
Arlington	24,000	720,000
Irving	24,000	720,000

Tax costs give Lewisville an advantage over the other locations, but a combination of all factors now will give a clearer picture.

Combined Costs Point to Irving or Lewisville

Because of the heavy cost of site preparation, Arlington's location requires the greatest first-year capital outlay, as shown in Table 3.

5

Table 3

Combined First-Year Costs for the Proposed Sites

Cost	Lewisville	Arlington	Irving
Lease	$115,000	$112,000	$105,000
Taxes	15,000	24,000	24,000
Site Preparation	40,000	55,000	40,000
Total	170,500	191,000	169,000

When the cost of site preparation, which is an expense that must be met during the first year, is prorated over the 30-year period, the yearly cost at Irving is slightly less than the cost at Lewisville. It is almost $9000 less than the cost at Arlington, as shown in Table 4.

Table 4

One-Year Costs and 30-Year Totals

Cost	Lewisville	Arlington	Irving
Lease	$115,500	$112,000	$105,000
Taxes	15,000	24,000	24,000
Site	1,333	1,833	1,333
One-Year Cost	131,833	137,833	130,333
30-Year Totals	3,954,990	4,134,990	3,909,990

It is obvious that Lewisville and Irving are more desirable than Arlington from a cost viewpoint. Because these two sites are about equal in terms of cost, the employee availability criterion coupled with the availability of Irving to the market area represented the determining factor.

6

Employee Availability Favors Irving

A supply of both skilled and unskilled workers is available
at all three locations. The wishes of current employees and the
possibility of procuring future employees were considered in the
analysis of employee availability.

Of the current employees surveyed, most of them live in the
North Dallas area. Some 86 percent indicated that they found
Irving more convenient than the other locations. At the same time,
Irving offers the same degree of new-employee availability as do
the other areas. Irving, therefore, offers the greatest opportunity
for the retention of current employees and possesses the needed
supply of workers for future company expansion.

Summary of Reasons Favoring Irving

Irving is recommended as the most desirable of the proposed
sites for the location of the Agri-Tech Company's new home. It
is in the heart of the market area, and it offers cost advantages
equal to or better than the other two sites. Finally, of great
importance, it is the site closest to the homes of Agri-Tech's
current employees.

7

EXERCISES AND PROBLEMS

1. In preparation for a Chamber of Commerce brochure to attract new industry to your city, you are requested to write a report on the quality of medical facilities of the city.
2. As department head supervising eight typists, you believe that all eight typewriters should be replaced. According to your records, three are four years old, three are two years old, and one was purchased eight months ago. Write a report to your boss describing the condition of the typewriters, drawing conclusions, and making recommendations.
3. The boss has approved your request to purchase eight new typewriters for your department. Obtain information about three makes of typewriters from your local office machines distributors. Then prepare a report to your boss, justifying your recommendation of one make of typewriter. Include sales or advertising materials in the appendix of your report.
4. Select some major company of interest to you, and investigate its methods of recruiting employees. When you have concluded your study, write a report revealing your findings. If your instructor requests it, submit first a detailed pre-project report describing your plan of research.
5. Select an interesting article or report from a business journal and, after reading it carefully, prepare a 150 to 200 word abstract of it.
6. Write a report entitled "Billboards in [your city]: well used or ill used." Make use of observational research to gather your data, and use library research and interrogational research to establish criteria.
7. The Atlas Home and Auto Supply Company plans to open a new branch in one of three locations—urban, suburban, or rural. About $500,000 is available for construction of the store and purchase of the land. As an independent marketing consultant, plan a study to determine where the store should be located.
8. You are to report on a study of the comparative qualities of three compact cars—C, P, and F. Prepare an outline of the entire problem. Show a clear statement of the problem, the qualities to be evaluated in selecting one of the cars as most desirable for a company using 20 cars a year, and the sources of information available to you. Prepare a possible Table of Contents page for the report. Also prepare a letter of transmittal.

9. Write a report on vehicle accidents in your state during the last 20 years. Use library research to obtain your facts and interrogational research to find out what is being done about the accident rate. You may wish to use charts, tables, and graphs.

10. Write a formal report with a body of about 15–25 double-spaced pages. Choose a topic broad enough to justify the length but one not so large that it requires volumes. Find a topic that involves a business problem. For example, you may know there is too great a turnover of employees in a certain store or shop. Or you may know of a shopping center that is losing its business to another area of town. Define your problem, clarify your purpose, and begin your research. Here are some other ideas you can use as a springboard for a topic:
    a. Opening of a restaurant or doughnut shop
    b. Development of a marina
    c. A program for hiring and training minority groups in a certain company
    d. Explanation for a certain policy or procedure—such as methods of communication used by a certain department store in collecting retail accounts
    e. Evaluation of two or three career areas. You might make use of this in your own specific career selection.
    f. A study, report, and recommendation on attitudes toward a certain troublesome problem, such as the opinions of a certain company's employees about wages, working hours, food services, or promotion plan

11. Observe a local service or facility and make recommendations for improvement. Here are some suggestions:
    a. Check-out service at a department store or supermarket
    b. Dining room arrangement and service
    c. Rest room facilities
    d. Duplicating service
    e. Grounds maintenance
    f. Parking lot
    Write a letter to the assumed manager, making recommendations.

12. Write an abstract of about 200 words on the report "Pyrolysis as an Alternative Method of Waste Disposal" on pp. 278–285.

13. The Diner's Choice cafeteria chain is considering opening a cafeteria near an existing cafeteria in your community. The chain wants to check the competition from the customer's viewpoint. You have been asked to make a survey of food

service at the existing cafeteria and to write a description of the service as it appears to the customer. Your report is to be strictly informative on the kinds of food served, including menus and prices; the physical arrangements for serving and dining; and the flow of traffic. Your report will come largely from observational research. Write the report in the form of a letter to the following:

> J. C. Benson, Vice President
> Diner's Choice Cafeterias
> 25 Townley Square
> Pittsburgh, Pennsylvania 15213

14. Write a report on the efficiency with which work is being done in a local store, office, or plant. You may wish to limit your scope to one operation—such as shipping, mailing, accounts receivable, maintenance, or duplicating. You may be able to write from past experience, or you may need observational or interview research.

    Make recommendations for improvement.

15. Select a local service or company and write a formal report to the manager or president on one of the following subjects. Investigate external sources, giving the reader the general principles and practices that he may wish to apply specifically.
    a. Staggering work hours in offices
    b. Developing a house organ
    c. Recruiting and training future executives
    d. Methods of supervising and training correspondents
    e. Proven techniques of employee relations
    f. Employee profit-sharing plans
    g. Handling customer complaints

11
Writing Various Kinds of Reports

As a report writer, you will be called upon to write many different kinds of reports. Business has many specific needs. There are periodic, project, progress, laboratory, field, library, inspection, or a combination of some types (such as laboratory–library), to name a few. They include such subjects as profit-and-loss statements, market analyses, stock averages, production figures, hours of work, progress on certain projects, employee turnover, evaluation of an ongoing process, agenda and minutes of meetings, summaries and abstracts. These and many other kinds of information are exchanged continually in carrying on business. However, with all these specific kinds of reports, how you handle the material of the report will depend upon one of two main purposes—to inform or to analyze.

THE TWO PURPOSES—INFORMATIVE OR ANALYTICAL

All of these specific kinds of reports can be classified into two kinds of reports according to purpose and objectives to be accomplished: (1) *informative* and (2) *analytical.* The analytical, in turn, breaks into two kinds: (a) those with interpretation and conclusions and (b) those that also include recommendations. So, your report may be informative, or analytical with conclusions, or analytical with recommendations. Which of these three purposes you serve in your report depends, of course, on what assignment you have been given (or initiate yourself).

Informative reports simply present data, with no attempt to analyze or interpret the meaning of the data or to make recommendations for action. The report writer will organize, classify, and present the material in an orderly way, but his purpose is fact-finding. Somebody else will use the facts of the report for making a decision or recommendation.

Analytical reports also provide information and, in addition, include analysis and interpretation. The analysis is the way we move from the facts of a situation to the conclusions that can be drawn from those facts. During analysis, we look for the relationships among the facts. The human mind can move with such lightning speed that we are not always exactly sure quite how we reached a conclusion. If your thought processes are valid, this speed may do no particular harm. But in the world of work, you often have to justify your conclusions and your decisions. Often you have to persuade someone to accept them. When such occasions arise, you need the analytical report—a rational way of showing your facts and how you sifted through them in reaching your conclusions and decisions.

If you go on to make recommendations, you must be all the more sure of your facts and conclusions. You are on the spot and there will be consequences, good or bad, if the recommendations are followed. And, of course, the reader wants his recommendations to be followed.

Here is an example of a straight informative report. The credit manager simply presents data to his superior, who will make recommendations in terms of this data. Since this is part of a report series, the reader has background knowledge, and so an introduction and terminal section are not needed.

TO: Kevin Milton, Vice-President   DATE: March 17, 1979

FROM: James Hallfield, Credit Manager

SUBJECT: Credit data on Betty and Bruce Nelson

The Nelsons were originally in the produce business, but
have shifted from that occupation. Over the years they
have been involved in real estate, owning apartment
buildings and commercial properties. We have no financial
statement at this time, but informal, but reliable sources
estimate a net worth in the medium six-figure bracket.

Our company last made a loan to Mr. and Mrs. Nelson on
July 23, 1973. This was for $95,000 on a commercial
building. The loan was paid in full with their personal
funds on January 24, 1976, about 11 1/2 years ahead of
schedule. The Nelsons have had savings accounts with
Southwest National since 1969. At the present time we
hold about $11,000 in savings, but the accounts have
ranged upward from that figure. Much of the savings
have been in certificates of deposit.

The Nelsons have maintained a good credit rating over the
years. One bank reports unsecured loans in high four to
low five figures, prompt repayment, with nothing now owing.
A checking account is maintained in low five-figure amounts.

We have little in the way of financial figures at this
time, but find that the Nelsons are highly regarded in
handling their financial affairs.

James Hallfield

In an example of an analytical report, Vice President Kevin Milton responds to the informative credit report from the credit manager, James Hallfield. Again, because of the report series, an introduction is not needed. The report consists of the text, which draws some conclusions, and the terminal section—the recommendations.

TO: James Hallfield   DATE: March 18, 1979

FROM: Kevin Milton

SUBJECT: Loan recommendations for Betty and Bruce Nelson

In your review of this loan, you should consider these facts:

1. Bruce Nelson contacted us late in February about making the
    proposed loan. At that time, he thought the terms which we
    might offer him were unacceptable. After he tested the
    market, he changed his mind and returned to the office to
    inform Thomas Kenmore that he would like to proceed with
    loan negotiations.

    A definite complication entered the picture in that Mr. Nelson
    and his wife were scheduled to leave the following day on an
    extended business trip to other parts of the country. The
    mechanics of handling the loan details, therefore, became
    somewhat involved, but we believe they can be overcome by
    coordinating the commitment letter through his attorney. If
    the loan conditions are accepted, Willard Parkinson has said
    he will fly the Nelsons back here to sign the various
    mortgage papers.

2. Mr. and Mrs. Nelson are making substantial cash investment
    of $250,000 in this transaction. Our experience with them
    has been A-1. And while we have not yet received their
    current financial statement, their reputation for taking
    care of their obligations is excellent.

3. The criteria of a good apartment loan are present: desirable
    location, quality construction, acceptable room layout and
    sizes, responsible borrower, market demand.

Our Loan Committee recommends a $800,000 loan under the following
conditions:

1. Rate: 9 1/4%

2. Service fee: $5,000 (or 1% of the loan if our counsel believes
    there's a legal basis for our doing so).

3. Term: 25 years. (The first payment would be delayed for one
    year with the loan to be amortized in 24 years.)

4. The present purchase agreement between Willard Parkinson
    & Son, Inc., and Betty Nelson will be rewritten to conform
    to new conditions.

5. Bruce Nelson will personally sign the mortgage note.

6. The repayment privilege will be 20% per year with a six
    months' interest penalty for anything paid over that amount.

7. Other normal loan conditions.

The main purpose of the following report is to inform—in response to a request for information. But a brief interpretation is
appended. Sales figures are tabulated, with a possible explanation
of the decrease in the one instance.

BLACK
   HOME AND AUTO   <u>Memo</u>
         SUPPLY

<u>TO</u>: William Wilton, General Manager   <u>DATE</u>: January 5, 1979

<u>FROM</u>: Paul Tarton, Sales Manager

<u>SUBJECT</u>: Sales by districts for month ending December 31.

Here are the figures of sales reported by districts for the month
ending December, 1978, which you requested in our telephone
conversation yesterday.

District	December Sales	December Sales a Year Ago
Jacksboro	$10,511	$12,314
Dayton	16,989	32,157
Newark	27,430	27,565
Athens	16,456	16,345

Sales dropped about 47 percent in the Dayton area and about
14 percent in Jacksboro. The other two districts held their
own. The Dayton drop may be partly explained, in my opinion,
by the fact that there is a new sales supervisor in the Dayton
area, and half of his sales force are inexperienced. This
does not mean that they are to blame for the decrease, but
they should be given a chance to prove how much they can
overcome the previous deficit. I shall do what I can to help
them.

REPORTS FOR VARIOUS JOB ASSIGNMENTS

Within the two large kinds of reports—informative and analytical—are the many specific kinds of reports. The report you write on the job is more likely to be designated as one of the specific kinds such as laboratory report, field report, inspection report, solution to a problem, or progress report. You might be told, for example, to "just get me the information on the subject" (informative), or you might be told to "try to come up with some solution," or "see what you can recommend" (both analytical). Often these are on specific assignments.

We can't illustrate all of the various specific kinds of reports, but we can give some examples of the more common ones that you are likely to deal with.

Investigative: Field

The investigative report deals with a specific problem or assignment. Something needs to be looked into, or a change is considered, and you are asked to come up with information and probably analysis. The report is usually analytical, for the reporter is considered somewhat of a specialist, who is qualified to get to the facts, to interpret them, and to make recommendations.

Two common kinds of investigative reports are the *field* and the *laboratory*. A field report relies heavily on observational and perhaps interrogational research. A laboratory report is more likely based on experimental research.

The field report is made following a visit to a specific site for a definite reason. It may present information about improving production methods in a department or a plant; the desirability of locating a new building, a bridge, a railroad, or a highway in a certain area; the damage done by a tornado or a fire; the advisability of marketing a certain area, etc. The information for the field report is gathered through such techniques as observing a situation or a condition, talking with people involved, perhaps both lay people and experts, etc. The report may include such parts as a discussion of background information, an account of the investigation, a presentation of facts, details, and results of the investigation, conclusions, and recommendations.

C O M M U N I C A T I O N S,   I N C.

Houston, Texas   77004

July 20, 1979

Bristol Electronics Company
3298 Arbor Avenue
Chicago, Illinois   60621

Attention: T.M. Timkins

Gentlemen:

As you requested in your letter of June 15, 1979, I have personally
inspected the communication site at Galveston, Texas, and submit
the following report.

Control Room

The control room is carefully supervised and everyone is well
trained in control facilities. The outage record and the logs
are kept accurately and up-to-date.

Power Supply

Transformers. The transformers are in peak operating condition.
According to the log, the two transformers operate at the same
time. One supplies the power and the other is a standby.

Auxiliary Switchover. The automatic switchover equipment works
perfectly. Standard tests were performed, and not once did the
signal lose phase from one transformer to the other.

Equipment Room

Converters. The converter equipment has an output with less than
3% distortion. A routine distortion check is made every hour
and recorded according to regulations. Very little outage occurs,
and no major outage has been recorded since the cable cut of
March 10, 1973.

Multiphase. The multiphase equipment is adequate with one exception.
The second branch is operating on auxiliary power with no backup.
A power supply has been ordered and should arrive by August 1.

Conclusion

The site at Galveston is one of the best in the Southwest. The
personnel are satisfied and no complaints were filed. The average
outages add up to about 25 minutes a week, which is the best record
in the Southwest.

Sincerely yours,

R. D. Benson

RDB: bt   R.D. Benson

Investigative: Laboratory

The laboratory report grows out of the carefully controlled conditions of good experimental research. This kind of report usually comes from a very special assignment, and an important decision is pending—such as going into the production of a new engine or changing equipment or materials.

The reader wants enough details of the experiment so he can evaluate the recommendation you make. But remember, you're the specialist; don't use specialists' language that he will not understand.

I M A G E,   I N C.

4028 Lakewood Blvd.
Cleveland, Ohio   44102

TO: William Bennett   DATE: May 4, 1979

FROM: Roy Allen   *R. a,*

SUBJECT: Test of new texoid scrimseal, Graph-X

The sample of scrimseal, Graph-X, was received on April 15 and was immediately taken to the laboratory, where imprints could be made. After a full week of continuous study and checking of the scrimseal sample, I have arrived at the following conclusions.

No pressure distortion whatever was found in any of the sheets checked. Corrective printing, such as adding detail, was found to be very effective. Line weight distortion on corrective scribing was kept to a minimum of a plus or minus two thousandths of an inch. Reprints were made quickly and easily with no pressure distortion.

From the results of the experiments with this new scrimseal, I recommend that a large supply be ordered and kept on hand at all times.

Activities: Periodic

An activities report keeps a central office informed about certain activities at the home location or at one of the branches or areas. Such reports are usually informational. Two common kinds of activities reports are the *periodic* report and the *progress* report.

Periodic reports are records of work or activities over a specific period of time—a day, a week, a month, etc. Their intervals are determined by management needs or customer requirements. They frequently build up from daily records or job reports to supervisors' periodic reports. Higher-level periodic reports pull together these other reports to present information to organizational officers or customers.

Progress reports are similar to periodic reports in that they also present information about past activities and they may be required at regular intervals. They are different in that they deal with changing or progressing conditions. The progress report presents information about work completed up to a point; the total work has not been completed. Often several progress reports may be presented on work in progress before a final report can be made on work completed.

Because an activities report is a customary report, an introduction or terminal section is frequently unnecessary. The following periodic report on branch activities uses informal, memo format. The writer uses headings and numerical listings to make the information easy to grasp.

TO: Gerald Brinson   DATE: December 5, 1978

FROM: Tim Manson

SUBJECT: Southgate activities--November, 1978

Training Program

1. November 30 was the midway point of the second phase of the Midwest Credit Union training program. Training is progressing satisfactorily and on schedule. With the resignation of Jane Otis, we need to make a slight change in the program but don't expect any delay in the training. In fact, this termination will advance the training of Wilma Tolliver and Chris Thomas.

Promotional

1. I again talked with Jan King about financing new washers and dryers for all locations. I think we will close before December 31.

2. Bids on the Allis-Nelson project will be opened December 10.

3. Although a divided period, 2 vacations, and one prolonged illness have disrupted my outside business call activity, I have made it a practice to converse at least a little with every broker, real estate agent, insurance agent, and attorney that comes into the office. Although it is difficult to assess results from the little additional time and effort spent on this form of intra-office business development, numerous phone calls for loan information and a couple of loan commitments were a direct result of this activity.

Customer Complaints and Action Taken

1. An unusually high number of customers in November complimented us on the friendly and helpful service of our personnel.

2. I had one serious disagreement with a large savings account customer about his reluctance to reimburse Midwest for our check to him which contained an overpayment. He blamed Midwest for allowing this situation to happen and condemned our system for not catching this before issuing the check. He quizzed Ann Billings unmercifully until I intervened and put a halt to it. When he started swearing, I invited him to leave the office. He finally calmed down and left. A check was mailed to us a few days later, and his accounts are still intact.

Building, Equipment, and Grounds

1. We had the usual winter heating problem at Parkside Office--hot in the morning and cold in the afternoon. Blower fans are turned off at noon each day. We have told Hamilton Company of this situation many times, but they cannot correct the problem. We will consider another solution.

2. The outside clock does not keep correct time. Maintenance knows about the trouble and will correct it.

Problem-Solution

Often your report assignment will be to come up with a solution to a particular problem. You are asked to investigate, collect data, assess, and come up with a recommendation. This kind of report would be analytical. It might be with personnel, such as, "See if you can figure out a way to make the office staff happier at West Park." Your problem might be with work efficiency, such as, "What can we do to keep the work from piling up in the steno pool?" Or it might be with marketing, such as "I see that Little Furies are not turning over nearly as fast at Denton as they are at Jefferson and Millburg. What can we do about it?"

These are recognized problems or defined needs. Your recommendation will try to solve the problem or make improvements.

```
      Q U I C K
                              Memorandum
        P R I N T


  TO:   Carl Emmons                    DATE:  May 12, 1978

  FROM:  Bill Tappan    ⅃⅃

  SUBJECT:  Low Output by the Steno Pool


  The problem of low output by the steno pool can be corrected by
  installing a Victor 750 Collator.

  The bottleneck in the steno pool is in the Duplicating Center.
  I have observed the typists at work and inspected samples of
  their typing.  Whenever they are at their desks, they are fast
  and efficient.  There are enough workers for normal typing load.
  The problem is that several typists periodically must be called
  to the Duplicating Center to help assemble and staple pages.
  Whenever large numbers of copied pages must be collated, as many
  as four girls are needed for up to five hours.

  This situation not only crowds the duplicating facilities, but
  also leaves the steno pool severely understaffed.  The four new
  contracts our company has taken on will, of course, increase our
  work load--perhaps as much as 15 percent.  We just don't have the
  capacity, and, under present arrangements, the bottleneck will
  get even worse.
```

The Victor 750 Collator is the answer. With only one person
operating it, the Victor 750 can assemble and staple up to 1000
twelve-sheet documents in 60 minutes. Doing the same job now
manually takes two girls four hours.

Assuming that the 15% work-load increase lasts indefinitely, I
estimate that the Victor Collator, which costs $5975, will pay
for itself in close to 10 months. Even at our present work load,
it would take no more than 12 months.

I have fully compared the capacity and the construction of the
Victor 750 with the Olympia 100 Collator, the only other model
which even comes close to meeting our needs. Though the initial
cost of the Olympia is lower, I believe the Victor is a better
value. The attached comparison sheet supports this conclusion.
The data does not come from manufacturers' specifications. I
tested both machines personally in factory demonstrations.

The evidence, I believe, shows that if we install a Victor 750
Collator, the costly bottleneck in the steno pool will disappear.

Comparative Figures for Victor 750

and Olympia 100

COST	OLYMPIA	VICTOR
Basic Collator		
--without stapler	$4425	$5575
--with stapler	4925	5975
PAPER SIZE	8 1/2 x 11-14 only	anything from 3 x 5 to 11 x 17
NUMBER OF BINS	8	12
ASSEMBLING METHOD	staggered sets	piled sets
STACKING	yes	yes
COUNTER	yes	yes
SKIP DETECTION	yes (shuts off)	yes (shuts off)

FLOOR SIZE	30'' x 98''	27'' x 60'' (45% less floor space)
NO. OF OPERATIONS FROM LOAD TO RUN	20-24	4-6
NO. OF OPERATIONS FROM STOP TO NEXT LOAD	8-10	4-6
TOTAL NO. OF OPERATIONS	28-34	8-12
TEACHING TIME	60-90 minutes	15-20 minutes
ANNUAL MAINTENANCE	$375	$75-90

Proposal

The proposal report is a special kind of problem report. It is like the problem in that it analyzes a specific problem and tries to come up with a solution. It is different in that it is usually self-initiated rather than assigned, and the problem it is working on may not already be recognized by the reader. Such a situation calls for a special approach on the part of the report writer. You will have to make clear in your report that there really is a problem, and you will have to justify the solution you are recommending. You will have to be especially convincing.

In the following report, the director of the sanitation department of a city proposes to the city manager a better method of disposing of solid waste materials. The problem is made real, and the solution is persuasive.

PYROLYSIS AS AN ALTERNATIVE METHOD OF

WASTE DISPOSAL

Presented to

Mr. Jerry Wolfe

City Manager

City of Columbus

by

Gene Browning, Director

Sanitation Department

January 24, 1979

CONTENTS

ii

PYROLYSIS AS AN ALTERNATIVE METHOD OF WASTE DISPOSAL

Recommendation

    The Sanitation Department of the City of Columbus is responsible
for the collection and disposal of solid refuse in order to maintain
a clean, healthful city. The purpose of this report is to point
out the need for a change from our present disposal system in order
to meet objectives and standards and to use our budget effectively.
It is recommended that we implement a pyrolysis process with energy
production and recycling of products.

Background of This Report

    Problems with Present Landfill Method of Disposing of Refuse.
The City of Columbus has three landfills which are used for solid
refuse, and these are becoming filled. The problem is that one of
these landfills will be filled by the end of next year, and the
other two will be filled in three to five years. Since land prices
have risen and more land for another landfill is not readily
available, alternatives must be considered. Public opinion is against
landfills, and complaints have increased. The noxious gases and
leachate runoff are environmental hazards and limit the future use
of the land. Long range planning indicates that disposal costs in
landfills are likely to increase drastically in the future. It is
estimated that the cost of the land and preparation for a landfill
is approximately $3,000 per acre. For a landfill of five foot
depth to last 25 years, 8,200 acres would be needed.

    To buy 8,200 acres now would cost $10,446,000, with annual
payments of $417,480 over a 25-year period. At the end of 25 years,
another landfill would have to be found, at perhaps double the
1978 cost.

    Suitable land is not immediately available, but real estate
agents believe it can be found. Purchasing another landfill in
25 years may be impossible. This report considers alternative
methods of disposing of refuse.

    Objectives of Columbus Sanitation Department. The objectives
of the Sanitation Department must be kept in mind in any consideration of alternate methods of disposal, since any method must meet
these standards. The objectives are as follows:

1

1. To improve the environmental health of Columbus by proper
    disposal of solid refuse.

2. To provide a satisfactory physical environment by collection
    of solid refuse.

3. To implement a method of solid refuse disposal with a
    potential for resource recovery better than the present
    landfill.

4. To contribute to national goals by conservation of energy
    through materials recovery from solid refuse.

Criteria Used for Alternative Methods. In keeping with the
objectives of the Sanitation Department and the budgetary restrictions of the City Government, the following criteria were used in
considering alternative methods of solid waste disposal:

1. Economics

2. Technical requirements

3. Legal restrictions

4. Energy recovery and recycling

5. By-products of the method

6. Disadvantages

7. Advantages

The client groups affected by this analysis are the residents of the
city and suburbs and the commercial enterprises.

Alternative Methods of Disposing of Refuse

The following are the alternative methods of disposing of solid
waste:

1. Composting

2. Incineration

3. Sanitary landfill

4. Anaerobic fermentation process

5. Pyrolysis with energy recovery

2

Composting is the biochemical degradation of the organic fraction of solid waste material which makes an end product, a humus-like substance that can be used for soil conditioning. A landfill is also necessary for the non-compostables. The following are factors that limit the use of this method: the composition of the refuse, land availability, size of the community, the need for secondary disposal, and the existence of a viable market for the end product.

Incineration is a system of burning for reducing solid, liquid, or gaseous combustible waste to CO_2, other gases, and noncombustible residue which must be deposited in a landfill. The limiting factors of incineration are the characteristics of the refuse, secondary land availability, the detrimental production of air pollutants, and the characteristics of the waste-waters and residues produced during the process.

Sanitary landfill is limited by the decreasing available sites, costs of transporting waste to the site, decomposition of the residue at the site with production of gases that are public nuisances and even severe hazards, migrating water which may lead to pollution of surface water and ground water systems, lack of adequate cover materials, nuisances caused by odors, blowing papers, and disease carriers. Additionally, the increase in environmental protective standards increases costs. According to a 1978 national survey, only five percent of all landfills are properly operated.

Anaerobic fermentation process has potential; however, it has not been applied in full-scale development to solid waste.

Pyrolysis refers to the process of decomposing organic compounds through the application of heat. Destructive distillation is carried out in an oxygen-free environment. With front-end separation to recover valuable resources from the refuse and with energy recovery during the pyrolysis, this method is recommended as the most beneficial.

Application of Criteria to the Pyrolysis Method

The economics of the pyrolysis method indicates that the initial cost of the land and plant with a 1000-ton per day capacity would be $14,742,000. Operating costs would be $5.72 per ton. Assuming that all the by-products are recovered or utilized, a revenue of $4.67 per ton would be obtained. This would make the net cost $1.05 per ton. There is also a potential for profit, as some operations have demonstrated. Initial cost would be high; however, the potential for recovery of materials, energy, and pollution-free air in the years ahead would greatly reduce cost.

3

Technical requirements for the plant consist of a feed preparation area leading into the pyrolyzer. There would be a front-end separation of glass and metal and a conventional pyrolysis system to recover the energy in the form of heat, oil, gas, and a glassy aggregate. The critical factors in the process are the heating rate, temperature, and waste composition. There would have to be some gas input from the area in starting the process. Fortunately, we are in an area rich in gas, and so there is no great problem.

Legal aspects to be considered are the environmental agency's decisions that obnoxious gases are not to be expelled into the air. In the pyrolysis process, all the products are contained, and the gases are used to sustain the process. Noise may be an issue, but a plant such as this or any other method of disposal is limited in its proximity to residential areas.

The energy recovery and recycling process of pyrolysis is in keeping with the Resource Recovery Act passed by Congress in 1970.

The by-products of the pyrolysis are gases with an energy range from 10 to 17 Btu's per ton, which is sufficient to provide heat for the pyrolysis. The solid residue, a glasslike aggregate, can be used in road construction. The fuel oil with low sulfur content is equivalent to 75 percent of Number 6 oil on a volumetric basis. Total pyrolyzed refuse weight reduction would be 75% and volume reduction would by 95% from original waste material with front-end removal of glass and metal. This glass and metal can also be recycled. The system has great efficiency.

The disadvantages of pyrolysis are the initial high cost, the need to be close to a supplemental gas market (in our region, this is not a problem), and the possible difficulty of establishing markets for some products.

The advantages are the complete recovery of usable products from solid refuse, the self-sustaining gases to perpetuate the pyrolysis process, potential for an industrial park through which the end-products could be marketed (this could be farmed out), potential for revenue profit, and the simplicity and flexibility of the operating process.

4

Pyrolysis Meets the Objectives of the Sanitation Department

Objective number 1 is effectively met because pyrolysis would improve the environmental health of Columbus. There would be no noxious gases or leachate run-off and no exposed refuse for vermin.

Objective number 2 is not affected particularly by pyrolysis because the refuse still has to be collected in a similar manner, no matter what method of disposal is used.

Objective number 3 is met by pyrolysis most satisfactorily because it is a better method of refuse disposal than the present landfills that have several shortcomings already enumerated in this analysis.

Objective number 4 relates to nationwide goals of energy conservation. Pyrolysis would very definitely contribute since it would change solid refuse into usable end-products that would substitute for natural gas products.

Summary of Reasons Favoring Pyrolysis

These findings are presented with the realization that to recommend this system to the public will require their understanding of the potential improvements. The initial high cost will be offset by the reduced cost when the operation is underway. The total value of this system will be very cost-beneficial. Portions of the area adjacent to the plant may be farmed out for different parts of the recycling process, and a recycling park could develop. Such a project would additionally reduce cost.

The alternative methods listed, though somewhat cheaper initially, have several flaws and do not provide the energy recovery and recycling benefits which pyrolysis provides. All require additional landfills, which increase their cost.

5

Bibliography

Durnay, Arsen, and Franklin, William E. The Role of Packaging
in Solid Waste Management 1966 to 1976. Rockville,
Maryland: U.S. Department of Health, Education, and
Welfare, 1969.

Golueke, Clarence G. Biological Reclamation of Solid Wastes.
Emmaus, Pennsylvania: Rodell Press, 1977.

Greenberg, Michael R., et al. Solid Waste Planning in
Metropolitan Regions. New Brunswick, New Jersey: Center
for Urban Policy Research, Rutgers University, 1976.

Pavoni, Joseph L., Heer, John E., Jr., and Hagerty, D. Joseph.
Handbook of Solid Waste Disposal. New York: Van
Nostrand Reinhold Company, 1975.

6

EXERCISES AND PROBLEMS

1. Prepare a report for your boss, who told you, "I keep getting the impression that our people are spending too much time on the coffee break. Maybe the thing is getting out of hand. Give me a report and tell me what you think we should do." Note that both observational and interrogational research are feasible.
2. Select some situation within your school or business which you think should be changed. Write a brief memo report to your superior describing the situation and recommending specific changes.
3. As an exercise in clear writing, write directions for a visitor on how to get from the airport to the recommended motel and on to your place of business. He will rent a car at the airport
4. Describe a small problem and solve it.
   Suggestions: Trash continually around the coffee area;
   Lights frequently left on in a store room, work room, or elsewhere:
   Food and beverage machines on the campus;
   Bulletin boards in a specific building;
   Unsatisfactory parking situation.
   Remember that you will have to persuade your readers that the problem is real and significant and that your recommendation will solve the problem.
5. As a practice in writing for your reader, write a definition for each of these terms. Write for the layman, a person who is knowledgeable but not especially experienced in the shoptalk of business.
   a. tensile strength
   b. Plymouth
   c. incremental return
   d. blue chip
   e. treasurer
   f. policy
   g. experimental research
6. Make a study of one of the following subjects. You will probably make heavy use of interview techniques.
   a. Consumer and management attitudes towards trading stamps
   b. The Chamber of Commerce's image to various parts of the community

c. Two different department stores—exclusive and general. You will compare and contrast such areas as prices, quality of goods, clientele, customer services, range of merchandise.

7. Analyze the structure, sentence style, logic, and graphics, in an article from a business magazine such as *Consumer Reports, Business Week, Changing Times,* or *Fortune.*

8. Investigate and report on trends that may be occurring in one of the following areas:
   a. The size of farms in the United States
   b. Consumption of different kinds of energy in the US
   c. Number of women in a particular job area, such as executive positions, industry, medicine, construction, law, or government

9. Write a report on the effective use in your city of one of the following: city parks, parking facilities, downtown shopping area, advertising media, or delivery services.

10. Recommend a location and facility for the Company's Annual Saturday Outing.

11. Recommend that a particular piece of company equipment should be replaced.

12. Write a market analysis in which you compare prices and quality of a particular product or type of store in the community. If you choose to write on a product, you may wish to use an item discussed in *Consumer Reports.*

13. As a field investigator for the home office, make an on-the-spot investigation of the orderliness and cleanliness of a large local discount house or supermarket. Write up your findings in a memorandum report. Be specific enough to support general conclusions.

14. Assume that you are manager of the Collinwood branch of the Morris Discount Stores. This is one of 15 outlets of the Morris chain. The chain handles a variety of family and home merchandise ranging from clothing and appliances through equipment for auto, garden, sports, and outdoors. You are allowed by company policy to donate in each 12-month period up to $4000 worth of merchandise to local, certified fund-raising organizations.

    Write a letter report to your general manager listing the store's contributions for the 12-month period just concluded. Include the items, their value, the receiving organization, and other relevant data. Assume any reasonable facts, data, and information which will make your report complete.

15. As sales manager of Ajax Sports, Inc., you are required to sub-

mit a monthly sales report to the general manager. In this report for May, you comment on the sales of your three major lines of athletic shoes: tennis, basketball, and track. Sales are reported in dozens of units sold. Figures are always compared with the sales for the same month last year as well as the previous month. Because of the season, basketball shoes have fallen off, and because of the recent nationwide interest in jogging, the line of jogging shoes has had a tremendous upswing in sales.

Your sales force has remained fairly stable, though you did add three trainees last month.

Although you do not report on sales advertising, you do believe strongly that the budget for newspaper and early evening TV commercial time should be increased by at least 20% to $130,000 a month.

Assume any reasonable facts, data, and information which will make your report complete.

16. You are head of a team of four who were given the job of conducting a survey of the cities of Canton, Akron, and Kent. Your project is to interview individuals designated by a random sampling to determine their reactions to front-engine drive compact cars as compared with rear-engine drive.

This is your first progress report and you have finished about half the survey of the first city, Canton. You find, however, that interviews run an average of 22 minutes (including travel) as compared to the projected 16. It is important for your team to stay on schedule, but to do so you would need another interviewer for the team. Under the present conditions, your team will be in Akron two days later than the original schedule called for. Assume all other necessary facts involved in your survey, and submit a progress report to your supervisor.

17. Assume that your company purchased the Motorcraft Company last year. One of the first projects was the renovation of the manufacturing plant with special attention to the cafeteria.

This is your second report, six weeks after the first report. During these six weeks the new loading dock has been redone, fluorescent fixtures have been installed throughout the factory area, and the cafeteria has been fitted with new furniture and equipment. Complete stainless steel cooking facilities were installed. Table tennis and billiard tables were purchased for the lounge area. Employee wash-up and locker areas were renewed.

Labor costs for the work should be reported. Materials costs for the project are handled through another department. You are about one week ahead of schedule.

You may assume any reasonable facts, data, and information to make your report complete.

18. Select one of the following subject areas in which you have the most special training or interest and write an analytical report.

   a. Market action of the past six months of the stock of three competitive companies listed on the New York Stock Exchange or the American Stock Exchange

   b. Customer relations at a local supermarket

   c. A current advertising campaign in print

   d. Programming policies and practices of a local television station

APPENDIX A

GLOSSARY OF TERMS

account payable a debt that is owed by an enterprise to someone else, and which hasn't been paid yet

account receivable a debt that is owed to an enterprise, for which payment hasn't yet been received

actuary a mathematician who calculates insurance risks and the premiums based on those risks

ad valorem Latin phrase meaning "according to value"—that is, not according to weight or number of units.

agent one who acts in another's behalf, such as an advertising agent or an independent sales representative

amortization reduction in a debt by periodic payments of the principal and interest

arbitration a method of settling disputes by having them mediated by an impartial third party

attachment a legal document authorizing the sheriff to seize a debtor's property for nonpayment of a debt

balloon payment a lump sum, usually large, payable at the end of a loan period after the periodic payments have been made

bankruptcy a legal means by which a debtor relinquishes claim to his assets and relieves himself of his financial obligations

bear market the stock market when prices are falling

bid   the price offered by a willing buyer

blue chip   a stock-market term for a stock whose products and financial record are of a high quality

boycott   a refusal to have commercial dealings with someone or some organization

bull market   the stock market when prices are rising

cartel   an agreement between companies of various countries to fix the world price on a commodity and thereby control the world market in that commodity

caveat emptor   Latin phrase meaning "let the buyer beware"

chattel   any property or right except real estate property

closed shop   a business firm within which all wage-earning employees are required to be union members

compound interest   interest that is due, calculated by adding to the principal the interest already earned

cooperative   a type of corporation set up to gain the benefits of large-scale operation, in which every member, regardless of the size of his or her investment, has a single vote

creditor   one to whom a debt is owed by another (by the debtor)

debtor   one who owes a debt to another (to the creditor)

demand   the amount of goods that buyers are ready to buy at a specified price at a given time

demography   the study of population and its characteristics—for example, age distribution, birth and death rates, and percentages of married/single, urban/suburban/rural

depletion   the decreasing value of an asset that is being reduced by being converted into a salable product—like oil in the ground

dividend   the earnings that a corporation pays out to its stockholders in cash, property, more securities, or any combination of these

domicile   in law, a person can have many residences, but only one domicile, the place he or she declares to be home

efficiency ratio   the ratio of ends produced (that is, output) to the means used to produce it (that is, input)

encumbrance   a claim—a mortgage, a lien, and so on—against a specific piece of property

entrepreneur   originally a French word, meaning "an enterpriser," or owner and operator of a business

equity   the amount of one's actual ownership in a piece of property—for example, one's equity in a $50,000 property may be $10,000

escalator clause   a provision in an agreement for adjusting a price if the cost of living or some other index rises

escrow   an arrangement by two parties to clear their transaction through a designated third party (the escrower) so that neither of the two

can take unfair advantage of the other or jeopardize down-payment
monies before the transaction clears

estate the total of one's property left at death

exclusive agent an agent who has sole rights to handle a product or
service within a designated market area

extrapolation estimation of a future value through projection of the
curve of past and present values into the future

featherbedding practices by labor unions to maintain or increase artifi-
cially the number of jobs at a company

Federal Reserve System a system of twelve central banks, created in
1912 and controlled by a Board of Governors in Washington, D.C.,
to which national banks must belong and in which they must keep
certain percentages of their assets to assure the security of their
depositors

fiscal adjective that means "pertaining to financial affairs"

fixed asset any property used in operating a business, which won't be
consumed or converted into cash during that business's operation

foreclosure the legal procedure by which a mortgage holder forces the
sale of property in order to recover the money owed him or her

franchise a right granted by a corporation, or by the government, to
someone to carry on a certain kind of business in a certain location—
for example, utilities companies are public franchises; your local
McDonald's is a corporate franchise

frequency distribution a distribution determining how many of each
item have the same value—for example, the frequency distribution
of kinds of automobiles sold in a week may be twelve full-sized,
fifteen compacts, three station wagons, and so on.

futures contracts whose fulfillment by delivery of the goods is not required until a specified time in the future; most commodity ex-
changes—wheat, coffee, pork bellies, and others—work on the basis
of "future delivery" contracts, or "futures"

gold standard the monetary system under which money can be converted into gold, and gold into money, at specified, fixed rates

goon slang term for a person hired by a company to intimidate its workers and hold their demands in check

Gresham's Law "Bad money drives out good"—when two kinds of
money circulate in the same economy, people hoard, melt down,
or export the more valuable of the two, thereby keeping the less
valuable money in circulation

gross national product (GNP) money value of the total output of goods
and services in a national economy during a given period of time,
usually a year

head tax a tax per person

hidden assets   assets carried on a company's books at less than their fair market value; the value of the "hidden asset" is the market value of the asset minus its book value

implied warranty   a warranty that a buyer can assume to exist when nothing to the contrary has been said by the seller

impounds   the money required to be put into an account to assure later payment (usually of taxes) when payment is due

inflation   a period when the purchasing power of one's money is falling

interest   the price paid for using someone else's money—usually stipulated as a percentage of the money being used (the principal)

interpolation   determination of an intermediate value by the plotting of a curve between two already determined points

inventory   all the salable goods on hand at a company or a list of those goods

jobber   same as "wholesaler" or one who buys in relatively small (that is, "job") lots for resale to a retailer

joint venture   a business transaction or project carried out by individuals who join together for that purpose

judgment   the decision a court makes in a lawsuit

Keynesian economics   a school of economics based on the thoughts of John Maynard Keynes (1883–1946); the school basically disagrees with classical economics in holding that an equilibrium (position of rest) can be reached even though some economic resources are unemployed; the remedy advocated is government intervention in one form or another

kickback   payment by someone of part of his or her earnings to assure himself or herself favorable treatment or to evade some requirement

lease or leasehold   a contract to possess something for a fixed period of time in return for payment of a certain sum of money

letter of credit   a letter authorizing that credit be extended to the bearer of the letter and assuring that the signer will pay the resulting debt

liability   a valid claim by a creditor against one's assets

line position   a line position in a company is any job—from president to laborer—that involves work on production, as distinguished from a staff position (See **staff position.**)

liquidation   turning one's assets into cash by selling them off

local option   the right of local communities (as provided by state constitution or legislative act) to regulate certain activities as it sees fit

lockout   the closing of a plant by an employer to enforce demands against employees or to avoid the employees' demands against him

margin   in commercial transactions, the difference between the purchase price paid by someone and the price he or she gets for it when it's resold

mats   short term for "matrices"—printing devices that serve as dies from which printing plates are made

maturity date   the date on which an obligation is due

maturity value   the amount that must be paid on the date the obligation is due

mean   the "average" that is computed by adding all the pertinent numerical items and dividing by the number of items. If these are the following values in a group—3, 6, 6, 6, 7, 8, 8, 9, 10—the mean is 7, the median is 7, and the mode is 6. (See **median** and **mode**.)

median   the "average" that is calculated by identifying the middle value in a group of numerical values—that is, there are the same number of items above the median as below it.

mediation   the process by which a third party (the mediator) attempts to bring two disputing parties into agreement

mixed economy   a national economy that has some characteristics of free enterprise and some of socialism (that is, governmental determination)

mode   the "average" in a series of items that is determined by identifying the value that occurs most frequently

monopoly   sufficient control of an industry or a commodity to be able to control or regulate its price

mortgage   a legal claim on a property, derived from having loaned money to the purchaser of that property

mutual fund   an investment trust whose managers decide which securities to buy and sell

nationalization   the acquisition and operation by the government of a business that was previously owned and operated privately

net sales   the total of all sales minus returned sales

nonprofit corporation   a corporation organized for charitable, educational, humanitarian, or other purposes not primarily aimed at making a profit

notary public   an official appointed by a state to administer oaths, certify documents, and perform similar functions

obsolescence   the decrease in value of something because of lessened demand or new invention, but not because of wear and tear

open-end contract   a contract that allows a buyer to order additional units, on the same terms, without additional consent by the seller

operations research (o.r.)   a term embracing all research that aims to quantify and analyze business data by scientific method and thereby guide the decision-making process

option   a contract that gives someone rights with respect to property, usually the right to buy it or sell it at a stipulated price

overdraft   a draft (or check) drawn in excess of the amount a person has on deposit in the bank

over-the-counter market   name applied to security transactions that take place outside an organized stock exchange, usually through local brokers

partition   in law, the division of property among co-owners; where division in kind is impractical, the whole is sold and the proceeds divided

par value   the value printed on the face of a stock or bond certificate, the stated value

patent   the exclusive right to an invention

peak load   in public utilities, refers to the time of the week during which the greatest consumption of electricity or gas occurs

per capita   Latin phrase meaning "by the heads" or "per individual"

perquisite   compensation or privileges over and above one's regular salary; now sometimes called "perks"

personal property or personalty   all one's property other than interests in real estate

petty cash   a cash fund kept on hand for small disbursements

piggyback service   the loading of motor-truck trailers onto railroad flat cars

portfolio   a term used to refer to all the securities held by one person or institution

power of attorney   a written instrument empowering someone else to act as your agent and signatory

prima facie   Latin phrase meaning "at first sight" or "on the fact of it"—prima facie evidence will carry a legal verdict if nothing valid is presented in rebuttal

pro rata   Latin phrase meaning "in proportion"

proxy   a written authorization designating someone else to cast your vote

quick asset   assets that can be turned into cash immediately with a minimum loss

quitclaim deed   a deed in which the grantor (the person giving the deed) signs away whatever rights he or she has in a property, but without guaranteeing what rights, if any, he or she has

quorum   the number of persons legally necessary (in person or by proxy) to conduct a valid business meeting

rationing   any arrangement, usually under governmental regulation, limiting the quantity of product that can be purchased by a given class of buyers

real estate   an interest in land or things attached to land

rebate   a return of some part of the charges that have been paid out for a service or commodity

receivership the court's appointing a person to administer the affairs of a person or firm unable to meet its debts when they are due

registry the flag a ship flies, designating the country whose laws the ship is governed by

rescind in law, to revoke an action or an agreement

residence see **domicile**

retainer the fee charged by a professional person for services in a matter

right-to-work laws laws that outlaw closed shops

riparian rights the rights of an owner whose land abuts water to the land under the water

rolling stock in transportation, movable property such as trucks, locomotives, freight and passenger cars, and so on

royalties the money paid out per unit of goods sold to the person or company who owns or holds rights to the goods

salary money paid to an employee at a fixed weekly or monthly rate

scab derogatory slang term for a strikebreaker: someone who takes employment at a company when its regular employees are on strike

secondary boycott a boycott of someone who uses or sells the product made by the company who is the primary object of the boycott— for example, a boycott against supermarkets who sell grapes in order to harm their suppliers, the grape growers

securities collective term applying to all kinds of written instruments of investment value: mortgages, stocks, bonds, certificates of ownership, and so on

seniority preference given solely on the basis of how long someone has been on the job

slowdown a form of strike in which workers stay on the job but deliberately reduce their efficiency

solvency a business is solvent when its assets exceed its liabilities, and it can pay its debts as they become due

staff position a position in the company whose holder does not work directly in management, production, or distribution but gives specialized assistance to "line" employees

stock split the issuance of a number of new shares to replace each share of stock now outstanding

subcontract an agreement by which the party who has contracted to do a job gets someone else to do part or all of the work on that job

subsidy money granted, usually by the state, to support an enterprise or a program felt to be in the public interest

subvention a grant or subsidy

supply the amount of a good that sellers are ready to sell at a specified price in a given market at a given time

surcharge   a charge imposed in addition to another charge

surtax   a tax levied in addition to another tax

syndicate   any combination of persons or corporations joined to achieve a common business purpose

tariff   a customs duty or tax levied on goods as they enter (or leave) a country

title   evidence of ownership in something of value

trading down   action by a merchandiser in buying and selling cheaper goods in an effort to increase sales volume

trading up   handling goods of higher price in an effort to increase the profit margin per item

underwriter   anyone who guarantees to furnish a definite sum of money by a definite date to a business or government in return for an issue of bonds or stock; in insurance, one who assumes somebody's risk in return for a premium payment

unlawful detainer   legal device by which a landlord can have a tenant evicted when the tenant has overstayed the tenancy or broken the terms of the lease

value added   the difference between the purchase price of raw materials and the sale price of the product; in some places, value added is now subject to taxation—a value-added tax

vendee   the buyer of something

vendor   the seller of something

vested   a legal term to identify a right of immediate enjoyment or future enjoyment that cannot be alloted without consent of the party having that right

wages   the money paid to those who render their work on an hourly or daily basis

waiver   voluntary abandonment by a person of some or all of his or her right to something

wildcat strike   a strike called suddenly without the preliminary procedures called for by the union's contract with the company

windfall gain   a gain that was not foreseen

writ   a written order by the court directing a court officer to perform an act—for example, seizing a property

APPENDIX B

COMMON ABBREVIATIONS USED IN BUSINESS

abbr.	abbreviation
ac	alternating current
actg.	acting
A.D.	in the year of our Lord
ad, advt.	advertisement
Adm.	Admiral
ADP	Automatic Data Processing
AFL-CIO	American Federation of Labor and Congress of Industrial Organizations
Aly.	Alley
a.m., A.M.	before noon
Am.	American
amt.	amount
anon.	anonymous
approx.	approximately
Apr.	April
apt.	apartment

Arc.	Arcade
assn.	association
asst.	assistant
Atty.	Attorney
Aug.	August
Ave., Av.	Avenue
bbl.	barrel
B.C.	before Christ
B/E	bill of exchange
B/L	bill of lading
bldg.	building
Blvd.	Boulevard
Brig. Gen.	Brigadier General
Bro(s).	Brother(s)
B/S	bill of sale
bu	bushel
bx.	box, boxes
C	centigrade, Celsius
Capt.	Captain

cc.	carbon copy	Ens.	Ensign
cc, c.c.	cubic centimeter(s)	e.o.m.	end of month
cf.	compare	Esq.	Esquire
ch., chap.	chapter	E.S.T.	Eastern Standard
Cir.	Circle		Time
cm	centimeter	et al.	and others
cml.	commercial	et seq.	and the following
Co.	Company	etc.	and so forth
c/o	care of	Expy.	Expressway
C.O.D.	cash on delivery	Ext.	Extended, Extension
Col.	Colonel		
Comdr.	Commander	F	Fahrenheit
Corp.	Corporation	FBI	Federal Bureau of In-
C.P.A.	Certified Public Ac-		vestigation
	countant	fbm	board foot
Cpl.	Corporal	Feb.	February
cr.	credit, creditor	Fed.	Federal
C.S.T.	Central Standard	fig.	figure
	Time	fl. oz.	fluid ounce, fluid
Ctr.	Center		ounces
cwt	hundredweight	F.O.B.	free on board
		Fri.	Friday
dc	direct current	frt.	freight
D.D.	Doctor of Divinity	ft	feet, foot
D.D.S.	Doctor of Dental Sur-	Frwy.	Freeway
	gery		
Dec.	December	G., g	grain, gram(s)
deg.	degree, degrees	gal	gallon, gallons
Dem.	Democrat	Gdns.	Gardens
dept.	department	Gen.	General
dia., diam.	diameter	gi.	gill, gills
dol	dollar	gm	gram(s)
doz.	dozen	Gov.	Governor
dr.	debit, debtor	govt.	government
Dr.	Doctor, Drive	gr	grain(s), gram(s)
D.S.T.	Daylight Saving Time	gr. wt.	gross weight
E.	East	Hon.	Honorable
ea.	each	hosp.	hospital
ed.	edition, editor	h.p., hp	horsepower
e.g.	for example	hr.	hour
enc., encl.	enclosure	Hts.	Heights
Eng.	English	Hwy.	Highway

Ibid.	in the same place	mo.	month
id.	the same	Mon.	Monday
i.e.	that is	mpg	miles per gallon
in.	inch, inches	m.p.h.	miles per hour
Inc.	Incorporated	Mr.	Mister
Inst.	Institute	Mrs.	Mistress, title used be-
IOU	I owe you		fore the name of a
IQ	intelligence quotient		married woman
ital.	italic, italics	Ms.	feminine equivalent of
			Mr.—does not de-
Jan.	January		note marital status
Jct.	Junction	M.S.T.	Mountain Standard
J.D.	Doctor of Laws		Time
jour.	journal	Mt.	Mount, Mountain
Jr.	Junior	mtge.	mortgage
		mun.	municipal
kc	kilocycle, kilocycles		
kt.	carat, kiloton	N.	North
kW	kilowatt	Natl.	National
		N.B.	note carefully
l	liter	N.D., n.d.	no date
La.	Lane	No.	number
lat.	latitude	Nov.	November
lb	pound	nt. wt.	net weight
Lt.	Lieutenant		
LL.D.	Doctor of Laws	Oct.	October
long.	longitude	O.K.	all correct, approved
Ltd.	Limited	o.s.	out of stock
		oz	ounce
m	meter, noon		
Maj.	Major	p., pp.	page, pages
M.D.	Doctor of Medicine	par.	paragraph
mdse.	merchandise	pd.	paid
memo	memorandum	Ph.D.	Doctor of Philosophy
Messrs.	plural for Mr.	Pk.	Park
mfg.	manufacturing	pkg.	package
mfr.	manufacturer	Pkway.	Parkway
Mgr.	Manager, Monsignor	Pl.	Place
mi	mile, miles	Plz.	Plaza
min	minute, minutes	p.m., P.M.	afternoon
misc.	miscellaneous	P.O.	post office
Mlle.	Mademoiselle	ppd.	prepaid
Mme.	Madame	pr.	pair

Pres.	President	Sept.	September
pro tem	temporarily	Sgt.	Sergeant
Prof.	Professor	SOS	radio distress signal
P.S.	postscript	Sq.	Square
P.S.T.	Pacific Standard Time	Sr.	Senior
pt.	part, point	S.S.	Steamship
pt	pint	St.	Saint, Street
		subj.	subject
q.	question, quire	Sun.	Sunday
qt	quart	Supt.	Superintendent
quot.	quotation		
		tbsp	tablespoonful
Rd.	Road	tel.	telegram, telephone
recd.	received	temp.	temperature
Rep.	Republican	Ter.	Terrace
Rev.	Reverend	terr.	territory
R.F.D.	Rural Free Delivery	Thurs.	Thursday
rm.	ream, room	Trl.	Trail
rms.	reams, rooms	Treas.	Treasurer
R.N.	registered nurse	tsp	teaspoonful
r/min.	revolutions per minute	Tues.	Tuesday
		Tpke.	Turnpike
r.p.m., rpm	revolutions per minute	U.N., UN	United Nations
R.R.	Railroad, Right Reverend	U.S.A.	United States of America
R.S.V.P., r.s.v.p.	please reply		
		Via.	Viaduct
Ry.	Railway	vid.	see
		viz.	namely
S.	South	vol.	volume
Sat.	Saturday	V.P.	Vice President
sec.	second	vs.	versus
secy.	secretary		

APPENDIX C

GLOSSARY OF USAGE

As an educated user of English, you will be called upon to use different kinds of language at different times. Sometimes you may say, "It is I"; other times you may say, "It's I"; and still other times "It's me." All are proper if they fit the speaking or writing situation. The following table will help you to classify and select certain words and phrases according to the occasion.

Standard English

General English

General English is the central language, suitable for all occasions. It is also called *standard* and *informal*. This is the language spoken and written by educated people in their everyday communications. It includes all-purpose words such as "go," "look," "into," "the," "radio." It excludes nonstandard terms of slang, illiteracy, and extreme formality.

> As the first of the women's death sentences was read, two women jurors appeared to be blinking back tears. One wiped her eyes. However, when each was polled as to whether the verdicts were theirs, all clearly announced "Yes."
>
> (The Associated Press, *Los Angeles Times*, March 30, 1971, p. 1)

303

Formal

Formal English is the language of serious articles, reports, books, and addresses. It is usually written.

The computer makes possible a phenomenal leap in human proficiency; it demolishes the fences around the practical and even the theoretical intelligence. But the question persists and indeed grows whether the computer will make it easier or harder for human beings to know who they really are.

(Norman Cousins, "The Computer and the Poet," *Saturday Review/World*, July 23, 1966, p. 4)

Colloquial

Colloquial English is used in familiar and conversational writing and is not acceptable in most serious business letters. Examples of colloquial usage are: "Mrs. Higgins was mad" instead of "Mrs. Higgins was angry"; and "That was a funny thing to say" instead of "That was a strange thing to say." Most of the words labeled colloquial in this glossary should be avoided in business letters, except those that demand a familiar, personal tone.

Nonstandard English

Slang

Slang is a special type of group language that uses coined terms, new and unusual combinations, and metaphors. It is generally unacceptable outside the group. Examples of slang are "lousy" for "unpleasing" and "make a crack about" for "insult."

Beverly decided to split before that screwball customer freaked out.

Dialect

A dialect is a special type of group language confined to a locality or ethnic group. An example is the word "fetch" for "Go get and bring back."

I reckon you all better mosey along.

Illiterate

Words and expressions not consistent with the grammatical patterns of General English are considered illiterate. Obscenity, profanity, poor grammar, and misspellings are included here. Examples are "ain't" for "is not" and "he don't" for "he doesn't."

This glossary discusses a number of words and phrases that present usage problems. The list is not complete, but it includes the most common troublemakers. A dictionary will give detailed information on words and expressions not included here.

a, an	Use "a" before a consonant sound and "an" before a vowel sound.

a tree, a book, an oak,
a history book, an honest man,
a European, an American

aggravate	General meaning is "to make worse." Colloquial for "annoy" or "irritate."

GENERAL: The wet climate will *aggravate* his illness.
COLLOQUIAL: Don't *aggravate* Mr. Henson with your questions.

ain't, aren't I, amn't	Illiterate for "am not," "isn't," and "am I not."
alibi	Colloquial for "excuse"

COLLOQUIAL: He had no *alibi* for his impolite actions.
GENERAL: He had no *excuse* for his impolite actions.
GENERAL: The police accepted his *alibi* that he had been at home when the store was robbed.

almost, most	"Most" is a colloquial substitution for "almost."

COLLOQUIAL: *Most* everything was sold by noon.
GENERAL: *Almost* everything was sold by noon.

a lot, lots	Colloquial for "much," or "many." "Alot" is a misspelling of "a lot."

| | COLLOQUIAL: | I have thought *a lot* about your suggestion. |
| | GENERAL: | I have thought *much* about your suggestion. |

alright

"Alright" is a misspelling of "all right."

a.m., p.m. (A.M., P.M.)

Correct only with figures. Lowercase letters are more commonly used.

The guests arrived at 2:00 p.m. (not "in the p.m.")
The guests arrived in the afternoon.

among, between

"Among" implies more than two. "Between" implies only two. "Between" may be used with more than two when each is regarded individually.

He divided his fortune *among* his three sons.
He divided his fortune *between* his two sons.
Agreement was finally reached *between* the five contending countries.

amount, number

"Amount" refers to bulk or mass. "Number" refers to things that can be counted.

A large *amount* of clothing was left over.
A large *number* of garments were left over.

and etc.

Illiterate and redundant for "etc." "Etc." is an abbreviation of "et cetera" ("and" plus "other" things.)

anyone, any one

"Anyone" is a pronoun meaning "anybody." "Any one" is an adjective-pronoun combination that singles out one of a group. Use "anyone" if "any" is to be accented; use "any one" if the "one" is to be emphasized. "Any one" will usually be followed by "of."

He talks to *anyone* who will listen.
Any one of these errors is cause for dismissal.

anyplace	Colloquial for "anywhere."
	COLLOQUIAL: We couldn't find a taxi *anyplace*.
	GENERAL: We couldn't find a taxi *anywhere*.
any ways	Dialect for *"anyway."*
	GENERAL: We did not believe him *anyway*.
anywheres	Dialect for *anywhere*.
	He couldn't find the invoice *anywhere*.
apt, likely	"Apt" means "having a natural ability or tendency." "Likely" means "a probability."
	Ted was *apt* at learning to type. He is *likely* to become a good typist.
as	Dialect for "that." Vague for "because," "for," "since," "while," "why," or "whether."
	DIALECT: I don't know *as* I believe his story.
	GENERAL: I don't know *that* I believe his story.
	VAGUE: *As* the store was not busy, we played cards.
	IMPROVED: *Because* the store was not busy, we played cards.
	IMPROVED: *While* the store was not busy, we played cards.
as to	Vague for "about."
	He questioned us *about* (not "as to") his share in the profits.
at about	Contradictory. Use one or the other, not both.
	The ship will dock *at* noon. The ship will dock *about* noon.

awful, awfully   Colloquial and vague for "very," or "unattractive."

COLLOQUIAL:	His new clothes look *awful.*
GENERAL:	His new clothes are *unattractive.*
COLLOQUIAL:	He seems *awfully* sure of himself.
GENERAL:	He seems *very* sure of himself.

bad, badly   "Bad" is an adjective. "Badly" is an adverb.

He feels *bad* about his mistake.
He behaved *badly* at the party.

Colloquial in the sense of "very much."

The man needed a new suit *badly.*

being as, being that   Illiterate for "since" or "because."

NONSTANDARD:	*Being as* he had already read the book, he let me borrow it for a week.
GENERAL:	*Since* he had already read the book, he let me borrow it for a week.

bursted, bust, busted   Corruptions of "burst."

The dam *burst* and flooded the town.

As slang "bust" and "busted" have several meanings, such as "dismissed," "without money," "party," "arrested."

but that, but what   Colloquial for "that" in negative expressions.

COLLOQUIAL:	I do not doubt *but what* he can sell the piano.
GENERAL:	I do not doubt *that* he can sell the piano.

calculate   Dialect for "guess," "suppose," "think."

can, may	Interchangeable in colloquial questions and negations.
	Can I go with you? *May* I go with you?
	In General English "can" denotes ability; "may" denotes permission or possibility.
	May I go with you? It *may* rain on Friday. *Can* you operate the 3D Copier?
can't hardly, **couldn't hardly,** **won't hardly,** **wouldn't hardly**	Double negatives are illiterate.
	ILLITERATE: It was so dark I *couldn't hardly* see.
	STANDARD: It was so dark I *could hardly* see.
	STANDARD: It was so dark I *couldn't* see.
complected	Dialect for "complexioned."
	DIALECT: He was dark *complected.*
	STANDARD: He was dark *complexioned.*
complete	This adjective has no comparative or superlative form. A thing is either complete or not.
	The list of names is *complete* (not "more complete").
consensus of opinion	"Consensus" means "general opinion"; therefore, "of opinion" is redundant.
considerable	Illiterate when used as an adverb.
	ILLITERATE: The temperature dropped *considerable.*
	STANDARD: The temperature dropped *considerably.*
could of	Illiterate for "could have."
	They *could have* (not "of") left earlier.

criteria

Plural of "criterion."

He uses one *criterion* for judging credit customers.
We will have to form some *criteria* for giving pay raises.

data

The singular form, "datum," is not often used. "Data," the plural form, is often considered as a singular collective noun.

The *data* have not all been assembled yet.
The *data* has not all been assembled yet.

deal

Colloquial for "business," "transaction," "agreement," "plan."

Hillside Hotel offers a good *deal* for conventions.

differ from, differ with

"Differ from" means "to be unlike." "Differ with" means "disagree."

South American cowboys *differ from* those in North America.
I *differ with* him about politics.

different from, different than

"Different from" is correct. Avoid "different than."

His machine is *different from* mine.

don't

Illiterate as a contraction for "does not."

ILLITERATE: He *don't* mean any harm.
STANDARD: He *doesn't* mean any harm.

due to

Colloquial as a preposition for "because of" in an adverb phrase. General English when "due" is a predicate adjective.

COLLOQUIAL: *Due to* the rain the picnic was postponed.
GENERAL: *Because of* the rain the picnic was postponed.

GENERAL:	The postponement of the picnic was *due to* the rain.
each other, one another	Interchangeable, although some writers prefer "each other" when referring to two and "one another" when referring to more than two.
	Joe and Jim praised *each other.* The members of the accounting department praised *one another.*
enthuse	Colloquial for "become enthusiastic."
COLLOQUIAL:	Everybody was *enthused* about the holiday.
GENERAL:	Everybody was *enthusiastic* about the holiday.
equally as	Redundant. Omit "as."
	The two machines seemed *equally* efficient.
etc.	See "and etc."
everyone, every one	See "anyone."
everyplace	Colloquial for "everywhere."
COLLOQUIAL:	He looked *everyplace* for his wallet.
GENERAL:	He looked *everywhere* for his wallet.
exam	Colloquial shortening for "examination."
expect	Colloquial for "suppose," "think."
COLLOQUIAL:	I *expect* the shipment will arrive tomorrow.
GENERAL:	I *suppose* the shipment will arrive tomorrow.
extra	Colloquial for "very," "unusually."
COLLOQUIAL:	He seems *extra* happy today.

	GENERAL:	He seems *unusually* happy today.

farther, further

"Farther" usually applied to geographical distance, "further" to degree.

The town was *farther* than we had thought.
He refused to discuss it *further*.

female

Do not use as a synonym for "girl," "lady," or "woman."

figure

Colloquial for "believe," "think."

COLLOQUIAL:	I *figure* that is too big a job for him.
GENERAL:	I *believe* that is too big a job for him.

fine

Colloquial for "well" as an adverb. Vague as an adjective of approval.

COLLOQUIAL:	The computer works *fine* since the technician checked it.
GENERAL:	The computer works *well* since the technician checked it.
VAGUE:	He is a *fine* person.
MORE SPECIFIC:	He is a *likeable* person.

flunk

Colloquial for "fail."

folks

Colloquial or dialect for "relatives."

funny

Colloquial for "peculiar" or "odd." In General English, "funny" applies to the laughable.

gentleman, lady

Stilted for "man," "woman." Appropriate in the salutation to a letter.

get

Nonstandard for "understand" or "move emotionally."

I couldn't *get* what he was saying.
Music like that always *gets* me.

It is General English in idioms like *to get the better of, to get along with* (a person), *to get over* (an illness).

good   Illiterate as an adverb. Vague as an adjective of general approval.

ILLITERATE: He surely types *good.*
STANDARD: He surely types *skillfully.*
VAGUE: The movie was *good.*
IMPROVED: The movie was *interesting.*

good and   Colloquial as an intensive.

COLLOQUIAL: Jensen became *good and* tired of her complaining.
GENERAL: Jensen became *very tired* of her complaining.

guess   Colloquial for "suppose," "think."

COLLOQUIAL: I *guess* production was delayed by the strike.
GENERAL: I *believe* production was delayed by the strike.

gym   Colloquial shortening of "gymnasium."

had of   Illiterate for "had."

If he *had gone* (not "had of gone") he would have liked the demonstration.

had ought   Illiterate for "ought."

He ought (not "had ought") to have gone to the demonstration.

hanged, hung   "Hanged" applies to executions; "hung" to other situations.

The murderer was *hanged.*
The pictures were *hung* immediately.

In British English "hung" also applies to executions.

hardly   See "can't hardly."

herself, himself   Intensive or reflexive pronouns.

myself, yourself   Substandard when used for "she," "her," "he," "him," "I," "me," "you."

SUBSTANDARD: John and *myself* were selected.

GENERAL: I *myself* wrote the memo.

hisself   Illiterate for "himself."

in, into   "In" implies location within. "Into" applies to movement from without to within.

He is *in* the store. He walks *in* the store.
He walked from the street *into* the store.

individual, party   "Individual" is stilted for "person." The word refers to a single thing, animal or person. "Party" is illiterate for "person" or "individual" except in legal language.

STANDARD: We must respect the rights of the *individual.*

STILTED: I've seen that *individual* somewhere before.

STANDARD: I've seen that *person* somewhere before.

ILLITERATE: I know the *party* you are talking about.

STANDARD: I know the *person* you are talking about.

in regards to   Illiterate for "in regard to" or "as regards."

invite   Illiterate when used as a noun for "invitation."

irregardless	Illiterate for "regardless."
is when, is where	Illiterate in definitions.

ILLITERATE:	The bull market *is when* prices are rising.
STANDARD:	The bull market is the stock market when prices are rising.

just	Colloquial as an intensive.

COLLOQUIAL:	The fire in the paint department was *just* terrible.
GENERAL:	The fire in the paint department was terrible.

kind, sort	Singular words that can be modified only by "that" or "this," not "these" or "those."

CORRECT:	I prefer *this kind* of tennis racket.
INCORRECT:	I prefer *these kinds* of tennis rackets.

kindly	Avoid "kindly" for "please."

Please (not "kindly") fill out the attached form.

kind of, sort of	Colloquial as an adverb of degree, as "somewhat."

COLLOQUIAL:	He was *kind of* displeased.
GENERAL:	He was *somewhat* displeased.

kind of a	Nonstandard for "kind of."

What *kind of* flower is that?

lady, gentleman	See "gentleman, lady."
lay, lie	"Lay," "laid," "laid" are transitive verbs and take a direct object.

Lay the *book* down.
He *laid* the *book* down.

"Lie," "lay," "lain" do not take an object.

He *lies* down.
He *lay* there yesterday.
He *has lain* there often.

learn, teach   "Learn" means to get knowledge.
"Teach" means to give knowledge.

A good student *learns* more than a teacher is able to *teach* him.

leave, let   "Leave" is illiterate for "allow." "Leave" means to "depart from" or "cause to remain."

Don't *let* (not *leave*) him have his way.
He will *leave* town tomorrow.
Leave the book on the table.
Let me alone.

like   Colloquial for "as if," "as though."

COLLOQUIAL: He looks *like* he's angry.
GENERAL: He looks *as if* he were angry.

likely   See "apt."

locate   Colloquial for "settle."

COLLOQUIAL: He finally *located* in Montana.
GENERAL: He finally *settled* in Montana.
GENERAL: He *located* his business in Montana.

lots   See "a lot."

mad   Colloquial for "angry."

COLLOQUIAL: He was *mad* at me for spilling ink on his suit.

	GENERAL: He was *angry* with me for spilling ink on his suit.
math	Colloquial shortening for "mathematics."
may be, maybe	"May be" is a verb phrase. "Maybe" is an adverb.
	He *may be* the winner. *Maybe* he will be the winner.
might of	Illiterate for "might have."
	They *might have* (not *of*) had car trouble.
mighty	Colloquial for "very."
	COLLOQUIAL: Jack is a *mighty* good salesperson.
	GENERAL: Jack is a *very* good salesperson.
	GENERAL: A *mighty* smokestack towers over the power plant.
moral, morale	"Moral" as a noun means "lesson." *Moral* as an adjective means "right conduct." The noun "morale" refers to a state of mind.
	What was the *moral* of the story? Stealing is a *moral* situation. *Morale* has been high since Tim Conners left the department.
nice	Vague word of approval. Use a more precise word.
	VAGUE: He did a *nice* job of cleaning the supply room.
	PRECISE: He did a *thorough* job of cleaning the supply room.
no account	Colloquial for "worthless."

no place	Colloquial for "nowhere."

COLLOQUIAL:	That lazy salesclerk was *no place* around.
GENERAL:	That lazy salesclerk was *nowhere* around.

nowhere near	Colloquial for "not nearly."

GENERAL:	His report is *not nearly* finished.

number	See "amount."
off of	Colloquial for "off."

GENERAL:	The boy fell *off* the counter.

OK, O.K., okay	Colloquial for "all right."
one another	See "each other."
ought	See "had ought."
party	See "individual."
perfect	This adjective has no comparative or superlative form. Anything is either perfect or it is not.

His score is perfect (not "more perfect" or "most perfect").

phenomena	Plural of "phenomenon."
piece	Colloquial for "a short distance."

COLLOQUIAL:	She drove down the road a *piece*.
GENERAL:	She drove down the road a *short distance*.

plenty	Illiterate as an adverb meaning "very."

ILLITERATE:	I was *plenty* tired after taking inventory.
STANDARD:	I was *very* tired after taking inventory.

p.m.	See "a.m."

prof	Colloquial for "professor."
raise, rise	"Raise," "raised," "raised" are transitive verbs, requiring a direct object.
	He wanted to *raise* the window.
	"Rise," "rose," "risen" never take an object.
	He tried to *rise* from his seat to raise a window.
real	Colloquial as an adverb for *"very"* or other intensives.
	COLLOQUIAL: He seemed *real* sure of himself.
	GENERAL: He seemed *very* sure of himself.
said	Substandard for "previously mentioned.
	SUBSTANDARD: He got in *said* car and drove away.
	STANDARD: He got into the car I mentioned before and drove away.
same	Substandard as a pronoun except in legal language. The word "it" is preferable.
	SUBSTANDARD: So I paid him the money and got a receipt for *same*.
	STANDARD: So I paid him the money and got a receipt for *it*.
seldom ever, seldom or ever	Illiterate for "seldom," "seldom if ever," or "hardly ever."
	INCORRECT: He *seldom ever* watches TV.
	CORRECT: He *seldom* watches TV.
set, sit	"Set" is illiterate when used to mean "occupy a seat." "Set" means "place something in position."

CORRECT:	They *set* the box on the floor.

"Sit" and "sat" mean "occupy a seat."

ILLITERATE:	They *set* in the lounge most of the day.
STANDARD:	They *sit* in the lounge most of the day.

shall, will   Interchangeable as auxiliary verbs to form the simple future.

I will (shall) go.
You will (shall) go.
She will (shall) go.

should, would   "Should" is used as an auxiliary verb to indicate condition or obligation.

If they *should* arrive early, we will have to be ready.
I *should* have gathered more facts.

"Would" is used to indicate wish or customary action.

Mr. Jackson *would* always be at his desk early.
Would you please send a diagram?

should of   Illiterate for "should have."

He should *have* (not *of*) checked the order.

sit   See "set."

so   Vague as a conjunction or a transitional adverb. "Because," "since," or "so that" are more exact.

FAULTY:	I smelled smoke, *so* I looked in the lounge.
EXACT:	*Because* I smelled smoke, I looked in the lounge.
FAULTY:	We arrived early *so* we could be ready for the crowd.

| | EXACT: | We arrived early *so that* we could be ready for the crowd. |

"So" as an intensive must be followed by a qualifying clause of result (a "that" clause).

| | INCOMPLETE: | He was *so* angry. |
| | COMPLETE: | He was *so* angry *that* he could hardly talk. |

some   Illiterate for "somewhat." Colloquial for "unusual" or "remarkable."

	ILLITERATE:	The medicine made her feel *some* better.
	STANDARD:	The medicine made her feel *somewhat* better.
	COLLOQUIAL:	That police dog was *some* animal!
	GENERAL:	That police dog was an *unusual* animal.

someone, some one   See "anyone."

someplace   Colloquial for "somewhere."

| | COLLOQUIAL: | Those lost keys just had to be *someplace.* |
| | GENERAL: | Those lost keys just had to be *somewhere.* |

someway   Colloquial for "somehow."

	COLLOQUIAL:	He will raise the money *someway.*
	GENERAL:	He will arise the money *somehow.*
	GENERAL:	He will raise the money *in some way.*

somewheres   Dialect for "somewhere."

sort   See "kind."

sort of, sort of a   See "kind of."

strata	Plural of "stratum."
suspicion	Dialect when used as a verb meaning "suspect."
	We suspected (not *suspicioned*) that he was lying to us.
teach	See "learn."
theirself, theirselves	Illiterate for "themselves."
these kind, these sort	See "kind."
they	Vague and colloquial as an indefinite pronoun to mean people in general.

<table>
<tr><td>VAGUE:</td><td>At the YMCA, they treat people of all backgrounds alike.</td></tr>
<tr><td>EXACT:</td><td>At the YMCA, the members (or, the supervisors) treat people of all backgrounds alike.</td></tr>
</table>

thusly	A pretentious form of "thus."
true facts	"True" is redundant. All facts are true.
	These are the *known* facts. I suspect that what he reports as facts are not *truly* facts.
try and	Colloquial for "try to."

<table>
<tr><td>COLLOQUIAL:</td><td>They will try and finish the job on time.</td></tr>
<tr><td>GENERAL:</td><td>They will try to finish the job on time.</td></tr>
</table>

type	Illiterate for "type of." "Type" is not an adjective, but a noun.

<table>
<tr><td>ILLITERATE:</td><td>He does not like that type person.</td></tr>
<tr><td>STANDARD:</td><td>He does not like that type of person.</td></tr>
</table>

unique	"Unique" means "only one of a kind" and therefore cannot be compared.

	INCORRECT: I have never known a more *unique* person.
	CORRECT: He is *unique.*
want that	Illiterate for "want".
	ILLITERATE: He *wanted that* I should lend him ten dollars.
	STANDARD: He *wanted* me to lend him ten dollars.
ways	Colloquial for *"way"* or *"distance."*
	COLLOQUIAL: It's a long *ways* to Omaha.
	GENERAL: It's a long *way* to Omaha.
when	Incorrectly used to introduce definitions. See "is when."
where	Illiterate for "that." See "is where."
	ILLITERATE: I read in the newspaper *where* there is a famine in India.
	STANDARD: I read in the newspaper *that* there is a famine in India.
where . . . at	Illiterate for "where." Omit "at."
	INCORRECT: *Where* is the service garage *at?*
	CORRECT: *Where* is the service garage?
which, who, that	"Which" and "that" apply to things. "Who" and "that" apply to people.
while	Illiterate for "and" or "but." Vague for "although."
	ILLITERATE: Ann is a ceaseless typist, *while* I prefer to rest occasionally.
	STANDARD: Ann is a ceaseless typist, *but* I prefer to rest occasionally.

| | VAGUE: | *While* I disapprove of your method, I approve of your motive. |
| | IMPROVED: | *Although* I disapprove of your method, I approve of your motive. |

who   "Who" is used as a subject, or its equivalent, in its own clause. If the verb needs a subject, use *who*.

> He asked *who* I thought owned the place.
> He asked me *who* I thought I was.

whom   "Whom" is used as an object in its own clause. It is usually a direct object or an object of a preposition.

> I asked her *whom* she wanted to see.
> He asked me to *whom* he should give the check.

will   See "shall."

won't hardly   See "can't hardly."

worst way   "In the worst way" is nonstandard for *"very much."*

| NONSTANDARD: | Betty wanted a new job *in the worst way.* |
| STANDARD: | Betty wanted a new job *very much.* |

would   See "should."

wouldn't hardly   See "can't hardly."

would of   Illiterate for "would have."

> I *would have* (not *of*) arrived earlier if I hadn't had car trouble.

you   Vague and colloquial when used as an indefinite pronoun.

| VAGUE: | A person should value his friends, for you |

	never know when you will need them.
GENERAL:	A person should value his friends, for he never knows when he may need them.
yourself	See "herself."

APPENDIX D

PUNCTUATION

To End Sentences

1. *Statements:* Use a period.

    A storm broke three windows in the warehouse.
    The glasses you sent were defective.

2. *Questions:* Use a question mark.

    Does the radio operate on direct current?
    He asked, "When will you ship the suits?"

3. *Questions in a series:* Use a question mark after each question in a series that has the same beginning.

    What is the horsepower of the Watercraft Model? of the Sportsman Model? of the Ranger?

4. *Indirect Questions:* Use a period. These are not actually questions, but statements about questions.

    INDIRECT QUESTION: The driver asked where we wanted
                           him to put the drums.
    DIRECT QUESTION: The driver asked, "Where do you
                           want me to put the drums?"

5. *Commands and Requests:* Use a period for a standard directive and an exclamation point for an emotional statement.

STANDARD DIRECTIVE: Stop by and pick up your free gift.
EMOTIONAL STATEMENT: Don't park there!

6. *Courtesy Requests:* Use a period or question mark. Courtesy questions, often used in business letters, may end with either a question mark or a period. They are not really questions, which require a verbal answer, but imperatives that suggest an action answer. A phrase like "Will you" is often equivalent to "Please."

> May I have your answer this week.
> May I have your answer this week?

7. *Exclamations:* Use an exclamation point after words of emotional intent and after an ironical or emphatic expression:

> What an exciting project!
> How many times I have heard that excuse!
> Wow!
> Watch out!
> Congratulations!

Except in sales messages, the words themselves must convey the emotion. The exclamation point will not create the emotion; it will only signal the intent.

> "Look out!" Ann yelled. "Are you trying to spill the coffee?"

If the words themselves do not convey the emotion, the exclamation point is a poor crutch. Use a period, or revise the sentence.

QUESTIONABLE: It was hard to believe! "Honest John" was actually trying to cheat!

IMPROVED: It was hard to believe that "Honest John" was actually trying to cheat.

REVISED: What a shock! "Honest John"—I could hardly believe it—old "Honest" himself was actually trying to cheat!

To Separate Pairs of Main Statements

1. *Full break, stressing equal importance:* Use a period.

   She nodded and smiled all the time I talked. I could not, however, get her to buy the TV set.

2. *Separate statements, but two parts of one idea:* Use a comma with coordinating conjunction ("and," "but," "or," "nor," "for").

   She smiled and nodded all the time I talked, but still I could not get her to buy the TV set.

If one of the main statements contains a comma, you may for clarity put a semicolon at the major break between the two statements.

   We would like delivery on Friday morning at eight o'clock, but Thursday night at nine o'clock will be satisfactory.

   As we have told you, we would like delivery on Friday morning at eight o'clock; but Thursday night at nine o'clock will be satisfactory.

   We would like delivery on Friday morning at eight o'clock; but, if it is more convenient for you, Thursday night at nine o'clock will be satisfactory.

No comma is necessary when both clauses are short—usually no more than five words each.

   I like the company and the company likes me.

You may use a comma to separate very short main clauses that are not joined by one of the five conjunctions ("and," "but," "or," "nor," "for").

   They came, they saw, they bought.

3. *A semibreak, with close relationship:* Use a semicolon.

   He prefers a person with college training; I prefer a person with field experience.

   She nodded and smiled all the time I talked; however, I could not get her to buy the TV set.

The word "however" is a connective adverb, not a conjunction. It is preceded by a semicolon when used between main statements. Other connective adverbs include "still," "therefore," "also," "accordingly," "furthermore," "otherwise," "likewise," "yet," "so," "for example," "that is," "namely."

The clocks arrived too late for our weekend sale; therefore, we are returning them to you.

We have plans for expansion; for example, in January we will open a new store in Southmoore.

4. *Suspense or abrupt break:* Use a dash.

She nodded and smiled all the time I talked—still I could not get her to buy the TV set.

5. *Balance—the second statement echoes or amplifies the first:* Use a colon.

To make a sale adds to your commission: to make a customer adds to your future.

To Separate Introductory Elements

1. *To avoid confusion:* Use a comma. The subject begins the main idea of the sentence. Unless the subject of your sentence stands out clearly, put a comma after introductory elements to mark where the subject begins.

Yes, people of ability will get ahead in this company.

As long as I remained, the cashier watched me suspiciously.

Although the car was actually a wreck, the eager young man thought it was a bargain.

Having many people to see, the women canvassed the neighborhood ten hours a day.

To get the full benefit of our insurance plan, fill out and return the enclosed card.

The following sentences are clear without a comma.

In the show window stood three naked mannequins.

On Sunday he rests.

2. *For a double start:* Use a dash. Use a dash to separate a beginning list from a summary word.

Suits, sportcoats, shoes—these are on sale.

Oil, wheat, cattle—these are the state's main products.

When a list is not followed by a summary word but by the verb, a dash is not necessary:

Suits, sportcoats, shoes, and many other items are on sale.

3. *After the salutation in business letters:* Use a colon, unless open punctuation is used.

Dear Sir: Gentleman: Dear Mrs. Eidelstein:

4. *To introduce an item or a list of items:* Use a colon.

Success in business requires these qualities: hard work, intelligence, personality, and imagination.

This is what he said: "Choose a profession that you can give your heart to as well as your ability."

To Set Off Parenthetical Items

1. *Slight interruption:* Use a comma. The parenthetical material can be removed from the sentence without changing the meaning of what remains.

John Vielkind, who is head of the credit department, will get in touch with you.

Mrs. Thomas, speaking on behalf of the entire department, chose her words carefully.

A word or a group of words necessary to identify or distinguish the word they refer to are part of the main thought, not an interruption. Therefore, no punctuation is used.

The person who is head of the credit department will get in touch with you.

Any man speaking on behalf of the entire department must choose his words carefully.

Here are some typical slight interruptions:

DIRECT ADDRESS:	Joe, I believe you can handle the territory.
APPOSITIVE:	(A term restated in another way) James Henson, the new district manager, will arrive Tuesday.
SPEAKER IN DIRECT	"This engine," said the salesper-

QUOTATION:	son, "is the largest we build."
LOOSELY CONNECTED:	It was, to be sure, his first day on the job.
TRANSITIONAL EXPRESSION:	You will agree, however, that the merchandise was defective. We will begin our sale, therefore, on July 12.

A tightly connected expression is not set off by commas.

We will therefore begin our sale on July 12.

2. *Abrupt or violent interruption:* Use dashes.

Then Vic—good old high-pressure Vic—had not a word to say.

An interruption in full statement form, unless it is an idiom ("it seems to me"), takes dashes, not commas.

The committee decided—you may think it's a joke, but it isn't—that the resolution should be adopted.

Shall we—can we—increase our sales quotas?

3. *Nonemphatic, supplementary material:* Use parentheses. Some examples are explanations, restatements in different form, and letters in enumeration.

Three of our typists (Jean Stacey, John Terrell, and Mary Saunders) are demanding new typewriters.

Not one of our new employees (you'll not believe this, I'm sure) was absent during July.

Please send your check for fifteen dollars ($15.00) immediately.

4. *Incidental remarks made by someone who is quoting someone else:* Use brackets.

Johnson said: "Jake Benson, our company's founder, used to say 'Full steam ahead' [he meant "speed"] whenever the problems got heavy."

Lists and Series

1. *Any three or more items in a series:* Use a comma.

The engine is powerful, it is well built, and it is economical.

She grabbed her purse, jumped from her seat, and marched from the store.

Ted Smith, Bill Avery, and Mary Olson will make the trip to St. Louis with me.

For clarity, separate each item with a comma, including one before "and." In the example below, without the comma after the word "green," no one can tell for sure whether there are four choices, the last of which is white; or whether there are three choices, the last of which is a combination of green and white.

You have a choice of red, yellow, green, and white.

Commas are not needed for separation if all items are joined by *and*.

He worked and fought and cheated his way to the top.

2. *Two equal adjectives:* Use a comma. Equal adjectives modify the noun separately. Two adjectives are equal if their order can be reversed or they can be connected by *and*. They are not equal if each adjective in turn modifies the total idea that follows it.

EQUAL: We need an experienced, intelligent salesperson.

NOT EQUAL: We need an experienced car salesperson.

3. *Commas within items:* Use a semicolon at the major breaks in a series that contains commas.

The planning team is made up of Janet Wilson, a market research specialist; Thomas Crampton, an industrialist; and Jack Billings, a city councilman.

Some of our employees have worked overtime this week: Greene, 7 hours; Howard, 6 hours; Collins, 10; and Mitler, 4.

We sent reports to shareholders in Akron, Ohio; Baltimore, Maryland; Dallas, Texas; Richmond, Virginia; San Francisco, California; and Seattle, Washington.

4. *A series as a parenthetical group containing commas:* Use dashes.

Three problems—loafing, absenteeism, and theft—are costing us heavily.

Their scores—Mary, 21; Sally, 20; and Jo, 19—were the highest in a group of 300.

5. *A formally announced list:* Use a colon. Such words as "these," "those," and "the following" are signals. Use a colon only after a grammatically complete statement—with subject-verb-direct object or predicate noun.

The manager listed our problems as these: loafing, absenteeism, and theft.

To Set Off Final Items

Items tacked on to the end of your main statement can be separated from it by a comma, a colon, or a dash.

1. *Parenthetical items:* Use a comma. Final parenthetical items are not necessary to the direct line of thought and are often afterthoughts, such as modifiers and tag questions.

Jay Johnson was manager then, if I am not mistaken.
The police arrested Tim Riley, whom they charged with breaking and entering.
It's a great bargain, isn't it?

2. *Complimentary closing of a letter:* Use a comma, unless you are using open punctuation.

Sincerely yours,

3. *Formal announcement of something to follow:* Use a colon. The colon signals "Watch this space: special information to follow." Such words as "this," "these," "one" and "the following" are signals. In sentences, the colon is normally used after a full subject-verb-complement statement. Here are some typical patterns.

To announce that a word or a list will follow:

I am enclosing copies of the following: your original letter, our return letter, and your answer.
No Parking: Reserved for Vice President
For Sale: Three-Bedroom House

To stress an appositive or restatement of a term:

The success of the V-20 is due to the efforts of one man: Henry Hatton.
His eyes is fixed on one thing: promotion.

To introduce a long quotation:

This is what he advised us: "Choose a company with a ground floor—you can build the top floor yourself."

After the salutation of a letter:

Dear Miss Torrence:

4. *Informal introduction of summarizing word or emphatic words:* Use a dash.

He wanted to sit in the show window—a ridiculous notion.

She wanted only one thing out of her staff—hard work.

To Separate Parts

Parts of items must be separated by commas or a colon to prevent misreading and to give clarity.

1. *Dates:* Use two commas.

On June 6, 1976, we opened the new store.
On Thursday, June 6, 1976, we opened the new store.
At 1 A.M., Thursday, June 6, 1976, we opened the new store.

If no day of the month is given, the comma may be omitted.

In June 1968 he joined the company.

2. *Addresses:* Use two commas.

She lived in Oran, New Jersey, for two years.
She lived at 138 Main Street, Oran, New Jersey, for two years.

2. *Addresses:* Use two commas.

She lived in Oran, New Jersey, for two years.
She lived at 138 Main Street, Oran, New Jersey, for two years.

3. *Titles and Names:* Use two commas.

Ralph James, M.D., was appointed to the Advisory Commission.
Ralph James, Jr., was appointed to the Advisory Commission.

Ralph James, Jr., M.D., was appointed.
Ted Emmons, Credit Manager, will answer your letter.
American Dye Co., Inc., got the contract.
London Mills, Ltd., bid too high.

4. *Statistical material:* Use one comma to separate the hundreds from the thousands, the thousands from the millions, and so on, in numbers of more than four digits:

    1,845,233   57,828   3200

5. *To express "to" in ratios:* Use a colon.

    7:5   3:1

6. *To separate hours from minutes:* Use a colon.

    9:45 A.M.   4:30 P.M.

7. *To separate the initials of the typist from those of the person who dictated a letter:* Use a colon or slash.

    HBM:tb   HBM/tb

Ambiguous Meanings

1. *To prevent two words or figures from being read together:* Use a comma.

AMBIGUOUS: Inside business went on as usual.
CLEAR: Inside, business went on as usual.
              Whatever happens, happens.
              In 1975, 235 employees took vacations in August.

2. *To indicate when two words are connected:* Use a hyphen.

MEANING 1: guaranteed used cars (used cars that are guaranteed)
MEANING 2: guaranteed-used cars (cars that are guaranteed to have been used)

MEANING 1: 6 foot-soldiers (6 soldiers who travel by walking)
MEANING 2: 6-foot soldiers (soldiers 6 feet tall)

MEANING 1: 9 inch blades (9 blades each of which is an inch long)
MEANING 2: 9-inch blades (blades 9 inches long)

MEANING 1:   recover a couch (to obtain possession of a couch once more)
MEANING 2:   re-cover a couch (to cover a couch again)

Quotations

1. *To indicate direct quotations from a written or spoken source:* Use a pair of double quotation marks around the quoted parts.

   She asked, "What special items are on sale?"

   "What special items," she asked, "are on sale?"

   The dictionary says, "*Ain't* should be shunned by all who prefer to avoid being considered illiterate."

   Note that the parenthetical, unquoted part is left out of the quotation marks.

   "That's the price," he said, "such as it is."

   "That's the price," he said. "Take it or leave it."

2. *Quotations within quotations:* Use single quotation marks.

   The business manager said, "Believe me when I say 'A penny saved is a penny earned' is the best advice I ever had."

   Except in journalistic and British English, single quotation marks are never correct alone. Use them only within double quotation marks.

   INCORRECT: The customer thought 'darn' was a swearword.
   CORRECT: The customer thought "darn" was a swearword.

3. *A series of sentences by one speaker:* one set of quotation marks.

   The manager said, "Sit down, gentlemen. I'm dictating a letter. I should be finished in about four minutes. Please wait."

4. *More than one quoted paragraph:* Use quotation marks before each paragraph and only at the close of the last paragraph.

   A pertinent section of *The Communist Manifesto* reads as follows:

   "Centralization of credit in the hands of the State, by means of a national bank with State capital and an exclusive monopoly.

"Centralization of the means of communication and transport in the hands of the State.

"Extension of factories and instruments of production owned by the State; the bringing into cultivation of waste lands, and the improvement of the soil generally in accordance with a common plan."

5. *Other punctuation with quotation marks.*
Periods and commas go inside quotation marks.

He called the Spring Sale a "flop."

The common expression, "dog eat dog," refers to Darwin's theory.

Semicolons and colons go outside quotation marks.

He came to the door and said only one thing: "She quit"; then he left.

Dashes, question marks, and exclamation points go inside quotation marks when they are part of the quote and outside when they are not part of the quote.

He asked, "Would you buy another one?"

Didn't General Smiley say, "I'll keep us out of war"?

We heard him cry "Fire!"

If the mark applies to both the quotation and the whole sentence, use it only once.

Did she ask, "How many accidents can we afford?"

Titles

In handwritten and typed letters and papers, underlining takes the place of italics.

1. *Publications and works of art.* In works issued separately, use italics for titles of books, plays, magazines, newspapers, bulletins, pamphlets, paintings, musical compositions, and movies.

Theory of the Leisure Class	the *New York Times*
Beethoven's *Fifth Symphony*	*Playboy* magazine
The *Sound of Music*	the *Mona Lisa*

For parts of other works, use quotation marks for titles of short stories, poems, essays, subdivisions of books, articles in a magazine, songs in musicals, and movements of symphonies.

Hawthorne's short story "Dr. Heidigger's Experiment" from *Twice-Told Tales* contains a lesson for the businessperson.

The article "Priorities for the Eighties" appeared in the *Businessman's Weekly.*

2. *Ships, trains, aircraft:* Use italics.

the *Queen Elizabeth*   the *Santa Fe Flyer*
the United Airlines' *Sky King*

3. *The.* Do not underline the word "the" unless it is part of the title.

The Red Badge of Courage   the *Saturday Review*

4. *Historical documents and events, books of the Bible:* no italics or quotation marks.

He memorized The Sermon on the Mount from the book of Matthew.

He quoted from The Declaration of Independence, which is a Revolutionary War document.

Possessives

1. *Singular nouns:* Add an apostrophe and an *s.*

the driver's side   a day's wait   a woman's rights

2. *Plurals ending in s:* Add only an apostrophe.

the clerks' coffee break   three days' wait
the Joneses' house   two dollars' worth

3. *Singular nouns ending in s or z sound:* Add an apostrophe and an *s* or only an apostrophe, whichever form you prefer.

the boss's desk   James' hat   James's hat

4. *Indefinite pronouns:* Add apostrophe and *s.*

anybody's guess   everybody's responsibility

5. *Plurals that do not end in s:* Add apostrophe and *s.*

men's suits   children's dresses

6. *Compound expressions used as a single noun:* Add apostrophe and *s.*

his brother-in-law's car
the Director of Budget's parking space
Thomas and Hedges' sale
somebody else's seat
Jack and Bill's customers (same customers)

Special Words

1. *Words used as words:* Use italics (underline) or quotation marks. You have a choice. However, be consistent in using the method you choose in a single piece of writing.

   The word "receive" is often misspelled.
   The word *receive* is often misspelled.

2. *Letters and numbers used as words:* Use italics.

   The *a* and the *o* in the sign looked alike.
   He doesn't dot his *i's* or cross his *t's.*

3. *Foreign words that are not commonly used in English:* Use italics. Check the dictionary for confirmation.

   femme fatale, tempus fugit
   menu, rodeo, blitz

4. *Words used in special context:* Use quotation marks. These words include definitions, single quoted words, words out of normal context (such as slang in standard writing), and nicknames.

   He defined "ego" as "awareness of one's self."
   Mr. Jackson did not appreciate having his Jaguar referred to as a "hot rod."
   His favorite customer is John "Tiny" Benson.

5. *In spelling out compound numbers from twenty-one to ninety-nine:* Use a hyphen.

   one hundred and twenty-eight   thirty-one
   ninety-seven

6. *To express fractions that precede a noun:* Use a hyphen.

   a two-thirds interest   a three-fourths majority

Fractions not followed by nouns are not hyphenated: two thirds of the numbers.

7. *To avoid an awkward union between the prefix or suffix and the root of the word:* Use a hyphen.

re-enter	un-American	shell-like
semi-invalid	bell-like	de-emphasize
re-address	pre-inventory	

8. *With the prefixes all-, ex-, half-, quarter-, self-, and the suffix -elect:* Use a hyphen.

all-American	quarter-turn	half-awake
ex-soldier	self-sufficient	President-elect

9. *To connect two or more words used as a single adjective preceding a noun:* Use a hyphen.

a blue-green sweater	an up-to-date record
a well-balanced diet	a do-it-yourself kit
an attention-getting device	

The hyphen is omitted, however, when the first word of the modifier is an adverb that ends in *ly* or when the qualifying words follow a noun:

a freshly prepared solution

the diet is well balanced

a record that is up to date

10. *With compound words or expressions:* Use a hyphen. Check the dictionary to see if words should be written solid *(blackberry)*, hyphenated *(tough-minded)*, or open *(high school)*.

jack-of-all-trades

a middle-of-the-roader

brother-in-law

11. *The past tense of coined words:* Use an apostrophe and *d*.

O.K.'d   X'd out

12. *Plural of numbers, letters, and words used as words:* Add an apostrophe and *s*.

7's	Q's	1960's	C.O.D.'s
11's	T's	&'s	IOU's

He used too many *but's* and *if's*.

The 1930's were the Depression years.

Omission of Words

1. *Omission of words from a quotation:* Use an ellipsis (three spaced periods).

   > Mr. Akins said, "We are sure . . . that the building will be ready by July 1 for a grand opening.

   For an ellipsis at the end of a quotation use four periods, one to indicate the end of the sentence.

   > Mr. Akins said, "We are sure, with good evidence, that the building will be ready by July 1. . . ."

   If the omission overlaps beyond one sentence, use four periods, one for the period between the sentences.

   > Mr. Akins said, "We are sure . . . that the building will be ready by July 1 for a grand opening. . . . or a sale."

2. *Omission of words in a patterned series:* Use a comma.

   > One of the men who was injured is a lathe operator; the other, a toolmaker.
   > Nancy scored 98 on the speech test; Sally, 110.

3. *To avoid repetition of a root word:* Use a hyphen.

   > short- and long-run objectives
   > first-, second-, and third-class mail

Special Emphasis

1. *Emphatic pause before an important word or phrase:* Use a dash.

   > The secret of his success is—hard work.
   > We can't say Edwards is not an effective salesman—he is the second highest in sales.

2. *To indicate emotional force for a phrase or statement:* Use an exclamation point.

   > Make your reservations now!

3. *Emphatic restatement:* Use dashes.

His decision—the best decision—was based on years of experience.

Compare the price—$159—with the cost of rental.

We are concerned with one thing—satisfied customers.

4. *To pinpoint specific words:* Use italics.

She couldn't understand that *to want* is not *to get.*

5. *To hint at a double meaning:* Use quotation marks.

our "happy" office force   (Hints that the force is not happy)

out for "lunch"   (Suggests that the reason for being out is something other than lunch)

INDEX

345